LANGUAGE AN

Dorothy S. Strick
Donna E. Alvermann and N
ADVISORY BOARD: Richard Allington,
Anne Haas Dyson, Carole Edelsky, Mary Ju

MW01069638

continued

For volumes in the NCRLL Collection (edited by JoBeth Allen and Donna E. Alvermann) and the Practitioners Bookshelf Series (edited by Celia Genishi and Donna E. Alvermann), as well as other titles in this series, please visit www.tcpress.com.

Black Immigrant Literacies

Intersections of Race, Language, and Culture in the Classroom

Patriann Smith

Foreword by Shondel Nero

TEACHERS COLLEGE PRESS

TEACHERS COLLEGE | COLUMBIA UNIVERSITY
NEW YORK AND LONDON

Published by Teachers College Press,® 1234 Amsterdam Avenue, New York, NY 10027

Copyright © 2023 by Teachers College, Columbia University

Front cover photos: Teen by Iiona Virgin via Unsplash, signs by carrotmadman6 via Flickr Creative Commons, map by NOAA Central Library Historical Collection.

Library of Congress Cataloging-in-Publication Data is available at loc.gov

ISBN 978-0-8077-6896-9 (paper)
ISBN 978-0-8077-6897-6 (hardcover)
ISBN 978-0-8077-8202-6 (ebook)

Printed on acid-free paper
Manufactured in the United States of America

Contents

Foreword

My doctoral dissertation research almost 30 years ago emanated from the presence of a young Black man ("Charles") from my home country (Guyana—the only officially English-speaking country in South America) in my English as a second language (ESL) class at a private university in Brooklyn, New York. Charles's presence in my class was a surprise mostly because it unearthed and forced me to seriously question a set of assumptions about language, migration, race, pedagogy, and assessment that up until that point I had not. Some of the questions I was asking at the time included: What is the basis for determining native speakership of English, especially given the globalized nature of English? Should students from the Anglophone Caribbean be considered native speakers of English? Did Charles's race and immigrant status affect his placement in an ESL class? How should teachers effectively address the needs of Caribbean English speakers in terms of language, literacy, and assessment?

Through my evolving research and practice over time, it became clear that the linguistic questions around Charles's (mis)placement were really proxies for much deeper ones concerning ideologies and structures, in the United States and around the world, embedded in societies and education systems as legacies of slavery and colonization. These ideologies comingle race and language such that racism and linguicism are essentially one and the same, often intersecting with classism; create hierarchies of named and standardized languages tied to Eurocentric norms, privileging white speakers of any language while marginalizing others; and normalize monolingualism when, in fact, multilingualism is the norm in the world.

In this book, Patriann Smith takes direct aim at this global colonial legacy through the experiences of Black Caribbean immigrant youth and her own immigrant experience, inviting us into a much needed critical conversation on the topic. It makes perfect sense that Smith engages what she calls Black immigrant youth "authentic narratives" to tackle the challenges and possibilities of literacies in the 21st century because this group's lived experience reflects the generative intersection of race, language, literacy, and migration resulting from colonization, and is fertile ground to reject the essentialist, pathologizing frames often accorded their lives and those of all marginalized people.

The book troubles and extends the past 30 years of language and literacy research that has taken us through sociocultural, critical, intersectional, translingual, transnational, decolonizing, and anti-racist turns to address the education of marginalized populations in the United States and elsewhere, especially the rapidly increasing population of immigrants. Informed by Rosa and Flores's (2017) *raciolinguistic* perspective, Smith centers the race and language of Black immigrants (Caribbean and African) to simultaneously high-light their unique experiences; counter their relative invisibility in U.S. literacy discourses, subsumed under the African American umbrella; *and* dispel the model minority myth that pits Black immigrants as "better Blacks" against African Americans (a white suprema-cist, colonial trap). But Smith does not leave us mired in the colonial past. She brilliantly harnesses the challenges of colonial "entanglements" of race, language, and identity and re-frames them agentively, as part of her argument for reimagining education and literacies. Thus, she proffers a nuanced and rigorously researched Black immigrant literacies frame-work to provide an avenue to centralize race in the teaching of Black immigrant youth and to give them an opportunity to thrive. It is informed by intersecting insights from already existing lenses in the field—*racial, diasporic, and transnational literacies*—so for literacy scholars, the book offers a rich contribution to the conversation.

The narratives of the two focal Caribbean youth in the book lay bare their struggles and joys of "becoming Black," "becoming immigrant," and "unbecoming native speak-ers." But they are agentive voices. Through their own words, we see how they come to their own racial, linguistic, and cultural awareness, skillfully navigating their various selves across time and place. The narratives make Smith's case for engaging racial, dia-sporic, and transnational literacies as a way to expand the traditional binaries in literacy research, which are premised mostly on white, monolingual, monocultural, U.S.-based norms.

This book is a fresh corrective to these norms, fully attuned to the complex, global-ized world of the 21st century. Smith speaks to every audience that has a role in the edu-cation of Black youth—teachers, parents, peers, community members, administrators, policymakers. Every chapter ends with critical questions for research and pedagogy, ac-companied by a rich array of strategies and resources. Smith makes it clear, though, that her framework is no panacea. "It is not enough to read," she says. She feels that teachers and the entire educational system have a moral responsibility to act on behalf of Black youth to counter the institutionalized racialization they face daily and give them oppor-tunities to thrive. I agree.

In the 30 years since Charles became the catalyst for my research on Caribbean im-migrants, a coterie of critical language and literacy researchers and practitioners have troubled, contextualized, and enriched the issues raised by this population to move us forward. Smith is a forceful voice among them. This book invites you into the conversa-tion with honesty, grace, and love.

—*Shondel Nero*

REFERENCE

Rosa, J., & Flores, N. (2017). Unsettling race and language: Toward a raciolinguistic perspective. *Language in Society, 46*(5), 621–647.

Acknowledgments and Dedication

A book centering Blackness, immigration, *and* languaging, all of which remain under direct attack in and beyond the United States, could be birthed, at last, only through undying persistence and the overwhelming support of community. *Black Immigrant Literacies: Intersections of Race, Language, and Culture in the Classroom* is born today because of the fortitude of the ancestors whose blood runs through my veins and the never-ending commitment of those who daily surround me. A love note to Black immigrants everywhere—my heart is joyful to represent the voices of the youth who trusted me with their stories.

I begin this dedication page by acknowledging the Father of my Life—the God who guides my heart and who pens the words through me—my Lord and Savior, Jesus Christ. Through God, I was fortunate as I wrote this book to have the support of an amazing African American doctoral student, research assistant, and Graduate Student Success fellow—*Shawn*. And through God, I came to be blessed, as a Black immigrant mother and scholar, to work with the most amazing Black immigrant and transnational youth along my life's journey. Special thanks to each of you who were part of this shared journey with me and who made this scholarship possible. I am tremendously grateful to God for working through you, and through so many, to help me tell your stories.

I am deeply grateful, and dedicate this book, to my dearest and most precious daughter, *Karice*. Karice is the first Black immigrant child who taught me how to see the world with new eyes, as she sacrificed so much of her childhood, migrating from her homeland Trinidad and Tobago to St. Lucia, and then back again, before her journey with me to the United States. You were so willing, so brave, so joyful, and so fearless, Reese, having to be so much while being so little. It is only because of those sacrifices you made as a child that we survived this immigrant journey almost a decade ago—you and I together—when I arrived, clueless yet determined, in the United States from the Caribbean. You taught me how to understand and to accept what it means to "become immigrant," to unbecome a "native" English speaker, and to "become Black" (Ibrahim, 1999). You taught me also how to experience what I have referred to as racialized entanglements (P. Smith, 2022c) with grace and with dignity even while vehemently advocating for yourself and for me, with firm conviction. Thank you, my dearest daughter, for your joyful spirit.

I dedicate this book also to my amazing nieces and my nephews—*Gheryl, Jaeda, Jayden, Jainy, Zain, Ella, Bella, Nathaniel*, and our newest addition who just recently graced the world with her presence, *Destiny*. The continual sharing of your lives here in the United States and "back home" in the Caribbean remind me daily of what it truly means to be "at home." This book is for all of you for whom I imagine a future where your gifts are as powerfully positioned as your dreams, a future where the realities you create surpass the limitations placed on Blackness.

It has been so fulfilling also to have the guidance of the scholarship and wisdom of my fellow Black, Latinx, Asian, Indigenous, white, and other immigrant, international, and multilingual friends, teachers, scholars, and community in the United States. What would I have done without my dearest sisters, brothers, loved ones, friends? I stand on the shoulders of so many giants.

My heart is overflowing with gratitude for my fellow Black *immigrant* and *transnational* friends, teachers, scholars, and community in the United States as well as my fellow Black Caribbean and African teachers, scholars, and community across the globe, whose perspectives are infinitely connected to this work and to the vision of solidarity that we hope for within, across, and beyond the Black community. You made this work possible. Thank you.

I also wish to thank, and dedicate *Black Immigrant Literacies: Intersections of Race, Language, and Culture in the Classroom* to, my father *Patrick*, who passed away not long before I began penning this work. As a Black immigrant to Trinidad and Tobago from St. Lucia, and a descendant of African slaves, you too crossed borders—although a bit later in life—to give so much to me, my siblings, so many students, and the world. Daddy, thank you for giving the best of yourself and for teaching me to live a life of conviction, peace, forgiveness, and bravery—for teaching me to get up every time I fall and to aspire to live a life of integrity. I could not have completed this book without the resilience of mind, body, soul, heart, and spirit that you instilled in me. I honor your legacy through this work. Rest well.

Sincerest thanks go out also to my Mother Dear, *Mary Anna*, whose sacrificial life is the only reason I am here today, as a scholar, with an opportunity to write and advocate through this work. Mummy, this book is for you too because, as a former Black/Indian immigrant, you crossed the U.S. borders from the Caribbean, and St. Lucian-Trinidadian borders as well, to give everything to me and to your children. Even now, so many thousands of miles away after returning home, you continue to do so. You taught me how to face the storms of life with calm, with poise, with dignity, and with resilience of character. I did face many storms while writing, right up until the proofing of this book, but you reminded me daily to persevere. I am so grateful to you for your inspiration and to the wisdom of our Indian and African ancestors for gifting you to the world so I could be here to write today. I honor you through this work. Thanks, Mummy.

I cannot help but mention my dearest mentor, friend, and "second mother," *Dr. Hyacinth Evadne McDowall*, whom I met in the predominantly Afro-Indian country of Trinidad during my formative years after migrating from St. Lucia as an adolescent. Dr. McDowall, herself a Black St. Vincentian who had migrated with her mother to Trinidad as a child, was an avid believer in the humanity of Black brilliance, Black joy, and Black life. Dr. McDowall was the first to introduce me to "literacy" as a field as I embarked on my college years—taking up then the occupation of teaching as a Black immigrant adolescent. It is because of Dr. Mac's "adoption" of me as a teacher trainee at the then-Caribbean Union College (CUC) in Trinidad during my formative years that my path was orchestrated such that I was led to embark on a journey with English language arts and then literacy. This all would lead ultimately to my emerging life's work and to this book. *Dr. Mac*, this one is for you too. You always said to me as a young adult, *"Don't worry, Pat, you see this brain that God gave you, no one can take it away."* I infinitely owe my deepest thanks to you for reminding me of the power of the mind—my mind, when I had no capacity to see the brilliance of Blackness and of humanity. To my "third mother," *Christiana Muoh*, a Black Nigerian and past colleague at CUC, whose African wisdom consistently has guided me for the past 2 decades since our years in college together as Black immigrants in Trinidad, I am so grateful to you for inspiring, for teaching, for caring. Thank you.

I acknowledge and dedicate this book to my Black ancestors brought to the Caribbean as slaves, who, like those in the United States, fought to the death for a freedom and for a future that they saw, by faith, for me and for so many of my Black brothers, sisters, and others. Thank you for your tremendous sacrifice, ancestors. Penning these insights is possible only because you gave your lives, and everything, through faith. I thank and dedicate this book also to all the Black immigrant ancestors across the globe who have gone before, to the Black immigrant children and youth of the world who are currently here, and to the Black immigrants to come. To my Indian ancestors, I thank you too, for I see your wisdom, beauty, goodness, and truth shining through me every day.

On a final note, to all the parents of Black immigrant children and youth who now call a new world home, somewhere across the globe, know that I remained infinitely inspired to write because of your sacrifice. As a single parent, I know fully well what it takes to leave your home so you can give your children "a better life." And I know the struggle of wanting better for you and for your children. I want you to know that "I see you." I dedicate this book to you, as you continue your journeys of finding connection, joy, peace, and community, crossing virtual and physical boundaries across the globe.

Through this book, may you find *or be* the best (home)schools and teachers for your Black immigrant or transnational children. May your dreams and those of your children be fulfilled and may you never be deterred by any new world's attempts to define you. May you and may they infinitely know and preserve with pride, the power and brilliance that you inherently possess, and may you all seek to bring out this light in others whom you meet on your migration journeys. May you always live with a presence that is made beautiful daily by the beautifully imaginary futures you wish to create. Know always that no matter what you face, God holds each of you in the palms of His glorious hands.

CHAPTER 1

Introduction

> No one could see the line, but I always felt it. I always knew it was there. Two separate parts of me, living and moving together in one body. Part African American. Part Nigerian. I always felt like a fragment, like a piece of something larger. But never quite whole. Split. Black on both sides.
>
> —Lakeya Omogun, 2021

The first time I read the quote above from Dr. Lakeya Omogun, assistant professor at the University of Washington and author of the blog post *Black, on Both Sides, Living Between My Nigerian and African-American Identities*, I felt it. It wasn't just Dr. Omogun's quote, but her entire blog that drew my heart in, reflecting how she came to consolidate the various parts of her life as a Black "American," a Nigerian, and an "African immigrant." As an Afro-Caribbean immigrant myself, with a daughter who migrated to the United States as a child, I was drawn to Lakeya's effortless depiction of the tensions that many Black immigrant youth face with literacies and their lives, in the United States and elsewhere (e.g., Brazil, Dominica, Ghana, Haiti, Jamaica, Nigeria, Somalia, St. Lucia)—tensions that persist regardless of where the Black multilingual child is from. I read Lakeya's blog and thought, "I can see so many of the myriad stories of my daughter and of Black immigrant youth with whom I have worked, in here!" I also thought how freeing it must have been for her to engage with the nuances, the tensions, the freedoms, and the possibilities that this blog allowed.

Reading Dr. Omogun's blog reminded me of comedy artist, and South African Black immigrant to the United States, Trevor Noah, who often describes how race, immigration, and language work together to inform so many of his experiences. It reminded me also of the African American rapper Drake, whose recent use of Afrobeats and specifically Jamaican Patois made it clear that he is inspired by the languaging of Black immigrants and of Afro-Caribbean and African nationals. The blog also brought to mind a recent *Subtitle* podcast episode featuring Guyanese-born New York University expert on Caribbean Creole English, Dr. Shondel Nero. In the episode, "The Future Sound of Black English," Dr. Nero describes using Englishes as a Guyanese, as a student growing up with British English, and also as an American (Theuri, 2022). She describes migrating to New York, where she expected to hear the Black American English that she had heard via music while in the Caribbean but instead heard numerous Black Englishes from Caribbean countries and African countries, such as Nigeria, working together in the languaging of the populations there.

These musings caused me to wonder—How could I continue to share stories of youth who lived like Dr. Omogun, Trevor Noah, and Dr. Nero, many of whom currently function as "immigrant" or "transnational" and constantly grapple with what it means to be racialized linguistically as Black in America? And in what ways could I open up to other teachers, many of the invisible Englishes, languages, and stories of Black immigrant youth whom I knew while also retaining their authentic and heartfelt voices? How could I do this in ways that showed their joyfulness, resilience, and the versatility with literacies that had so impacted my personal and professional life?

This book emerged as a response to wonderings such as these, which I have felt stirring for almost a decade. I had a desire to share with teachers, educators, and others who work in schools, how we might help to bridge the many invisible literacy barriers that often persist in alienating Black immigrant youth from their peers in U.S. schools. I describe how educators can center, affirm, and develop Black immigrant literacies in ways that allow *all* students to engage with and honor these literacies. To do so, I draw from the research concerning how Black border-crossers are (re)positioned as immigrants in the United States. I also draw from the languaging and Englishes of Black immigrants, as well as the ways in which these linguistic assets are erased while they are racialized.

Using what I have referred to as *authentic narratives* (P. Smith, 2022d) based on the transcripts of my conversations with Afro-Caribbean youth and guided by the framework for Black immigrant literacies (P. Smith, 2020d), I describe how teachers, educators, and other stakeholders can (a) teach and reach the *whole* Black literate immigrant, (b) use literacy and English language arts curriculum as a vehicle for instructing Black immigrant and all youth, (c) foster relations among Black immigrants and their peers through literacy, and (d) connect parents, schools, and communities for success with Black immigrant literacies, in solidarity.

I come to this work as a former teacher of students in the Caribbean, as a current teacher-educator, and as one with personal experiences as a Black immigrant. I bring to this work also my experiences as the single-parent mother of a Black immigrant daughter, and my experiences as a scholar-educator focused on Black immigrant literacies, a portrait that I paint in the *Classroom Caffeine* podcast episode titled "A Conversation with Patriann Smith" (Persohn, 2021) and in the *VoicEd Radio* podcast episode titled "A Transraciolinguistic Approach for Literacy Classrooms" (Zaidi & Hurley, 2021).

THE FRAMEWORK FOR BLACK IMMIGRANT LITERACIES

The framework for Black immigrant literacies is a useful premise for showing how educators can center, affirm, and develop Black immigrant literacies. It is useful because it functions as a vehicle for bridging barriers between Black immigrant and Black American youth and between Black immigrant and other youth. The framework was developed based on intersecting insights from three lenses that already exist in the field—diaspora literacy, racial literacy, and transnational literacy. It is presented as a basis for demonstrating how partial understandings still persist regarding the literacies of Black immigrant youth.

Diaspora literacy refers to the ability of Black people to develop an understanding of their "story" of "cultural dispossession" while reading "a variety of cultural signs of the lives of Africa's children at home and in the New World" (Busia, 1989, p. 197). *Racial literacy* frames an understanding of racism in America by considering race "as an instrument of social, geographic, and economic control of both whites and blacks" with which power is intertwined even as race intersects with numerous other factors (Guinier, 2004, p. 114). *Transnational literacy* denotes the "written language practices of people who are involved in activities that span national boundaries" (Jiménez et al., 2009, p. 17) as well as literacies and language practices of transnational youth that emerge as "transnational understandings" (Skerrett, 2012, p. 387).

The intersection of the lens of diaspora literacy, often used to examine the literacies of Black American youth; the framework of racial literacy, often used for both white and Black American populations; and the notion of transnational literacy, typically used to understand the literacies of youth who cross geographical and virtual borders, provides a basis from which to better understand Black immigrant literacies. Through these three lenses that undergird the *Black immigrant literacies* framework (P. Smith, 2020d), I accomplish three interconnected goals:

1. Use diaspora literacy to address the divisions that persist between Black immigrants and their Black American and other African peers;
2. Use racial literacy to address distinctions that exist in how Black immigrants come to understand race in relation to Black American and other peers;
3. Use transnational literacy to illustrate how racialized language and personhood intersect with being a border-crosser for Black immigrant youth in ways that create differences in how they enact literacies as compared with their Black American and other peers.

By using these lenses to foreground the framework for Black immigrant literacies, I provide an avenue for practitioners to centralize race in the literacy teaching of Black immigrant youth and their peers by considering five elements. These five elements of the Black immigrant literacies framework, which I have proposed elsewhere, are:

1. The claim to the struggle for justice;
2. The myth of the model minority;
3. A transraciolinguistic approach;
4. A focus on local–global;
5. Use of holistic literacies.

The *claim to the struggle for justice* allows for emerging understanding through intentional and adept communication between Black immigrants and Black Americans about the distinctive historical experiences surrounding slavery that they have endured in what has evolved into a white supremacist context that inadvertently frames their ability to lay claim to the struggle for justice.

The *myth of the model minority* facilitates a critical understanding of the ways in which a meritocratic model minority myth, as applied to Black immigrant youth, is steeped in divide-and-conquer racial politics that sustains interracial divisions between Black immigrant youth and their Black American peers and other minoritized immigrant populations.

A *transraciolinguistic approach* creates opportunities for youth, teachers, and parents to discuss and to leverage metalinguistic, metaracial, and metacultural understanding as youth keep learning and acknowledging their "not knowing" about race. This not knowing is often present because they have migrated from countries where there is a majority population that is Black or reflects predominantly people of color.

The *local–global* instantiates a rethinking of the global (e.g., in students' home countries) through their lived experience with the local (e.g., in the United States). The local–global recognizes duality and hybridity in how racialization is implicitly embedded in the "postcolonial" structures of youth's home countries as they encounter its explicit enactment through hegemonic whiteness and individual racialized encounters within countries such as the United States.

And *holistic literacies* (re)purpose literacies as holistic, as opposed to fragmented based on a privileging of literacy performance on tests. Through holistic literacies, youth use language, multiliteracies, and cross-border shifts to function as "language architects" (Flores, 2020) and as "raciosemiotic architects" (P. Smith, 2022e) who reread and rewrite text and their worlds (Freire & Macedo, 1987). They do this by using Englishes and broader semiotic resources across their lifeworlds, across home and school, based on an understanding of inescapable racialized tensions (P. Smith, 2020d).

AUTHENTIC NARRATIVES

The *authentic narratives* I employ to tell Black immigrant stories are based on the transcripts of my conversations with Afro-Caribbean youth as part of an Institutional Review Board (IRB)-approved study (2016–2019). These narratives—*stories captured and presented chronologically, relying strictly on participant voices based on transcribed data as they were told*—function as a basis for the scholarship presented, and reflect my firsthand encounters with Black immigrant youth. I had these conversations with youth in my role as coadvisor and later as advisor for the designated southwestern university's Caribbean Student Association in which the students were enrolled. The authentic narratives emerged as I engaged *with* the students naturally in community, responding to their needs. Specifically, these vivid stories of a Jamaican and a Bahamian immigrant youth, both of whom identified as Black, are presented later in ways that preserve participant voices fully, richly, and holistically. The stories represent how the youth engaged with me freely in my multiple roles as scholar, educator, single parent, scholar-mother, confidant, and friend, during our ongoing and emerging participation in the Caribbean Student Association over the course of our 4 years together.

My use of authentic narratives was informed by research concerning the narrative method as articulated by Dr. Jerome Bruner (1987). Here, transcript narratives function as autobiographical accounts (Emig, 1977) told by youth themselves about their lives. I also was guided in part by Dr. Anthony J. Onwuegbuzie's "critical dialectical pluralism" approach (Onwuegbuzie & Frels, 2013). This approach is described as "centered on the assumption that social injustices permeate all levels of society" (p. 9). The use of authentic narratives thus is steeped epistemologically in critical integrated research and informed methodologically by the narrative research paradigm. This was aligned with my goal to make visible how I had lived with and understood the Black immigrant youth by

> conduct[ing] research wherein an egalitarian society is promoted and sustained for the purpose of advancing both universalistic theoretical knowledge and local practical knowledge, and to conduct culturally progressive research. (Onwuegbuzie & Frels, 2013, p. 9)

Specifically, drawing from certain elements of this critical dialectical pluralistic approach, the research study that informs the insights presented later emerged through interaction with participants as guided by Onwuegbuzie and Frels (2013). This research allowed participants to have a

> co-equal say in what phenomenon should be studied; how research should be conducted to study this phenomenon; which methods should be used; which findings are valid, acceptable, and meaningful; how the findings are to be disseminated and utilized; and how the consequences of such decisions and actions are to be assessed. (p. 9)

I served as a research-facilitator who "assume[d] the role of democratic facilitator and consciousness raiser, or cultural broker, between the participant-researcher(s) and entities that have power over them" (Onwuegbuzie & Frels, 2013, p. 9). In doing so, I allowed the authentic narratives to emerge as an approach through which to present complete, holistic, and vivid insights into the lives and literacies of Black immigrant youth.

The authentic narrative approach is based epistemologically on the notion that to know about youth, and particularly those who are racialized, particularly as Black, requires a simultaneous understanding of their "pasts," "presents," and "futures," (P. Smith, in press). This approach mirrors how Sankofa has been used to describe the experiences of Black immigrant youth by acknowledging that knowing their literacies and languaging requires an understanding of the situatedness of these elements in contexts across time (Watson et al., 2014). It also aligns with the Literacy Futurisms Collective-in-the-Making (2021) framework, which emphasizes the importance of ancestral knowledge in the experiences of students of color.

Coined at the intersection of the biographical, autoethnographic, phenomenological, and narrative traditions, authentic narratives—based on a critical dialectical pluralistic paradigm—offer an opportunity to "see," to "hear," and to "be with" Black immigrant youth in ways often disallowed by limitations imposed Eurocentrically by journals, dissertations, and scholarship at large. These impositions often are invoked under the guise of having "too much raw data" and with a preference for imposing researcher interpretations on the lived experiences of participants. In turn, they tend to distort participant intentions and/or obscure opportunities for readers and listeners to themselves bring additional understandings to the raw data presented in published research.

Considering the above, I chose authentic narratives to portray the literacies and languaging of the youth in this book in order to disrupt the ways in which written scholarship tends to erase the deeply interwoven connections of literacies that reflect the full lives of youth. I chose this approach also because I wished to resist the urge to "thematize," almost into oblivion via analysis, "raw data" obtained from youth during research. Avoiding the trap of obscuring who youth of color really are and what they can do, I use this method to interrupt the tendency to "retell," "revoice," and "rewrite" stories about the literacies of racialized youth, often in the absence of complete stories that are their own, and that often do not tell us exactly what they meant to say (P. Smith, 2022d).

The authentic narratives serve as a compelling opportunity for teachers and educators to have firsthand experiences with the voices of youth. Because the authentic narratives of youth are presented alongside interpretations provided based on these narratives, they open up conversations that transcend the discussions I present. In doing so, they allow for considerations that can inform how teachers, educators, parents, and others see beyond what I learned about the languaging of Black immigrant youth on the page, as they too engage with numerous representations of what it means to be Black, immigrant, transnational, and human. "Sitting with me" to read the original stories of youth themselves, it is possible for any audience to insert their own voices into the meaning-making of the youth who trusted me with these sacred narratives. Insights based on each authentic narrative and aligned with elements of the Black immigrant literacies framework (P. Smith, 2020d) provide a way to discuss how teachers and educators can use the literacies and languaging of Black immigrant youth as a vehicle for bridging barriers and thus for expanding the possibilities present in all students' literacies.

A CALL TO TEACHERS, EDUCATORS, SCHOOLS, AND POLICYMAKERS

Teachers, educators, and schools whose populations include Black immigrant students are invited to "think with" and to "see through" the lenses of the Black immigrant literacies framework. It is possible to do this by engaging with the storying of authentic narratives and encountering the myriad of nuances presented by Black immigrant youth. The understandings obtained will prove useful for thinking about how instruction is designed and leveraged with Black immigrant youth in relation to, as well as in the absence of, their Black American, immigrant, white, and other minoritized counterparts. Particularly in situations where Black immigrant peers operate in classrooms with white youth, it is possible to use the considerations presented in the Black immigrant literacies framework to avoid typical assumptions about how Black youth approach literacy tasks that are often different from those presented in their home countries. It is also possible to see how they experience tasks that are often steeped in cultural nuances about which they may not have prior knowledge.

Teachers are invited, through the ideas presented, to be intentional about enabling Black immigrant youth to process the unique demands of being repositioned linguistically, racially, and culturally as "border-crossers." They can do this by understanding how Black youth experience being subsumed as part of the overall Black population in the United

States and by working with them via mechanisms such as *a transraciolinguistic approach* (see P. Smith, 2019). Teachers are invited to allow multilingual and Black immigrant youth to "educate up" so they can provide teachers, peers, schools, and parents, over time, with insights into the distinct assets they possess. Teachers also are positioned to tap into the unique challenges faced by this population as they navigate practices of educational settings within their home countries and those within a new world.

Schools, policymakers, institutions, and the broader society, in common with teachers, are asked to be morally responsible for the literacy education of Black immigrant youth (see Willis et al., 2022 on CARE[1]) by reimagining ELA/literacy standards, classrooms, and schools. By understanding the educational and literate experiences of the often-invisible Black immigrants whose narratives are presented, students and youth in the elementary, intermediate, and higher grades can be empowered to critically examine how similarities persist across racialized practices in their countries and the United States. The insights presented enhance the capacity of multiple stakeholders to support youth as they navigate differences in how racialized systems affect them locally in the United States and broadly across the globe.

Overall, the various elements of the Black immigrant literacies framework can be considered as building blocks. The first two constructs (i.e., claim to the struggle for justice and myth of the model minority) are based on developing awareness and understanding. The latter three (i.e., a transraciolinguistic approach, local–global, holistic literacies) illustrate what youth should be able to do as they engage in "pursuits" (Muhammad, 2020) through their literacies. Elements of the framework are not meant to occur in prescribed stages or in isolation from one another, as Black immigrant youth are individuals, unique and with a myriad of experiences, who present their individual ways of adjusting to race through literacies in their own way and time.

I caution against using this framework as a "catch-all" approach or a way of essentializing Black immigrant youth. The Black population is not a monolith, and each child has a unique story (see Adichie, 2009, on avoiding the dangers of a single story). Rather, I view this modest step as an invitation through which to more carefully consider how practitioners can better meet the needs of this unique and largely invisible yet racialized population; additionally, I see it as a mechanism to engage with what I refer to as *immigrant of color literacies* (P. Smith, 2020d). Using the framework flexibly and not prescriptively, those who work with Black immigrant youth have the opportunity to notice how essentializations often accompany their literacy use as they attempt to navigate novel racialized settings.

I have grown and learned about Black immigrant children and youth as a Black immigrant mother, scholar, teacher, and educator working across multiple countries and states—St. Lucia, Trinidad, Barbados; Florida, Illinois, Texas. I have done the same across multiple universities—University of Illinois at Urbana Champaign, Texas Tech University, University of South Florida, the University of the West Indies. I now invite teachers and educators to grow and learn about Black immigrant children and youth as well. Through the Black immigrant literacies framework, there is promise for healing dichotomous wounds that have prevailed across Black/African immigrant, Black Caribbean immigrant, Black American, Black Latin American, and/or other racially and linguistically distinct subpopulations for so many generations. With its complementary use alongside other emerging and established frameworks in the field, parents, schools, and communities can come together in solidarity across racial, linguistic, and cultural lines to support Black immigrant youth as they leverage their language, including Englishes and other semiotic resources in ways that allow them to maintain a sense of personhood so crucial to their well-being.

ENVISIONING IMAGINARY FUTURES WITH
BLACK IMMIGRANT LITERACIES

In 2019, for the first time, the demographics of the United States reflected a majority non-white population under the age of 16. Of this population, according to the Pew Research Center, "46.8 million people in the United States identified their race as Black, either alone or as part of a multiracial or ethnic background" (Tamir, 2022). In 2022, one in 10 Black people living in the United States were identified as immigrants (Tamir & Anderson, 2022). And by 2030, the United States will face a demographic turning point. Racial and ethnic groups will continue to function as the primary drivers of overall growth because of the unanticipated decline in the country's white population. In addition, immigration will continue to overtake natural births as the main source of population growth for the country. By 2060, the nation's foreign-born population is projected to rise to 69 million from 44 million in 2016.

Amid these projections, Black residents in the United States—both native and foreign born—are expected to continue to function as one of the major nonwhite groups accounting for the growth of the nation. At the same time, people of African descent are increasingly represented across the world, with a quarter of the Earth's population expected to be African by 2050 (Ferris, 2015; United Nations, Department of Economic and Social Affairs, Population Division, 2015). Notwithstanding, at the time this book was being written, a report from the United Nations human rights experts conducted by the Working Group on People of African Descent, in the *St. Lucia Times*, highlighted the ways in which discrimination impacts Black boys and girls worldwide as they fail to be considered as children even by the law (Editorial Staff, 2022).

There is no greater time than the current moment to understand how to address Black immigrant literacies in and beyond U.S. schools. Demographic shifts continue to occur nationally and globally, and Blackness as well as racialization become further complicated in relation to immigration and languaging. The insights presented in this book function as a unique opportunity for learning how to dismantle essentializations, address nuances, and create emerging solutions that support the growing Black immigrant and transnational student population. With these shifts, there will be an opportunity to bridge barriers that often remain invisible, but are very much present and pervasive, within the Black immigrant population (e.g., Afro-Caribbean, African, Afro-Latin American) and between Black immigrant youth and their peers (e.g., African Americans, white, Latinx).

Relying on the framework for Black immigrant literacies, communities and schools in the United States will better allow stakeholders to advocate for the literate needs of all youth by understanding how Black immigrant literacies position these youth in relation to peers. They will be poised to do so by understanding the numerous emerging and subtly racialized nuances present in defining the self, as shown in Dr. Lakeya Omogun's story, Trevor Noah's comedy, and Dr. Shondel Nero's podcast. Schools beyond the United States also have the opportunity to create pathways such as those that engineer liberatory Caribbean imaginaries (P. Smith, 2022c). In doing so, they can free youth to read and address race in their own contexts where the pervasive impact of racialization lingers but often is overlooked. The Black immigrant literacies framework represents a pursuit of solidarity (Martinez, 2017), silencing invisibility (P. Smith, 2020d) and enhancing how literacy tools are used to build bridges for mutual understanding, relational healing, and well-being (Smith, 2022a).

OVERVIEW OF THE CHAPTERS

Black Immigrant Literacies: Intersections of Race, Language, and Culture in the Classroom consists of six chapters, the first of which is this Introduction. Chapter 2 outlines the rationale for reenvisioning the literacies of Black immigrant youth. Chapter 3 presents a discussion of the elements of the framework for Black immigrant literacies, followed by the significance of these elements for teachers, educators, and parents of all youth. In this chapter, I also discuss diaspora literacy, racial literacy, and transnational literacy as intersectional and theoretical bases for the Black immigrant literacies framework and explain why this framework is useful for reenvisioning the literacies of all youth. Chapter 4 presents the first authentic narrative, that of an Afro-Caribbean Jamaican immigrant youth, Chloe (who identifies as Black), reflecting her interactions with Black American, African, and white peers. Insights identified based on the authentic narrative are aligned with the framework for Black immigrant literacies and inform the specific recommendations made for teaching Black immigrant youth. Chapter 5 presents the second authentic narrative, that of an Afro-Caribbean Bahamian immigrant youth, Ervin (also self-identifying as Black), reflecting his interactions with Black American, African, and white peers. Insights identified, based on the authentic narrative and aligned with the framework for Black immigrant literacies, guide recommendations for teachers to use literacy and English language arts curriculum that meets the literacy needs of Black immigrant youth. These insights, based on the authentic narrative, also allow for recommendations to be made about how teachers can foster positive relationships among Black immigrant youth and their Black American, white American, and other immigrant peers—through literacy. Chapter 6 discusses how parents, schools, and communities can use the Black immigrant literacies framework across racial, linguistic, and cultural lines to partner in solidarity, as they help Black immigrant youth relate to other students, and thrive.

NOTE

1. Willis et al. define the CARE acronym as Centered in Black Students; Awareness of Anti-Blackness, Historical Knowledge, and Political Knowledge; Racial Justice; and Expectations of Personnel in School Districts, Schools, and Classrooms.

CHAPTER 2

Reenvisioning the Literacies of Black Immigrant Youth

Black immigrant youth can be described as first-, second-, or third-generation immigrants to the United States who identify as Black and who have family origins in Africa, the Caribbean, or elsewhere. Also functioning often as transnationals, Black immigrant youth and their parents have long been identified as an overlooked and invisible population (Bryce-Laporte, 1972). Yet, as has been shown (P. Smith, 2023a), Black immigrants have been significantly represented in the United States since the second half of the 20th century, given the influx of Black immigrants from the Caribbean, Latin America, and sub-Saharan Africa during this time (Jackson, 2007).

A BRIEF HISTORY AND DEMOGRAPHICS OF BLACK IMMIGRANTS IN THE UNITED STATES

The increasing presence of Black immigrants in the United States occurred in what can be described as two phases—the pre-World War II 1900 to 1930 phase when large numbers of Black immigrants arrived, and the post-1965 phase following passage of the Hart-Celler Act (the Immigration and Nationality Act of 1965), as well as corresponding changes in immigration policy across Europe and the United States. Immigrants in the pre-World War II phase came primarily from the Caribbean region, Canada, and Cape Verde. Initially, those in the post-1965 phase came primarily from the Caribbean—Jamaica, Haiti, and Trinidad and Tobago. However, current trends indicate that despite the Caribbean accounting for the largest number of Black immigrants in the United States, African immigrants continue to represent the largest increases documented among this population (Bryce-Laporte, 1972; Jackson, 2007). This trend corresponds to the upsurge in research on Caribbean immigrants as depicted in the literature around the 1990s. That upsurge is also partly responsible for the limited research on African populations in the United States at that time (Dodoo, 1997).

As of 2019, Black immigrants who originated primarily from the Caribbean or Africa accounted for 88% of all Black foreign-born people in the United States. With the Caribbean functioning as the largest origin source of Black immigrants in the United States, according to Pew Research Center, just under half of the foreign-born Black population (46%) are documented as having been born in the Caribbean region (Tamir,

2022). Of this Caribbean foreign-born Black population, Jamaica and Haiti are the two largest countries of origin, "accounting for 16 percent and 15 percent of immigrants, respectively" (Haughton, 2022). By contrast, African immigrants—described as those born on the African continent—make up 42% of the overall foreign-born Black population, having reflected an exponential growth of 246%, from 600,000 in 2000 to 2 million in 2019 (see P. Smith, 2023a for the original depiction of this literature and the material presented in the two sections that follow).

INTERSECTIONS SURROUNDING BLACK IMMIGRANT YOUTH AS A "NEW MODEL MINORITY"

Many students from the Black immigrant population tend to be regarded as a *new model minority* and as *designer immigrants* (Kasinitz, 1992; Kperogi, 2009; Simmons, 1999). New model minority perceptions of Black immigrants tend to be pervasive because of claims of "immigrant superiority" (Sowell, 1978) and because Black immigrants have long been perceived as having socioeconomic advantages over their Black American peers. These perceived advantages have been examined and were documented across the Black community in the United States between 1910 and 1940 (Tillery & Chresfield, 2012). Scholars assert that the Black press in the United States then had offered an accurate portrait of the socioeconomic advantages of West Indian immigrants relative to native-born Blacks. Yet, research comparing the earnings attainment of male African immigrants, their Caribbean-born counterparts, and native-born African Americans as of 1990 has shown that African Blacks then earned more than Caribbean and African American Blacks, when certain variables were controlled (Dodoo, 1997). And more recent research that examined how race, ethnicity, and teacher discrimination impacted academic performance for Nigerian and Black American adolescents has debunked the prevailing indication of African immigrant youth as a new model minority (Onyewuenyi, 2018; Ukpokodu, 2018).

New model minority perceptions of Black immigrant youth continue to be pervasive in spite of such emerging evidence because these youth often are perceived as achieving considerably better academic performance than their African American counterparts (Ukpokodu, 2018). Such perceptions persist because Black immigrant students tend to come from countries where the official language spoken is English, despite their typical status as bilingual, multilingual, bidialectal, or multidialectal (Winer, 2006; Zong & Batalova, 2019). Much of the model minority narrative, in turn, emerged partly because the United States maintained a racial structure that made it difficult for Black immigrants to have cultural self-determination and self-representation for most of the 20th century. Subsumed within the African American population on their arrival in the United States, Black immigrants who tried to distinguish themselves from native-born African American peers were often viewed as divisive and ethnocentric (P. Smith, 2020b).

Yet, much like their Black American counterparts, Black immigrant youth have been identified as facing a significant number of challenges with academic performance (Gilbert, 2008; Kumi-Yeboah, 2018; Ukpokodu, 2018). For instance, many dialect-speaking Caribbean students have been described as lacking proficiency in the academic

English language of the United States based on differences in language structure, pronunciation, and vocabulary (Pratt-Johnson, 1993). Similarly, certain West African students have been shown to lack the academic language and literacy background and requisite English language skills for U.S. classrooms (de Kleine, 2006). Beyond this, Black immigrant students often are assigned to English as a Second Language (ESL) classes despite the official language in their countries being English and their familiarity with nonacademic English (Obeng & Obeng, 2006). The perceived challenges with language often are thought to arise because Black immigrant youth's repertoires represent great linguistic variation, much of which is reflected by the Creole speech used in their writing (Clachar, 2004). Yet their categorization based on what Clachar (2003) describes as the "generic" notion of "ESL learner ... to include all but native speakers of Standard English, seems to disguise the complex differences between learners of Standard English as a second dialect and ESL learners regarding literacy challenges" (p. 271). Beyond the above, Black immigrant student performance in relation to language on certain academic literacy measures, such as the Program for International Student Assessment (PISA), has been registered repeatedly as lower than the norm (e.g., P. Smith et al., 2019, 2022, 2023).

Black immigrant students' academic challenges often emerge as a function of the distinct linguistic backgrounds of their home countries, many of which reflect corresponding racial and cultural nuance. For instance, although often phenotypically racialized and labeled as Black, Black immigrants frequently do not fit into neat racially, ethnically, linguistically, and culturally distinct packages. In fact, as Clemons (2021) observes, ethnoracial formations often prevent such neat distinctions. Notwithstanding, using labels here only for the purpose of discussion, it is helpful to note that *English-speaking immigrants* often come from Caribbean countries such as Jamaica and Trinidad and Tobago and sub-Saharan Africa, *French-speaking immigrants* often migrate from Caribbean countries such as Haiti, and *Spanish-speaking immigrants* from Caribbean and Latin American countries such as Cuba, Brazil, Puerto Rico, and the Dominican Republic.

Immigrants who come from English-speaking countries are often Black and thought to possess better English language skills (Zong & Batalova, 2016), and frequently are the target of linguicism, where power and privilege accompany a version of the English language they do not speak (Agyepong, 2013; Awokoya, 2009; Nero, 2006; Skutnabb-Kangas, 1988). Their language is discriminated against in many instances because of "raciolinguistics" (Alim, 2016) and "raciolinguistic ideology" (Rosa & Flores, 2017)—where race and language work together as a basis for delegitimizing them in schools (P. Smith, 2019).

Those who come from French-speaking countries such as Haiti, a country accounting for more than a quarter of all Black English learners (ELs) in the United States, are often Black and officially classified as limited English proficient (LEP) or as ELs (U.S. Census Bureau, American Community Survey, 2013). Black immigrants from Haiti bring their experiences of operating under what some have called "French hegemony," where Creole and Creole culture are marginalized. Haitians are educated with the expectation that they will be useful to countries other than Haiti, and Haitians who have become educated are taught to dissociate from their Haitian identity (Delva, 2019; Fanon, 1961/1963). Moreover, despite the adoption of Kreyòl as an official language of instruction in Haiti (Prou, 2009), many migrate to the United States from a system of Catholic education that engineered congregational schools whose alienation, racism, and autocratic and violent rule were steeped in Westernization and whose oppression marginalized the Vodouist and Creole-speaking Haitian population (François, 2016). Notwithstanding, Black immigrant Haitian youth have been shown to resist raciolinguistic ideologies, rely on Haitian faith literacies, and use their multiliteracy practices as tools for (re)constructing identity (Omogun & Skerrett, 2021).

Black immigrants who come from Spanish-speaking countries of Latin America and the Caribbean, such as Brazil and the Dominican Republic, are often either Black, Latinx, or Black Latinx and speak varying degrees of English, Spanish, and/or French. This forces them to contend with an idea of *Latinidad* (Latinx identity) that often does "not include people who look like them while also living with the stigma of Blackness that is perpetuated by other Latinos, including family members" (Hordge-Freeman & Veras 2020; Nolasco, 2020, p. 2).

Overall, besides Englishes, the diversity of language use among Black immigrants in the United States has seen a predominant representation of Spanish (Clemons, 2021; Hordge-Freeman & Veras, 2020) as well as French Creole and French (Cooper, 2020) within an increasingly significant Black EL population. The Black EL population is most visible in Maine, Vermont, and Mississippi, with the primary countries of origin for this population being Haiti, the Dominican Republic, Kenya, Ethiopia, Somalia, Mexico, Congo, Tanzania, and other parts of Africa (U.S. Department of Education, Office of English Language Acquisition & White House Initiative on Educational Excellence for African Americans, 2015; U.S. Department of Justice & U.S. Department of Education, 2015).

A recent study points to the outperformance of Black ELs in comparison to their peers, suggesting that this functions as a counterexample to the typically touted achievement gap that affects Black, and thus Black immigrant, youth (Shockley, 2021). Yet my colleagues and I have argued, using Milner's (2012) notion of an "opportunity gap," that achievement gap narratives inequitably encourage linguistic comparisons of Black and racialized students against standardized norms determined to be acceptable based on the performance of white peers (P. Smith et al., 2019). We urge instead a rethinking of these comparisons based on achievement that often foster divisive rhetoric among racialized subpopulations.

Such rethinking allows for research to examine Black immigrant youth—mostly from the Caribbean and Africa—and how they reflect numerous ethnoracial and ethnolinguistic variations holistically through their literacies as they migrate from their home countries and arrive in the United States. Acknowledging that they are forced to reconsider how they previously have used Englishes and languaging in their home countries, as well as how they have discriminated against nonstandardized Englishes in academic settings in these countries, becomes more important than measuring them against a white standard (P. Smith, 2019; P. Smith et al., 2019).

In response to the nuances that Black immigrant youth present, Nero (2000) has suggested that the literacy needs of Caribbean bidialectal students be addressed by focusing on their classroom practices, teacher preparation, deconstructing ESL/English dichotomies, and disrupting linguistic attitudes. Milson-Whyte (2018) has further argued for pedagogical strategies to help Caribbean Creole-speaking students master linguistic practices in U.S. classrooms, by eliminating stigmas associated with their language, enriching their linguistic identities by helping them develop pride regarding their Creole heritage, and engaging them in linguistic practices such as "code-meshing and translingualism" (p. 1).

These strategies have been touted as capable of supporting Black immigrant youth whose broader bicultural socialization, ethnic identity development, and mental well-being, are all part of their process of learning how to live in the United States. The strategies appear useful because these youth become part of an often-homogenized discourse that tends to reinforce their longstanding invisibility (Bryce-Laporte, 1972), limiting the awareness of their challenges and the academic support they receive in schools.

Understanding how to address the academic achievement of Black youth also has been fostered through lenses such as assimilation theory and cultural ecological theory, which help to distinguish Black immigrant, second-generation, and nonimmigrant youth (Hudley, 2016; Kim, 2014; Malcolm & Mendoza, 2014; Morrison & Bryan, 2014). Notwithstanding, there is a need to draw simultaneously from the fields of sociology, literacy education, and linguistics, among others, to better understand and attend to how race, language, and migration intersect in addressing the literacy needs of Black immigrant youth. It is also important to do so in ways that address tensions persisting between Black immigrant and Black American peers (Daoud et al., 2018; Jackson & Cothran, 2003; Okonofua, 2013). At the same time, there is a need to disrupt the invisibility of Black immigrants with clear attention to race (e.g., Braden, 2020; Nalubega-Booker & Willis, 2020; Skerrett & Omogun, 2020).

This emphasis on race in relation to migration and language both within and beyond the Black immigrant population is justified given historical indications in the United States through which literacy has functioned as a vehicle for exclusion of Black people and people of color in general (Smith & Warrican, 2021b). One such example is visible in the United States' historical restriction of naturalized citizenship to "all free white persons who have or shall migrate into the United States as of 1790, a legislation that proved to be racially discriminatory even while touted as 'radically inclusive'" (Jacobson, 1998, p. 22). Accompanying this restriction was the Immigration Restriction Bill, sponsored by Henry Cabot Lodge in 1895 and passed in 1896, which "required immigrants to show knowledge of reading and writing in their own language, for admission to the United States" (Curthoys & Lake, 2006, p. 219).

More recent indications highlight how race plays a major role in the discrimination faced by Black immigrant youth, and observations demonstrate how race and language intersect to typically motivate such discrimination (e.g., Hotchkins & Smith, 2020; Nalubega-Booker & Willis, 2020; Skerrett & Omogun, 2020). Intersectionally addressing how race, language, and migration affect the literacies of Black immigrant youth can become possible by disaggregating the needs of these youth from broader discourses within which they often are subsumed (see Njue & Retish, 2010; P. Smith et al., 2019; Waters, 1994). In doing so, it is possible to effectively disrupt the tendency to use academic (literacy) success as a key basis for designating the model minority status of Black immigrant youth. This practice not only obscures challenges they face with such discrimination, but also fails to allow them to portray their literacy practices beyond those valued by schools (P. Smith, 2019, 2020b, 2020d, 2022a).

A focus on assets that racialized immigrant youth already possess is justifiable given the tendency to emphasize, in the research, how immigrants' academic achievement can be enhanced even while their social and emotional literate well-being often remains unaddressed. We know now more than ever about the potential effects of language and literacy as social determinants of the health of immigrants, given how they create "cultural barriers and financial difficulties" that function as obstacles to accessing and comprehending health information (Kreps & Sparks, 2008; U.S. Department of Health and Human Services, Office of Disease Prevention and Health Promotion, 2022). Identifying and centering literate assets of the Black immigrant student population in the United States is thus well warranted considering the tendency of schools, organizations, communities, and the larger society to function based on deficit as well as assimilationist approaches that often require Black immigrants to adapt to and adopt norms of the societies into which they often are subsumed. These concerns can be addressed by providing educators with clarity about the ways in which the literacies of Black immigrant youth can be (re)envisioned while also attending to key factors such as race.

LANGUAGING AND ENGLISHES OF BLACK IMMIGRANTS: A SELECTIVE REVIEW

The languaging of Black immigrants in the United States has a brief but substantive history. As far back as 1961, following *Brown v. Board of Education* (1954), which seemingly functioned as a precursor to educational equity for African Americans, research has been undertaken to explore the languaging of Negroes and whites. For instance, according to Barth (1961), who examined language use by Blacks in comparison to whites, "social experiences through which words take on meanings for these Negroes [are] differentiated from those experienced by whites," and "words associated with these settings [have] systematically different meanings for members of the two racial categories" (p. 69). At the same moment in the history of America, emerging analyses of white versus Black language use revealed semiotic uses involving languaging by Blacks such as "cut[ting] their eyes" and "suck[ing] their teeth" that were not reflected by whites. Researchers showed then how whites were often ignorant of the meanings of gestures such as these, especially when Blacks directed them to whites. Researchers explored how gestures, when used by people racialized as Black—an element I have referred to as raciosemiotic architecture (P. Smith, 2022e)—represented African "survivals." They also considered how these gestures were visible across the Caribbean, the United States, and Africa (Rickford & Rickford, 2015).

This research has had implications for Black immigrants who were subsumed, then as they are now, within the overall Black population. As often observed, *Brown v. Board of Education* did not, however, yield true equity (Baugh & Welborn, 2008). During the decades that followed *Brown v. Board of Education* and to this day, African American students (and it can be extrapolated, Black immigrant as well) were disparaged, suspended, diagnosed as learning disabled, and placed in speech pathology remediation labs because of "talking while Black" (Wheeler, 2008, p. 176). Instances in 1979 such as the "Black English case," *Martin Luther King Junior Elementary School Children v. Ann Arbor School District Board*, led to rulings such as those by Judge Joiner ordering the school to "take appropriate action to overcome linguistic barriers" faced by multilingual students (described then as vernacular-speaking) in mainstream classrooms (Labov, 1995, p. 46).

In response, among the scholars whose research informed the early focus on the languaging of the Black immigrant population in the United States is Dr. Shondel Nero. In her seminal work, "The Changing Faces of English: A Caribbean Perspective" (2000), published more than 2 decades ago and drawing attention to the linguistic needs of Afro-Caribbean students in the United States, Nero described how globalization of Englishes, when considered by individuals of Caribbean heritage, raised concerns about the native/nonnative speaker dichotomy. In turn, she showed how this dynamic served as a basis for inviting teachers in the United States to expand how bidialectalism was addressed in classrooms relative to Caribbean Creole English (CCE).

Nero's focus on CCE emerged at approximately the same time that Caribbean educators and scholars were continuing to work toward consensus around the shared goals and visions for Creole linguistics in the region. During this period, ministers of education within the Caribbean Community (CARICOM) advanced a position paper based on the 1993 CARICOM Ministers of Education and Culture Standing Committee in Barbuda. Through this paper, CARICOM illustrated a vision to cultivate pride in students' home language and build competence in what was regarded then, as it is now, the official language of school, "Standard English" (B. Bryan, 1997).

The simultaneous focus on language of Caribbean populations beyond the United States, primarily *sans* race as well as in the racialized context of the United States where a Black–White binary prevailed, led to calls for sociolinguists (Myhill, 1988; Rickford, 1985; Wolfram, 1971) to address Black linguistic heterogeneity in the United States in ways that reflected the nuances presented by Black immigrants. Having focused extensively on the linguistic diversity of populations racialized as Black (i.e., often African Americans), these calls increasingly invited sociolinguists to address the heterogeneity and complexity of language use across Black populations and across generations (i.e., first-generation Black immigrants, second-generation Black immigrants) in ways that reflected Black immigrant Caribbean and other Englishes (Blake & Shousterman, 2010; Bryce-Laporte, 1972). Alongside these calls have been invitations to preserve the tribal languages of indigenous students, many of whom belong to American Indian, Alaska Native, and Native Hawaiian communities and are often themselves "mixed-race" due to their entanglements with the African American community (Aguilera & Lecompte, 2008).

Since then, the continued acknowledged complexity of Black English (i.e., Plantation Creole)—or *Black Englishes*, to be more precise—has allowed for analyses illustrating the similarities among American and Caribbean/West Indian Englishes (e.g., African American English; Jamaican Englishes; Surinamese Englishes; Cameroonian and Nigerian Pidgin Englishes; Papiamentu—Afro-Iberian/Afro-Portuguese languages of

Aruba, Bonaire, and Curaçao; West African languages, West African Portuguese Pidgin, Taki-Taki [or Sranan Tongo] and the Saramaccan of Surinam; Black Dutch of the Virgin Islands; and Sierra Leone's Krio) (Birmingham, 2015; J. L. Dillard, 1972; Rickford & Rickford, 2015; Scott et al., 2008). More recent research also indicates how the language use of populations such as the Afro-Seminole corresponds largely to the Gullah speakers of the Georgia and South Carolina coast and the Sea Islands and to language use in Hughes, Seminole, Okfuskee, and Okmulgee Counties of Oklahoma, as well as potentially in Florida and the Bahamas (Hancock, 2015). Further, there is continued evidence presented of the lineage of Atlantic Creoles in relation to languages native to West Africa (Holm, 2015) and examinations that show significant divergence in what authors refer to as Negro Nonstandard English (R. Smith, 1980; 2015).

Global Englishes

Global Englishes, a concept representing the fluid nature of Englishes and extending beyond the nation-based approaches of World Englishes, increasingly explains variations in Englishes and their use across nation states (Kachru, 1992; Rose & Galloway, 2019). Across the globe, this concept functions as a way to describe the linguistic practices of youth who leverage numerous representations of English across their linguistic repertoires (García & Wei, 2015; Rose & Galloway, 2019). For Black immigrant youth in the United States, who often come from the Caribbean and from Africa, linguistic orientations such as "Caribbean Englishes," "French Creole," "West African Pidgin Englishes," and "Black South African Englishes" have helped to clarify the language differences that Black youth leverage when they migrate to the United States (see P. Smith, 2016, 2017).

Caribbean Englishes

Caribbean Englishes (CEs), also known as dialects of English, have functioned as part of the World Englishes model and operate along an English/Creole continuum. They sometimes are referred to by natives of the Caribbean as "English" and by others as Caribbean English Creole (Carrington, 1992; Pollard, 1993). World Englishes is based on the idea that three concentric circles, "inner," "outer," and "expanding," explain the ways in which Englishes are used across the globe. The inner circle of Englishes involves those Englishes that are spoken predominantly in Anglo-Saxon countries such as the United States, Australia, and Canada; the outer circle describes Englishes often seen in countries colonized by Britain such as Bangladesh, India, and those in the Caribbean; and the expanding circle represents Englishes learned as a foreign language in countries such as China, Indonesia, and Nepal. In this "three-circle" model, Englishes are said to be based on national identity. The World Englishes model has been extended recently to consider the notion of "cross-circle Englishes," which considers how users of Englishes interact beyond geographical borders and national identity, as well as how this process occurs for individuals of color (Canagarajah & Said, 2011; Kachru, 1992; P. Smith, 2020a; Smith et al., 2018).

As part of the World Englishes model, Caribbean Englishes function as outer circle Englishes and may be standardized (e.g., Bahamian Standardized English) or nonstandardized (e.g., Trinidadian English Creole). Standardized CEs, defined as the closest to standardized Englishes (i.e., similar to standardized American Englishes), often are referred to as the King's English, or simply as English. Nonstandardized CEs, on the other hand, commonly referred to as dialects of English, are denoted as Creoles, or Patois, but also sometimes as English or the King's English, particularly when used in comparison to dialects based on languages other than English (e.g., French Creole). Caribbean multilingual teachers of previously migrated Black Caribbean immigrant youth typically are speakers of both standardized and nonstandardized CEs and sometimes engage in self-marginalization by privileging standardized over nonstandardized Englishes (Carrington, 1992; Milson-Whyte, 2014).

Caribbean Englishes are particularly visible in the English-speaking Caribbean where Standard English functions as a dominant and official language despite countries' bidialectal, bilingual, and multilingual nature. In this region, Caribbean nationals speak many nonstandardized Englishes, including 35 Creoles and 15 indigenous languages (Simmons-McDonald, 2006; Voice, 2011). Students possess predominantly nonstandardized English linguistic backgrounds (Warrican, 2009; Winer, 2006), and English-related Creoles and vernaculars have been said to interfere with their literacy performance (Bogle, 1997; Craig, 1999; Miller, 1989).

The challenges encountered by Caribbean youth arise in a context where Caribbean English speakers often self-identify as Standard English speakers and lay claim to the [standard] language despite using *non-Standard English* varieties (Warrican, 2009; Warrican et al., 2019). CE speakers thus move back and forth between denigrating and celebrating their non-Standard English varieties (i.e., "attitudinal schizophrenia"), a process involving linguistic practices that have been described as code-switching, code-meshing, and more recently, translanguaging (see García & Kleyn, 2016; Kachru & Nelson, 2001; Young & Barrett, 2018). As they do so, CE speakers' Standard English ideology allows them to be intentional about using Standard English in formal settings because it promises upward mobility and social status (Nero, 2006; Winer, 2006). However, they also adhere to local non-Standard English varieties in informal contexts as symbols of national identity (P. Smith, Cheema, et al., 2018; P. Smith et al., 2022; St. Hilaire, 2011).

Often absent from such discussions, nonetheless, is an attention to racialization and how it functions as encoded within the structures and systems of the Caribbean curriculum and across the West Indian society, writ large. In fact, as Davies (2013) observes, there has been a longstanding tendency to disregard the existence of racism in the Caribbean despite its presence as an international phenomenon. This phenomenon, she shows, functions structurally and socioeconomically as a system that is presented in varied ways based on historical and cultural instantiations that are related to place. Similarly, Windle and Muniz (2018) observe how issues of race are silenced in Brazilian public education through prevailing discourses that tend to reflect racial democracy and mixing, but appear to overlook the politicization of Afro-Brazilian identity (see also Anya, 2016).

Even so, scholars such as Williams (2016) point to Caribbean populations' emerging use of postcolonial literatures as a basis for self-consciousness; for awareness of "psychological dispossession," "colonial exploitation," and "cultural fragmentation"; and for critiquing the inheritances of colonial rule. And others, such as Bristol (2012), have highlighted, through colonial critique, the ways in which educational practices have been extended from an era of colonial rule to the current day, requiring a continued "emancipation from slavery" (p. 47).

Notwithstanding, there remains a marked tendency, made visible through studies such as those examining colonial-era curricula like the *Royal Readers* textbooks in Grenada, West Indies, to overlook racialization, in particular, and its intersection with languaging (Joseph, 2012). There is also an inadvertent and corresponding preservation of colonial legacies through such lack of attention to race in the Caribbean context. For instance, Joseph (2012) shows, through a careful analysis of three stories presented in the fourth volume of the *Royal Readers*, how a number of implicit and often "unrecognizable" elements of "ideological whiteness," included in the textbooks by the colonial authorities, fostered subjugation and sustained a hold on their imperial power. It remains unclear whether mechanisms such as racial equity audits are conducted in the selection and approval of Caribbean textbooks and curricular materials for use in schools.

West African Pidgin Englishes

West African Pidgin English (WAPE) is used to refer to the Englishes used by West African speakers who form part of the primary population that migrates from Africa to the United States. Examinations of the grammar of WAPE students in the United States have indicated that a majority of students were designated as limited English proficient and categorized as ESL learners. The West African students examined were portrayed as lacking the English language skills required in classrooms. English grammar appeared to present a challenge to students and often led to their LEP and ESL designations, while organizational structure, punctuation, and spelling proved difficult, primarily to students placed in low-level ESL courses. Indications that very few of the students experienced interrupted formal education suggest that, for WAPE-speaking students, their WAPE language background serves as a critical factor that further compounds their social and cultural adjustment challenges. The confirmation that many students in the study had received ESL instruction for years without transitioning to a higher level is an indication that this instructional context was ineffective (de Kleine, 2006).

Advances in researching African English in recent years have led to calls for translingualism to be considered by teachers who work with immigrant students in schools and in the broader U.S. society. For instance, scholars have drawn from World Englishes and from the 1974 resolutions of the Conference on College Composition and Communication, as well as the 1996 Universal Declaration of Linguistic Rights, which invited students to be empowered through owning their languages. Specifically, Kigamwa and Ndemanu (2017) call for attention to the "historical and sociolinguistic realities of African immigrants' English speech and how these realities impact African immigrant acculturation in their host country" (p. 468). These innovations have been touted as key to addressing Black immigrant youth's continued "struggles with cultural and linguistic differences, stereotypes and marginalization in the school environment, low expectations from teachers, and adjusting to new schooling practices" (Kiramba et al., 2020, pp. 83–84).

Black Immigrant Englishes, Entanglements

Based on historical notions of the use of these Englishes, Black immigrant youth were thought to use variations of standardized versions of Englishes depending on their contexts. We now know, given evolving notions that demonstrate how translanguaging occurs with Englishes, that each Black immigrant youth brings their unique linguistic repertoire, via translanguaging—their very own way of using all the languaging they possess—to the classroom (P. Smith, 2020a). We know also that speakers of "English-based Creoles" and Creoles with "Standard English varieties" often reflect a shift that occurs in both directions as individuals use Creoles and standard varieties along the Creole continuum (Clachar, 2005).

We have come to understand, too, more recently, the ways in which race, language, and immigration intersect while Black immigrant youth are using these Englishes to evolve with their personhoods, as legitimate literate beings (García & Wei, 2014; Nero, 2014; P. Smith, 2020b, 2022a). These understandings, which have invited us to consider the ways that racialization, languaging, and migration together influence the Englishes of Black immigrant youth, have been critical to reenvisioning the assets they possess. They also have been crucial to seeing Black youth's relationship with Englishes not as one where they manipulate language as an element that is external to them, but in ways that show how the languaging of their Englishes is as much a part of them as the hair that we can see on their heads.

As I observed in my recent talk based on entanglements as informed by transdisciplinarity and steeped in quantum physics, "(Dis)Entanglements of Racialized Englishes and Peoples Across 'Black' and 'White' Worlds," and in my presentation at the Literacy Research Association Conference titled "Towards a Methodological Shift for Examining Racialized Entanglements: Interrupting Raciolinguistic Erasure for Transraciolinguistic Justice," youth racialized as Black remain entangled with the Englishes that they manipulate as part of their unique linguistic repertoires (P. Smith, 2022c, 2022d). These entanglements emerge in unique ways between Englishes and racialized migrants in much the same way that they occur in unique yet similar ways between Englishes and racialized Caribbean nationals (see Pennycook, 2021, for a discussion of entanglements of English).

I have shown that the entanglements constantly are being redefined in dynamic spaces between Englishes and racialized Black bodies based on institutional and local norms of schools and organizations within and across global contexts. What this means for Black immigrant youth is that their Englishes are not separate from who they are, or vice versa. My previous research about Jaeda, a Black immigrant youth operating in the United States, confirms that the rejection she faced in response to her languaging, as well as the type of Blackness she portrayed, meant that she felt rejected as a person too (P. Smith, 2022b). In other words, in line with the notion of personhood described by Rosa and Flores (2017) from "a raciolinguistic perspective," it is not possible to reject the Englishes of Black immigrant youth without rejecting their Black personhoods, as a youth's personhood is intimately entangled with the Englishes they use.

This entanglement of the self with language and its potential effects increasingly is observed in the field of health. In the case of Black immigrants, it exacerbates the risk for challenges with health and mental well-being based on intersectionally leveraged discrimination against their language, culture, and ethnicity (Alegría et al., 2017). Such challenges continue to present themselves among Black immigrant populations, given the emphasis placed on using their Englishes for certain types of *success* in literacy—what we often refer to as "academic success." Specifically, as I have shown, Black immigrant students

> seemingly escape the label of "underperformer" (ascribed to their African American and to certain immigrant peers) but at the same time they are subjected to raciolinguistic and monoglossic ideologies based on institutional norms that delegitimize their personhood, linguistic repertoires, and literacies, creating potential challenges for their well-being. (P. Smith et al., 2022)

It is becoming increasingly clear that the embodiment processes that allow for entanglements of Black immigrant youth and their Englishes (as well as other semiotic resources that they manipulate) are even more critically important for teachers to address in schools because they impact the health, affect, and well-being of Black (immigrant) youth. There is a need to understand that when teachers manipulate a child's Englishes, they are, in fact, manipulating the child, and vice versa. Social isolation and health disparities associated with COVID-19 and the recent unrest accompanying the racialization of Black people across the globe make it even more important for teachers to engage with these understandings about how such entanglements unfold in literacy and ELA classrooms.

Creating a foundation for acknowledging entanglements of Black immigrant youth and their Englishes, the Black immigrant literacies framework allows for these youth to develop their literacies in relation to their local contexts within the country of destination (i.e., the United States), their global contexts (i.e., the countries from which they originate), and their abilities as language architects who leverage a wide range of literacies (i.e., holistic literacies) that extend beyond mere academic literacy success.

It is often impossible, though, for many youth to acknowledge, as well as use, their literacies intentionally in agentive ways if they are largely unaware of them and of how their racialization, migration, and languaging are intersecting. It also can be a challenge for them to use these literacies in relation to themselves and to others (e.g., Black, Latinx, white) in a new land without support from teachers to guide them. Schools, teachers, organizations, communities, and the broader society thus have a unique opportunity, through the Black immigrant literacies framework, to support Black immigrant youth grappling with these complex entanglements that link them to Englishes in unique ways in and beyond U.S. schools. Through this framework, they are positioned to pursue the use of the "authenticated knowledge[s]" that draw directly from youth's lives (see Willis, 2022b, para. 3).

PEER INTERACTIONS IN THE BLACK
IMMIGRANT EXPERIENCE

Much has been written about comparative experiences of Black immigrant popula-tions in relation to their immigrant and nonimmigrant peers. There is less scholarship about designed initiatives that foster interactions among these individuals with a focus on building solidarity and much more descriptive indicators of how Black subpopula-tions engage differentially across the racial, linguistic, generational, and cultural spec-trums. In the emerging research that focuses on addressing the tensions existing among Black immigrants and their African American peers, it has been shown that there are opportunities for building relationships among these populations and for engendering interpersonal connections.

One such study examining 75 individuals who have led such initiatives, as well as a corresponding review of approximately 50 pedagogical resources developed and used by these individuals, reflects successes and also limitations. The successes are identified as the resulting spaces for interacting as subpopulations address their differences and oper-ate based on analyses that brought about their shared understandings. Successes also have been noted in the form of transformation intrapersonally, as well as interpersonally. Key limitations identified by scholars include "immigrant-centricity in relationship-building efforts and a reluctance to engage immigrants in conversation about their relationships to whiteness, Blackness, and racial hierarchies in the United States and in their countries of origin" (Stuesse et al., 2017, p. 245). The use of an "anti-racist, African Americanist framework" reflected in Steinberg's (2005) "standpoint of [the] black figure, crouched on the ground as others pluck fruit off the tree of opportunity" (p. 43) suggests that Black immigrants may be enjoying the opportunities created by African Americans. The indi-cation that identifying as immigrant in relationships creates challenges for interpersonal conversations, and that engaging in discussions about Black immigrants' proximity to whiteness proved to be difficult, confirms indications that interactions remain strained across Black immigrant and Black American populations.

Other studies focusing on the use of "ethnicity" and "culture" by Black immigrants as opposed to "race" have pointed to the ways in which this preference tends to reinforce the imposed notions of cultural inferiority often attached to Black Americans in the United States. Scholars such as Pierre (2004) observe that the use of "ethnic" uniqueness often espoused by Black immigrants allows for a situation where race is made irrelevant, while at the same time it positions biologically influenced notions of race as "culture." Pierre asserts that distinguishing Black immigrants from their African American peers in this manner perpetuates "cultural racism" and thus rejects "ethnicity theory" or dis-tinctive Blackness of immigrants that does not sufficiently attend to power relations and to subjugation based on race.

Such calls that invite attention to racialization, even while Black immigrant youth's cultural backgrounds are made visible, seem applicable to recent recommendations made by Daoud et al. (2018). They suggest a disaggregation by ethnicity in studies of Black col-legians to gain a clearer understanding of how diversity of their backgrounds influences their academic motivation. The authors made these suggestions while examining the social identity, academic identity, and college-going aspirations of Black immigrant and Black American students.

REENVISIONING THE LITERACIES OF
BLACK IMMIGRANT YOUTH

Black immigrant youth tend to have their academic literacies emphasized in schools while their invisible literacies are overlooked. This approach to their literacies obscures how they effectively use their entire literate repertoire across home and school contexts to meet varying demands of these contexts. There is a need to transition from the dichotomy of academic literacy versus invisible literacy to a view of holistic literacies of Black immigrant youth. This view of holistic literacies centers literacy as inclusive of practices not often valued in classrooms and by schools (P. Smith et al., 2022; Street, 1995). Yet the reliance on holistic literacies by Afro-Caribbean, English-speaking people is in fact consistent with the literary traditions of Caribbean nationals such as Jamaican American writer Claude McKay and St. Lucian Nobel Laureate Sir Derek Alton Walcott, both of whom, in and beyond their home countries, emphasized the productive aesthetics of songs, poems, plays, films, or novels as a theme of the Caribbean experience (Davies, 2013).

Contrary to holistic literacies as the norm, many ideas about literacy tend to focus on separating literacy capacity so that it is either-or (P. Smith, 2023b). This is the case, for instance, with the notion of "academic literacy," which for decades has operated as distinctly different from "invisible literacy." Academic literacy tends to refer to "the ability to communicate competently in an academic discourse community," to read, evaluate information, present, debate, and create knowledge "through both speaking and writing" (Wingate, 2018, p. 350). Through this process, literacies are emphasized that involve "engaging with, producing, and talking about texts that have currency in primary, secondary, and postsecondary education" (Morrell, 2002, p. 72). Despite being characterized as "never anyone's mother tongue, even for the privileged classes," academic literacy functions as an expectation for every student in specific academic discourse communities (Wingate, 2015, p. 11). Such communities in the United States, many of which function based on monoglossic ideology, tend to privilege what is known as academic language—specialized "content-specific vocabulary and complex sentence structures" (Flores, 2020, p. 23; see also Flores, 2013).

In addition, academic discourse communities often privilege just one language—English—and also have been shown to prefer just *one* form of standardized English in the United States—Standard American English (i.e., white [American] mainstream English; see Baker-Bell, 2020). In doing so, often they inadvertently exclude other standardized English linguistic repertoires (e.g., Jamaican Standardized English, Trinidadian Standardized English). These practices hold strong because monoglossic ideologies that value one language and that undergird academic literacy teaching go against a heteroglossic perspective. This perspective allows students the linguistic flexibility to easily manipulate English dialects—both standardized and nonstandardized—as well as their other home languages (e.g., García, 2009; P. Smith, 2016, 2020d; Wiley, 2014).

In contrast to academic literacy, *invisible literacy* typically is considered to mean the informal and functional knowledge and skills put into practice across home and school contexts. Invisible literacy practices allow students to draw from their home languages and dialects in ways that emphasize a heteroglossic norm, using language for literate practices with which they are familiar in the home or beyond classrooms, and that tend to be disregarded in schools. Since students' home languages are thought to predict their academic success and literacy learning in schools, attending to invisible literacy practices based on their language use beyond schools has been described as crucial. Even more important has been the creation of spaces within schools where invisible literacies of students are identified, used, and extended (Dyson, 2003; Kiramba, 2017).

Although invisible literacy practices are perceived as critical to students' academic literacy development, limited opportunities are available for youth to draw from their invisible literacies in schools (Dyson, 2003). In addition, students often fail to receive sufficient academic literacy support because of the faulty view that their home languages draw from "non-academic language," which, in comparison to academic language, is viewed as "less specialized and less complex" (Flores, 2020, p. 23; see also Flores, 2013; Kiramba, 2017). Because monoglossic ideology continues to be more popular than a heteroglossic norm, school-valued literacy continues to be preferred in academic discourse communities, posing an increasing challenge to the literacy success of students from a range of diverse populations (P. Smith, 2019; Wiley, 2014). Youth whose academic literacy success tends to be preferred over their entire literate repertoires, are further discouraged from leveraging their *funds of knowledge* in literacy classrooms (Moll et al., 2005; Razfar, 2012). Many such youth are "dialect" speakers (Nero, 2014); English learners and bilingual learners (Brooks, 2015, 2018; Kiramba, 2017); international, transnational, or immigrant students (De Costa, 2014; Jiménez et al., 2009; Rubinstein-Ávila, 2007; Skerrett, 2012; Watson et al., 2014); or students of color (P. Smith, 2019). Thus, they find themselves challenged by the monoglossic standardized English norms of academic literacy in schools despite possessing versatility with language that a heteroglossic norm provides (Darvin & Norton, 2014; García, 2009; P. Smith, 2022b).

For Black immigrants who have been described as a new model minority (Ukpokodu, 2018), these tensions are even more visible. As demonstrated earlier in this chapter, the languaging and Englishes of Black immigrant youth vary greatly. It is clear that what we often describe as their academic language and literacy practices seem to matter, but their invisible literacies and home languages often are overlooked. This happens because the standardized literacy assessments that help to portray Black immigrants as a model minority draw from academic language and literacy practices that reflect monoglossic language norms privileged by schools (i.e., one language, Standard English). For instance, African immigrant students' Black and African identities can "simultaneously act as a source of privilege and struggle, socially and academically" in schools, and while "African students are perceived as model minorities by teachers, counselors, and peers," some of them reflect grade point averages that often do not match this perception (Agyepong, 2019, pp. i–ii).

If we rethink how Black immigrants use language and view them as "raciosemiotic architects" and as "language architects," we can reenvision them as individuals who "manipulate language" and semiotics "for specific purposes" (Flores, 2020, p. 25). We also can be cognizant of how they do this in the face of racialization while capitalizing on language practices with which they are most familiar and disrupting the idea that their academic literacy is more valuable that their invisible literacy practices (Canagarajah, 2006; Flores, 2020).

In other words, such a perspective repositions Black immigrant youth's academic literacy success as their learned ability to use language "architecturing" already deployed in the home (i.e., invisible literacy) in ways that allow them to navigate (un)familiar expectations of school (i.e., academic literacy). From this vantage point, the focus is not to define Black immigrant youth based primarily on certain elements of their linguistic repertoires (i.e., what the field has described as their academic literacies) while overlooking other significant components (i.e., previously referred to as invisible literacies). Rather, it is possible to consider how these youth effectively leverage their holistic literate repertoires across home and school contexts in ways that meet demands across these contexts (Flores, 2020; P. Smith et al., 2022; Watson & Marciano, 2015).

Reenvisioning literacies in this way as a basis for exploring and addressing Black immigrant literacies is consistent with the notion of multiliteracies, which shows how "metalanguages [are used] to describe and interpret the design elements of different modes of meaning" (New London Group, 1996, p. 83). The approach allows for equally emphasizing all modes of meaning-making—tactile, gestural, spatial, visual, written, audio, linguistic, and synesthesia—that Black immigrant youth use to negotiate a range of discourses as they integrate "a variety of texts forms associated with information and multimedia technologies" (New London Group, 1996, p. 61; see also Kalantzis & Cope, 2012). Transcending the dichotomy present in an "invisible–academic literacies" dynamic for Black immigrant youth through multiliteracies allows for a holistic view of *all* student literacy practice. It also facilitates an understanding of how they draw simultaneously from linguistic and semiotic resources to make meaning through their often raciolinguicized literacies—"raciosemiotic architecture" (P. Smith, 2022) and to legitimize the self.

Bridging the gap between academic and invisible literacies by using the framework for Black immigrant literacies is important because youth can then be seen as having the capacity to make decisions about language use as part of their literacy repertoires based on the context in which they operate. Bridging this gap also enables teachers to rethink students' supposed unfamiliarity and/or incapacity with the norms surrounding meaning-making with what we often describe as "school texts." Teachers can then see literacy teaching as facilitating students who bring their "already-present literacies" (Watson & Marciano, 2015, p. 39) to classroom and school contexts. Considering Black immigrant youth as language architects frames students as "already understanding the relationship between language choice and meaning through the knowledge that they have gained via socialization into the cultural and linguistic practices of their communities" (Flores, 2020, p. 25).

A consolidated view of literacy that transcends the dichotomy between academic and invisible literacy provides an avenue for holistically considering the literacy practices of Black immigrant youth and presents educators with an avenue for addressing the literacies of all youth. In adopting such an approach to literacy, I invite those who interact with Black immigrants to better understand how to address their literacy needs while also helping to bridge gaps between these youth and their Black American and other peers (see P. Smith, 2016, 2017; P. Smith, Cheema, et al., 2018; Thornton et al., 2013).

SUMMARY

Careful to avoid pitting one group of Black youth against the other through dichotomous intraracial ideologies that create negative ways of thinking about one's racialized counterparts—Black, White, or otherwise—this chapter challenges the idea of Black immigrant youth as a new model minority. Subsequently, the chapter justifies the need for providing teachers and educators with guidelines for addressing the literacies of this largely invisible population. The chapter has shown how Blackness, immigration, and Englishes intersect in ways that challenge educators to think strategically about the literacy instruction and lives of Black immigrants as well as all youth. Highlighting the ways in which their Englishes function as well as the tensions that often persist in describing the literacy performance of this population, I invite teachers and educators to use the framework for Black immigrant literacies to move toward approaches to literacy teaching based on holistic understandings of literacy that center on, and are not oblivious to, race, even while extending beyond it.

QUESTIONS TO CONSIDER

1. How does the vast landscape of social media—TikTok, YouTube, Instagram, Facebook—illustrate distinctions among languaging based on race used by African American, African, Afro-Caribbean, and Afro-Latin American immigrant students?
2. What does social media reveal about the distinctions presented?
3. How do these distinctions help to better clarify the literacies within and across the Black populations in and beyond the United States?
4. What changes can be made to how literacy and English language arts curriculum is presented to K–12 students based on understandings of these distinctions?
5. What changes can be made to teacher preparation programs and coursework that include attention to distinctions in preparing teachers for addressing the myriad forms of diversity within the Black population?
6. What changes can be made to how institutions address well-being for all K–12 students based on understandings of shared experiences of Black immigrants?

CHAPTER 3

The Framework for Black Immigrant Literacies

Black immigrant youth's literacies often are considered in relation to the linguistic challenges faced. As indicated earlier, race is less central to this focus on language. So is migration in relation to racialized language. It is becoming increasingly important to use intersectionality (Crenshaw, 1991) to identify raciolinguistic ideologies in addressing linguicism that undergirds the languages (e.g., Englishes) of Black youth upon migration. These ideologies suggest that race influences language and language influences race, causing certain racialized speakers to be regarded as inferior when they use language (Rosa & Flores, 2017). In turn, there are novel opportunities to better understand the role of these ideologies for informing how schools support the literacies of all racialized immigrant populations (Alim, 2016).

As indicated earlier, one such opportunity is captured in the framework for Black immigrant literacies. In this chapter, I describe the elements of this framework and show how diaspora, transnational, and racial literacies have been integrated to serve as a basis for clarifying the framework. Together, these three lenses—diaspora, transnational, and racial literacies—form a foundation for demonstrating how teachers in classrooms can leverage the literacies of Black immigrant youth as assets in schools. The lens of *diaspora literacy*, often used to examine the literacies of Black American youth; the framework of *racial literacy*, often used for both white and Black American populations; and the notion of *transnational literacies*, typically used to understand the literacies of youth who cross geographical and virtual borders, all provide a basis from which to better understand Black immigrant literacies. Understanding how these lenses operate together is useful for identifying how they are presented in subsequent chapters to clarify the complex ways in which Black immigrant literacies function. But first, it is important to understand each element of the framework.

ELEMENTS OF THE BLACK IMMIGRANT LITERACIES FRAMEWORK

The Black immigrant literacies framework, which I proposed elsewhere (P. Smith, 2020d), allows researchers and practitioners to centralize race by considering the following when instructing Black immigrant youth and the populations within which they are subsumed (see Figure 3.1). The framework consists of five elements:

Figure 3.1. Framework for Black Immigrant Literacies

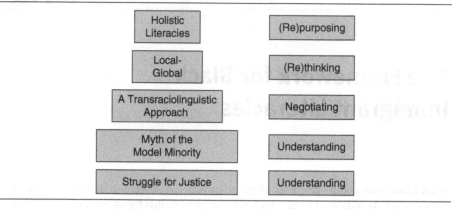

1. Claim to the struggle for justice;
2. Myth of the model minority;
3. A transraciolinguistic approach;
4. Local–global;
5. Holistic literacies.

Claim to the Struggle for Justice

The first component of the framework, *laying claim to the struggle for justice*, allows for emerging understanding through intentional and adept communication between Black immigrant and Black Americans about the distinctive historical experiences surrounding slavery that they have endured in what has evolved into a white supremacist context that inadvertently frames their ability to lay claim to the struggle for justice. This process requires Black students from American and immigrant populations to engage in literate practices that explore and extend their understandings of what it means to all be racialized as a result of and despite the differences in their histories. The process uses literacy to engender a sense of understanding about the ways in which Black American and Black Caribbean populations operate as descendants of slaves, many of whom were separated at the Caribbean border upon being brought to a new land. It creates, via multiliteracies, a solidarity across African, Black American, and Black immigrant populations by facilitating an understanding and hope for shared justice based on the history of colonization faced by Black peoples across the diaspora. In doing so, it allows all Black youth to leverage literacies with and as advocates for one another in ways that reflect their shared understandings of how they are all positioned to lay claim to the struggle for justice.

Myth of the Model Minority

The second component of the framework, *addressing the myth of the model minority*, facilitates critical understanding of the ways in which a meritocratic model minority myth, as applied to Black immigrant youth, is steeped in divide-and-conquer racial politics. This politics sustains interracial divisions between Black immigrant youth and their Black American peers and other minoritized immigrant populations. Disrupting the model minority myth requires Black students from American and immigrant populations to engage in literate practices that explore and extend their understandings of what it means to have certain groups of Black youth be designated as superior and others designated as inferior. It uses literacy to engender a sense of understanding about the ways in which Black American populations have been made to seem inferior to Black Caribbean and Black African populations only because these immigrants seem to function in ways that are accepted by the dominant population in the United States.

Addressing the myth of the model minority creates, via multiliteracies, a solidarity across African, Black American, and Black immigrant populations by facilitating an understanding that there is no better Black group and that any efforts to applaud certain Black immigrants in ways that denigrate their Black American counterparts also is designed to present all Black peoples as inferior. In doing so, this element of the Black immigrant literacies framework allows all Black youth to leverage literacies with and as advocates for one another in ways that reflect their shared understandings of how rejecting the model minority myth positions African Americans as legitimate in their own right.

A Transraciolinguistic Approach

The third component of the framework, *a transraciolinguistic approach*, which I have proposed elsewhere (P. Smith, 2022b), creates opportunities for youth, teachers, and parents to discuss and leverage an approach based on "transraciolinguistics," referring to that which exists simultaneously between, across, and beyond various representations of raciolinguistics. Transraciolinguistics was informed in part by "raciolinguistics," which suggests that race and language work together such that race influences the construction of ideas about language and language influences the construction of ideas about race (Alim, 2016; P. Smith, 2019). It was also informed by "a raciolinguistic perspective," which calls for a focus on both the individual and the global in addressing how race and language are intertwined (Rosa & Flores, 2017). A transraciolinguistic approach uses "an intersectional and critical lens to center race by supporting racial, linguistic, and cultural assets presented by immigrant and transnational students of color in classrooms" (P. Smith, 2022b, p. 545; see also P. Smith, 2019, 2020b, 2022a).

I have described a transraciolinguistic approach as using "metalinguistic, metaracial, and metacultural understanding of past experiences with race and language, and by extension, culture, to determine how to function effectively within non/academic settings in ways that do not completely sacrifice" their personhoods (P. Smith, 2019, pp. 299300). In transraciolinguistics, students simultaneously engage in thinking about their thinking about race (i.e., *metaracial*), thinking about their thinking about culture (i.e., *metacultural*), and thinking about their thinking about language (i.e., *metalinguistic*) across their interrelationships with diverse others. This approach as part of Black immigrant literacies can be leveraged through opportunities presented for developing metalinguistic, metacultural, and metaracial understanding (i.e., meta-understandings) as youth keep learning and acknowledging their "not knowing" about race through an iterative diagnostic and feedback loop (Guinier, 2004; P. Smith, 2020d).

For instance, a transraciolinguistic approach was reflected in the meta-understandings leveraged by a Black Afro-Caribbean immigrant, Jaeda, that led to flexibility on her part as she used language across multiple contexts. This approach was also visible in the meta-understandings reflected by this youth that led to duality with language while retaining her personhood. I have asserted that a transraciolinguistic approach allows Black youth to make sense of racialized experiences with language via metalinguistic, metacultural, and metaracial understanding through agency in literacy practice. An overview of a transraciolinguistic approach is presented in Figure 3.2 and in the VoicEd Radio podcast episode from the *Shifting Linguistic Landscapes* conference titled "A Transraciolinguistic Approach for Literacy Classrooms featuring Dr. Patriann Smith" (VoicEd Radio 2021).

Figure 3.2, which illustrates a transraciolinguistic approach, presents images of two individuals on the left and an image of one individual on the right. The two individuals on the left represent racialized students who use metalinguistic, metaracial, and metacultural understanding to navigate literate practices in their interactions with others. Similarly, the individual on the right represents a nonracialized student, who also is able to adopt and leverage such understandings with racialized students. The permeable equilateral triangle aptly denotes the transraciolinguistic space where students simultaneously use these three forms of understanding (i.e., metalinguistic, metaracial, metacultural) in interaction with one another. The broad permeable circle within which the triangle is located acknowledges that other forms of understanding (e.g., *metagendered, metareligious*) exist that influence how racialized and nonracialized students together make meaning through their many interactions with text and with the world.

Figure 3.2. A Transraciolinguistic Approach

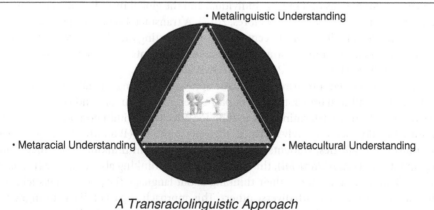

• Metalinguistic Understanding

• Metaracial Understanding   • Metacultural Understanding

A Transraciolinguistic Approach

Local–Global

The fourth component of the Black immigrant literacies framework instantiates a rethinking of the *global* through lived experience with the *local*. This is done by supporting a recognition of the duality and hybridity in how racialization is implicitly embedded in the "postcolonial" structures of youth's home countries as they encounter its explicit enactment through hegemonic whiteness and individual racialized encounters within the United States. This process requires Black students from American and immigrant populations to engage in literate practices that explore and extend their understandings of what it means to perceive a presence of race in the United States and its supposed absence in the home countries of Black immigrant youth. It uses literacy to engender a sense of understanding about the ways in which Black American populations have had to grapple with many explicit indicators of racialization in a world of predominant whiteness. This is often different from the experiences of their Black immigrant counterparts who seemingly have overlooked engagement with race because of how it often is encoded in the legislative, curricular, and other frameworks under which their home countries operate (see Warrican & Smith, in press).

This element creates, via multiliteracies, a solidarity across African, Black American, and Black immigrant populations by facilitating an understanding that racialization of Black bodies is present beyond the U.S. context. It also makes this racialization visible to all youth, particularly as it operates in varying degrees of silence in spaces such as Africa and the Caribbean. In doing so, connecting the local to the global allows all Black youth to leverage literacies with and as advocates for one another in ways that reflect their shared understandings of how their bodies, their languages, and their literacies are racialized by societies and systems in varied ways depending on context.

Holistic Literacies

The fifth component of the framework, *holistic literacies*, re(purposes) literacies as holistic (as opposed to fragmented based on a privileging of literacy performance on tests). In this way, youth use language, multiliteracies, and cross-border shifts to function as language and raciosemiotic architects who reread and rewrite text (including Englishes and semiotic resources in their lifeworlds) across home and school through languaging based on an understanding of inescapable racialized tensions. This process requires Black students from American and immigrant populations to engage in literate practices that extend their understandings of what it means to be literate and to succeed in life.

Typically, the idea of success for Black immigrants is based on how well they perform in schools, and this measure overly relies on what we call academic literacies as a mechanism through which youth define themselves. Instead, Black immigrant youth must understand that their literacies extend beyond just academic performance, and they must be allowed to explore the literate practices that engender their self-worth by drawing from linguistic and other semiotic resources that allow them to reflect their holistic literacies. This process—based on insights from the racialized literacies and lives of Black immigrant youth (Flores, 2020; P. Smith, 2022e) and reflected in language and raciosemiotic architecture—makes visible the ways in which racialization imposes on the multiple semiotic repertoires of youth. The process is also visible as youth agentively leverage literate practices across borders, which becomes central to meaning-making.

Holistic literacies as an element of the Black immigrant literacies framework uses literacy to engender a sense of understanding about the ways in which a lopsided view of success on the part of Black immigrant youth and by those who engage with this population creates challenges for their overall well-being. Engaging with holistic litera-cies also disrupts the broader narrative of Black immigrant youth's African American peers as underperformers in academic literacy simply because this population of Black youth often is viewed as engaging more readily with holistic literacy practices. Holistic literacies create, via multiliteracies, a solidarity across African, Black American, and Black immigrant populations by facilitating an understanding that recognition of academic literacy success on the part of Black immigrant youth does not necessar-ily translate into acceptance by institutions that often operate based on Eurocentric norms. Instead, it allows for the understanding that racialization of Black bodies still occurs—often even more so—in the academic spaces where any Black youth will claim to experience success.

By clarifying this dynamic, holistic literacies allow Black immigrant and American youth to leverage their literacies with and as advocates for one another in ways that allow them to support one another to create a balance in how they pursue literate prac-tice for well-being. Teachers who operate from this element of the Black immigrant literacies framework can engender such a balance by attending to how schools as well as Black youth are positioned to disrupt a lopsided pursuit of literate success in their classrooms. This charge can be taken up by all teachers regardless of the content area on which they focus.

INTERSECTIONAL LENSES UNDERGIRDING BLACK IMMIGRANT LITERACIES

To fully understand the framework for Black immigrant literacies, it is important to grapple with the languaging, including Englishes and broader semiotics of Black immi-grant youth, undergirding the framework and therefore to consider the intersectional lenses on which the framework is based. The three theoretical lenses undergirding the framework for Black immigrant literacies, as mentioned earlier, are diaspora literacy, racial literacy, and transnational literacy (see Figure 3.3; see also P. Smith, 2020d for the original depiction of the intersectional lenses presented next that undergird this framework).

Diaspora Literacy

Diaspora literacy is described as "an ability to read a variety of cultural signs of the lives of Africa's children at home and in the New World" and as Black people develop-ing an understanding of their "story" of "cultural dispossession" (Busia, 1989, p. 197). Diaspora literacy interrupts Black people's knowing of "our story in ways that are partial

Figure 3.3. Intersectional and Theoretical Basis for Black Immigrant Literacies

Black Immigrant Literacies

Diaspora Literacy
African people reading themselves into a new world.

Racial Literacy
The reading of race, contextually, in relation to power, and as intersectional.

Transnational Literacy
Reading, writing, and semiotizing (including languaging) across transnational boundaries.

and distorted" (King, 1992, p. 320; see also Clark, 2009; Fisher, 2006). It asks Blacks to repossess this story and thus Blacks' "cultural identity as 'Africa's children'" so that "human consciousness permits us to retrieve our humanity from distorted notions of the conceptual 'Blackness,'" which has, in turn, long functioned as an "alter ego of the socially constructed category of 'Whiteness'" (King, 1992, p. 321).

Through diaspora literacy, it is possible to examine and challenge "egregious racial stereotyping, inaccuracies, distortions, omissions, justifications and trivialization of un-ethical and inhumane social practices, including racial slavery" as reported in textbooks (King, 1992, p. 322). It is also possible to see how this approach was focused primarily on descendants of African slaves in America (i.e., Black Americans), who were expected to socially adjust, both in and beyond schools, to "model minority" immigrant and Eurocentric norms. For instance, in the critical ethnographic case study undertaken by Blaché (2022) with high school students, the author challenges Afro-Caribbean American students who hold "negative, deficit perceptions of all associated with Africa including themselves," through African diaspora literacy, to "(re)member" (C. B. Dillard, 2012) as they engage with Sankofan, an African-centered pedagogy.

While diaspora literacy is focused on Blacks being able to read themselves into a new world, the construct, if applied to Black immigrant youth, does not appear to readily con-sider how this reading occurs by the "voluntary Black immigrant" who may be either the descendant of slaves in the Caribbean (i.e., Black Caribbean immigrant) or the de-scendant of a family whose children were taken from Africa as slaves (i.e., African im-migrant). Diaspora literacy, because it appears to require the struggle for justice of the Black American as a basis for reading the world, seems to be one to which the voluntary immigrant often is unallowed to lay claim. This is because there is often a perceived su-periority associated with "model minority immigrant" status that creates intraracial ten-sions regarding how Blackness is positioned by such youth. In turn, attempts to apply diaspora literacy equally to Black immigrants often are regarded as attempts to equate the struggles for justice of African Americans with what often is perceived as a superior position occupied by Black model minority immigrants. Many of these immigrants are either African and have not undergone slavery, or descendants of slaves from the Caribbean who often are perceived as superior to their African American peers. As King (1992) observed about the situation within which she reviewed textbooks for state adoption decades ago:

> [It is the reification of the Euro-immigrant past] that naturalizes the particular social, and economic interests of dominant Whites by making the interests of newly arrived, non-White immigrants appear to be identical to theirs. Further, it suppresses the identification of these groups with Black Americans' transformative aspirations and historic struggles for justice (or with those of indigenous peoples). Hamilton [1972] contends that this divide-and-rule strategy is a characteristic of the new "unum" politics in California. As "minorities" become the "majority" there, manifestations of this strategy's effects are clearly evident in conflicts between non-White groups. (p. 326)

Despite these longstanding tensions and varied degrees of difference in the ways in which colonization stripped Blacks across the diaspora of economic, social, and moral dignity, and has come to operate largely on divide-and-rule politics, *in the end, trauma is trauma.* Black youth from Africa and from the Caribbean, much like Black American youth, have been shown to undergo significant challenges with largely racially motivated discrimination in the United States (Kumi-Yeboah & Smith, 2016; P. Smith, 2019, 2020b). Moreover, increasingly persistent anti-immigrant narratives, both nationally and globally, as well as national movements dedicated to the opposition of Blackness in the United States (Dancy et al., 2018; Sexton, 2018), such as those perpetuated in the state of Florida in 2023, reinforce the need for supporting Black immigrant youth literacies, much like those of their African American peers, which enable them to thrive.

A Black person, whether immigrant or American, is just that to everyone: *Black, and then otherwise* (see P. Smith, 2020b). And "racism—meaning the maintenance of, and acquiescence in, racialized hierarchies governing resource distribution—has not functioned simply through evil or irrational prejudice . . . [but also] has been an artifact of geographic, political, and economic interests" (Guinier, 2004, p. 98). The way in which the invisible population of Black immigrant youth uses literacy and language to navigate such racialized hierarchies and bridge identities as culturally and racially diverse Black immigrants remains largely unexplored and appears to be complex and nuanced (see P. Smith, 2019; P. Smith et al., 2022).

As King (2021) has observed recently, diaspora literacy emerged out of Black studies' original mission to produce knowledge that transforms consciousness and teach for social change while maintaining a connection with Black communities. As such, engaging explicitly and centrally with racialization as a basis for this process in ways that legitimately clarify Black immigrants' sense-making in the largely overt racialized context of the United States is critical if Black studies and diaspora literacy are to avoid impersonating other disciplines in the production of esoteric knowledge needed to establish legitimacy in schools and in the academy (King, 2021).

Racial Literacy

The term *racial literacy* was proposed as a response to "racial liberalism's individualistic and prejudice-centered view of formal equality," which was unable to consider differences across multiple interests of racial groups; this thus created a "white backlash" and "doomed both [Black–White] integration and the redistribution of resources" (Guinier, 2004, p. 114). According to Guinier, racial literacy presents a framework that is more dynamic than that of racial liberalism as a way to understand American racism. It implores us to rethink how race functions "as an instrument of social, geographic, and economic control of both whites and blacks" (p. 114).

Racial literacy is thought to be *contextual as opposed to universal*, so that individuals engage with "action and thought, between experimentation and feedback, between bottom-up and top-down initiatives" through "learning rather than knowing" via a process that is interactive where "race functions as a tool of diagnosis, feedback, and assessment" (Guinier, 2004, pp. 114–115). Racial literacy also "emphasizes the relationship between race and power" by reading race psychologically, interpersonally, and structurally, to acknowledge the significance of "individual agency" while remaining focused on how the forces of the institution and the environment both work to inform and represent this agency (p. 115). Guinier asserts that racial literacy "never loses sight of race" but also "does not focus exclusively on race" as it "constantly interrogates the dynamic relationship among race, class, geography, gender, and other explanatory variables" by avoiding assumptions that are based on individual prejudice and on individual victimhood to function as a basis for "monumental social change" (p. 115). The notion of racial literacy purports that "legal equality granted through the courts will not extirpate the distinctive, racialized asymmetries from the DNA of the American dream" (p. 116).

Bearing some resemblance to the notion of a raciolinguistic perspective (Rosa, 2016), which I have used previously (P. Smith, 2019) to examine raciolinguistic and monoglossic ideologies (García, 2009; Rosa & Flores, 2017) in the literacies and Englishes of a Black immigrant youth, racial literacy increasingly is used as a lens for examining literacies of teachers and students (e.g., Sealey-Ruiz, 2013; Skerrett, 2011). The tenets of racial literacy—*contextual as opposed to universal, relationship between race and power, lack of focus exclusively on race*—when considered in relation to Black immigrants, raise questions. Black immigrant youth, upon engaging with the U.S. context, might be said to adopt a frame of reference that focuses on context by learning rather than knowing. Yet, in the absence of a lived experience steeped in explicit and visible indications of how race and power function to maintain structural inequality, it is often the first time that race becomes central to the consciousness.

For the Black immigrant youth in the United States who do not appear (to others) to be white and who often have not functioned previously in a context where racialization is overtly present or is as explicit as the Black–White divide in the United States, there initially is also no "language for talking about whiteness" or race (Rogers & Mosley, 2006, p. 484; see also P. Smith, 2019). These youth, whose racial literacy often is challenged or largely absent, join a racialized society where they are positioned as immigrants who unfairly lay claim to affirmative action on the one hand (ABC News, 2020) and as "Black people [who] 'stole' the American dream" on the other (Guinier, 2004, p. 108).

Racial literacy, when considered within (an extended notion of) critical race theory (CRT) (Cabrera, 2018; Willis, 2018; Yosso, 2005), provides key opportunities to consider affordances for centralizing race in researching the literacies of Black immigrant youth. Through the extended notions of CRT (Cabrera, 2018)—(a) the intercentricity of race and racism, (b) the challenge to the dominant ideology, (c) the commitment to social justice, (d) the centrality of experiential knowledge, (e) the interdisciplinary perspective, and (f) hegemony of whiteness (new addition to CRT)—researchers can examine race by transitioning from its basis in capitalism (i.e., Gramscian Marxism) to its enactment through white supremacy (i.e., racial studies).

In such a context, race functions as

a marker of difference that, when mediated through a system of racial domination (i.e., White supremacy), attributes differential value to specific racial background . . . which creates and reproduces racial inequality. (Cabrera, 2018, p. 224)

As I have indicated previously:

. . . from such a perspective, researchers are afforded an opportunity to examine how Black immigrant youth's reading of the world becomes framed by Hegemonic Whiteness (see Willis et al., 2021; Willis & Smith, (Smith, 2021). This Hegemonic Whiteness, which is "the systemic and cultural means by which White supremacy is continually reproduced" (Cabrera, 2018) and where "cultural and discursive practices . . . serve to naturalize unequal social relations along the color line," functions in a "superstructure of White Supremacy" that attributes value to Whiteness "as a privileged, dominant, and frequently invisible social identity" (p. 223). By including as one of its key tenets, consideration of factors beyond race, racial literacy affords insight into how immigration [as a characteristic of Black immigrant youth] joins race at the table of Hegemonic Whiteness. Notwithstanding, the context from which white and Black Americans are primed to enact racial literacy, as described, remains distinctively different from that with which the Black immigrant is familiar. In other words, despite the affordances of racial literacy through an extended notion of CRT for centralizing race as a novel construct for the Black immigrant, Black immigrant youth bring a previously defined view of the world that is complex, nuanced, and largely different from that experienced by their Black American counterparts. This view must be accounted for in their attempts to read race. It is important, therefore, that even while drawing upon racial literacy, they also are supported in ways that allow them to bring to their social adjustment these often obscured, overlooked, untapped, and invisible lived experiences that deviate from mainstream American racialized contexts. (Smith, 2020d, pp. 22–23)

Transnational Literacy

Transnational literacy refers to "the written language practices of people who are involved in activities that span national boundaries" (Jiménez et al., 2009, p. 17). For scholars of transnational literacy, "transnationalism refers to the movement of people, media, language, and goods between distinct nation states, particularly that which flows in both directions and is sustained over time (p. 17; see also Portes et al., 1999). Literacies and language practices enacted by transnational youth emerge as "multilingual and multiliteracies practices are implicated in the formation of specific kinds of transnational understandings" that are "experienced as transnational knowledge-building transactions" (Skerrett, 2012, p. 387). They can include "the forms of literacy that are most privileged by school (reading and writing) as well as those (dance and art) that youth sometimes find only as avenues to develop in contexts outside school" and reflect interrelationships across the multiliteracies presented by youth, which foreground a shift in language occurring in tandem with a shift in multiliteracies and border crossing (p. 387).

The processes through which youth enact such literacies are multiple and varied. They include activities such as

> transmit[ting] funds to Mexico, China, and Nigeria; travel[ing] by bus to more than 30 cities in Mexico and 20 cities in the U.S. . . . communicat[ing] via telephone with about 100 far-flung nations and places . . . and opening a bank account . . . to send money to family members in Mexico without paying exorbitant rates. (Jimenez et al., 2009, p. 17)

Previous research has reiterated the need for integrating transnational and community literacies into the curriculum (e.g., Jiménez et al., 2009, 2015; Skerrett, 2012, 2015, 2016, 2017, 2020) in order to provide teachers with more elaborate understandings of students' lifeworlds (De Costa, 2010; Skerrett & Bomer, 2013), enable students to have a better understanding of their peers, build on the prior knowledge of students, and increase transnational youth's engagement in literacies, linguistic practices, and the learning of content associated with these practices (e.g., Horowitz, 2012; Lam & Warriner, 2012; Rubinstein-Ávila, 2007; Smith & Murillo, 2012).

For Black immigrant youth, the lens of "transnational literacies" (see P. Smith et al., in press, for discussion of the revised term) provides an opportunity to bring to the forefront their lived experiences that reflect literacies associated with shifts in border crossing. These shifts are simultaneously accompanied by transitions in the use of multiliteracies (i.e., linguistic as well as semiotic meaning-making processes) and students' leveraging of Englishes. When complemented by diaspora and racial literacy, such a lens provides an opportunity to understand how emerging literacies are mediated by previous and lived experiences. This lens also allows Black immigrant youth to read new lifeworlds in which their languaging is racialized even as they function as "Africa's children at home and in the New World" and as Black people developing an understanding of their "story" of "cultural dispossession" (Busia, 1989, p. 197). Through a lens such as this, educators can better understand how emerging literacies of Black youth who cross borders interrupt how they know their cultural stories, racially read the world, and reconcile partial and distorted stories that are often distinct from, but also intertwined with, those of their Black American peers.

Such an approach is consistent, to some degree, with my recent scholarship in which the theory of positioning (Harré et al., 2009) and a raciolinguistic perspective (Rosa, 2016) have been used to illustrate how the Black immigrant youth Jaeda reflected insights about her racialized linguistic and language practices while being positioned in relation to her Black American, white, and brown peers (P. Smith, 2019; see also P. Smith, 2020b; P. Smith et al., 2022). This research considered both individual trajectories and the relationship to global contexts used by Jaeda to navigate challenges with race and language in which she was positioned as called for by a raciolinguistic perspective (Rosa, 2016). I demonstrated that this adolescent adopted *a transraciolinguistic approach* that allowed her to wrestle with a sense of personhood even while seeming to "succeed" academically as an individual. According to this research (P. Smith, 2019):

> [A] transraciolinguistic approach can be described as Jaeda's metalinguistic, metaracial, and metacultural understanding of her past experiences with race and language, and by extension, culture, to determine how to function effectively within non/academic settings in ways that do not completely sacrifice her personhood. Specifically, Jaeda reflected a transraciolinguistic approach in the flexibility that she adopted as a young student and in the duality developed while retaining her personhood as an adolescent student. Developing a transraciolinguistic approach enabled Jaeda to make sense of her experiences based on both the global and local, and allowed her to continue to be agentive in her progress as a student. This progress was reflected in Jaeda's later enrollment as a member and leader of the Caribbean Student Association at her university. (p. 300)

I have explained further (P. Smith, 2020b) that:

> Through "metalinguistic" understanding, [Black immigrants] demonstrate awareness and control of linguistic elements (Herdina & Jessner, 2002) in their uses of standardized Englishes within the novel context of the United States that allowed them to be flexible in their negotiation of these Englishes for different purposes. Through "metaracial" understanding, [Black immigrants note] how standardized English is racialized and largely socially constituted (Martinot, 2003). Therefore, in many cases, they decide how they [will] individually oppose this racialization. Through "metacultural" understanding, the [Black immigrants] acknowledge the ways in which their race and standardized Englishes are associated with and transcend typical notions of these constructs within the cultural context of America (Sharifian, 2013). (pp. 139–140)

Using a transraciolinguistic approach, I illustrated how Black immigrants

> observe the ways in which monoglossic and heteroglossic ideologies intersect regarding their own standardized as well as U.S. standardized English norms, which enable them to develop and maintain a sense of agency about where and how they would use these, as well as their nonstandardized Englishes. (P. Smith, 2020b, p. 140)

APPLYING THE BLACK IMMIGRANT LITERACIES FRAMEWORK

The framework for Black immigrant literacies and its corresponding elements, developed with due consideration to the languaging and Englishes of these youth, has been presented here as a basis for understanding and interpreting the authentic narratives of youth to be presented later. The three theoretical lenses discussed—diaspora literacy, racial literacy, and transnational literacies—demonstrate how partial understandings persist regarding the literacies of Black immigrant youth. These lenses, when integrated, provide a basis for thinking in complex ways about how to leverage the literacies of Black immigrant youth to facilitate learning for all students in classrooms. By considering the foregoing lenses of diaspora literacy and racial literacy for understanding how transnational literacies emerge in the lived experiences of Black immigrant youth who engage in border crossing while becoming subjected to *racialized languaging* (Chow, 2014; P. Smith et al., 2022), teachers and educators are better positioned to address the literacies of this unique population and thus to affirm and honor their unique literacies, which often are subsumed within that of the Black American population.

QUESTIONS TO CONSIDER

1. What obstacles exist to developing a sense of a shared struggle for justice among various Black immigrant and native-born populations (e.g., Afro-Brazilian, Nigerian, Somalian, Ghanaian, Haitian, English-speaking Afro-Caribbean, African American)?
2. What provisions are made for Black immigrants whose identities deviate from predetermined norms (e.g., LGBTQIA, undocumented Black immigrants, mixed-race Black immigrants, Black immigrants who are also American, Spanish-speaking Black immigrants, French Creole–speaking Black immigrants, Afro-Indian immigrants, Afro-Latinx immigrants)?
3. In what ways can teacher preparation programs and courses redesign instruction to address the myth of the model minority that affects the sense of shared solidarity across Black immigrant and native-born populations?
4. How can schools and institutions use a transraciolinguistic approach to foster metalinguistic, metacultural, and metaracial understanding for all populations, including those presumed to be largely monolingual, monocultural, and monoracial?
5. What opportunities are available, through social media and otherwise, for enabling Black immigrants, and all students, to connect their local experiences with languaging to their global sources?
6. How does a focus on holistic literacies based on language and raciosemiotic architecture allow for a redesign of K–12 literacy and English language arts curriculum?

CHAPTER 4

Teaching Chloe, a Black Jamaican Literate Immigrant

Entanglements of Englishes, Race, and Migration

In this chapter, I present the "authentic narrative" of one Afro-Caribbean Jamaican immigrant youth, Chloe, who perceived herself as speaking Jamaican Creolized English, Jamaican Standard English, and Standard American English. I chose to focus on the authentic narrative of a Black immigrant from the Caribbean because even as the African immigrant population exponentially increases, data from the Pew Research Center show that the Caribbean continues to be the largest origin source of Black immigrants in the United States (Haughton, 2022; Tamir & Anderson, 2022). I also chose Chloe, someone from a majority-Black country, because Jamaicans often are thought to be one of the Afro-Caribbean populations with which most Americans can identify due to their place at the "center of cultural, racial and linguistic influence globally" (Devonish & Carpenter, 2020). Even so, as observed by Siegel (2020), "Jamaican Creole has achieved popularity everywhere but at home" (cited in Devonish & Carpenter, 2020), and it is not often acknowledged that "what it mean[s] to be a black Jamaican . . . depend[s] on the racial context of the receiving area" where one lives in the United States (Foner, 1985, p. 708). I chose 19-year-old Chloe because of the tendency to present the legitimate languaging of Jamaican and other English-speaking Caribbean students as "less than multilingual," a practice steeped in raciolinguistic ideology and which remains unchallenged in schools (Smith & Warrican, 2021b).

Historically, it has been observed that although Jamaicans encountered racial discrimination in the United States and Britain, they also seemed to have advantages living in specific areas, such as New York. This was because they were part of a larger Black population there that "cushion[ed]" them from "some of the sting of racial prejudice" and "provide[d] them with easier access to certain occupations and social institutions" (Foner, 1985, p. 708). That Chloe, a Jamaican, had lived in Dallas, Texas, during her elementary and middle school years is significant. Despite the increasing Black (including African immigrant) population in Texas, a state with approximately 13% Black or African American people—approximately 23.4 million—Chloe reports significant experiences with race-based trauma. Chloe's later transition to southwestern Texas, where the Black population is approximately 8%, means that her story is even more powerful. Juxtaposing Chloe's lived experiences in a Texas city with large numbers of Blacks against her residence in a

Texan city with so few Blacks demonstrates to teachers how being a racialized immigrant can create challenges Black immigrants' literacies across varied spaces and contexts.

I use Chloe's authentic narrative to illustrate her transnational experience with migration, racialized languaging, and Englishes, as well as her teachers' and peers' responses to her from childhood into adolescence and adulthood across elementary, middle, high school, and college, as a basis for discussing considerations for teaching this Black literate immigrant. As mentioned earlier, the authentic narrative is based on the notion of story. I describe the narrative as an authentic one because it emerged as a method preferred by the Black immigrant participants for telling their stories, as recommended by the "critical dialectical pluralist" approach (Onwuegbuzie & Frels, 2013). This method empowered participants to make the research-based decision regarding the form of data they preferred to be used in the study at this stage of the research process. The authentic narrative selected represents the transcription of Chloe's conversations with me during our engagement in data collection for a study on Black immigrant languages and literacies (see P. Smith, 2019; P. Smith et al., 2022). To protect the identity of the participant, the name Chloe is a pseudonym.

Chloe's authentic narrative (see the next section) forms the basis for discussing three insights that may persist regarding elements overlooked when teaching and caring for this Black immigrant child: (1) resources on which the Black immigrant draws while "becoming Black"; (2) resources on which the Black immigrant draws while "becoming immigrant"; and (3) resources on which the Black immigrant draws while "unbecoming a 'native' English speaker." I discuss each of the three insights in turn by highlighting how the authentic narrative illustrates specific elements of the Black immigrant literacies framework.

For the first insight, I will show how the "struggle for justice" and the "myth of the model minority" elements of the Black immigrant literacies framework are reflected. For the second insight, I will show how the "local–global" element of the Black immigrant literacies framework is reflected. For the third insight, I will show how the "holistic literacies" element of the Black immigrant literacies framework becomes visible.

Following this, I will highlight how teachers can use these elements of the Black immigrant literacies framework as a basis for literacy and English language arts instruction. In doing so, they can address the insights discussed above as well as other indicators when interacting with Black immigrant children and youth who may present similar and varied experiences. I also will include guiding questions for instructors who wish to engage teachers in thinking about the experience of Chloe as they plan instruction that caters to the experiences of Black immigrant youth.

CHLOE'S AUTHENTIC NARRATIVE: ENTANGLEMENTS OF ENGLISHES, RACE, AND MIGRATION: "YOU'LL NEVER HEAR HER SPEAK, LIKE BROKEN"

Childhood Years: "I Feel Like I Was Speaking English but, You Know, Broken Jamaican"

My name is [Chloe] and I am Jamaican American. I grew up in a family with my mom and sister. My mom always wants me to learn different languages. She put her money aside for me to go back to China and she wants me to be fluent in Mandarin. I am working on language all the time because she wants me to speak Spanish and Mandarin at the same time. She knows the whole of both. She knows Spanish, French, and something else.

I got to the United States when I was a baby. I would stay for school months and go back all summer and then come back for school and stay for the whole summer again, but the thing is me and my sister, we have language problems because my mom had a very thick accent like her family, so we started talking Patois all the time, so then we had to take English classes all the way up to middle school. I was in English as a Second Language classes but basically, like I feel I was speaking English, but you know Jamaican broken Jamaican; kids bullied me and my sister all the time.

I had a very good teacher though. She was very understanding, and she knew my mom. This teacher was white even though I went to an elementary school in east Dallas, which had a lot of Black kids and Hispanic kids. There're very different types. Very diverse. But my teacher understood. She always worked with me on reading. For example, there was a program, Reading Rainbow, and with the words lesson, she would always help me with the words because I would always spell it in [British] English, like "colour." . . . Like everything for me was British. So then, she helped a lot with that and then I got to middle school.

Middle School Years: "So Then I Started to Just Try to Talk Like Them, So Like Pronounced My Words Like How I'm Talking Now"

I went to five different middle schools.

In middle school, they pulled me out of the class in the middle of the day and said, "Oh, time for an hour of English." Ok, it was boring. I still remember how I did the keypad to spell out words and she said, "No. That's not right." I fixed it and I still get it wrong and then [I kept thinking] I'm going to [have to] do it in a test. Then I still got it wrong. So, it wasn't really helping me. I would be pulled out of class, not getting the teacher's instruction and still not getting any benefit from being out of the class. I would say my words, but then I started to say my words different from how I was writing. My speaking was changing, but the writing was not. Even today I still spell "colour" the same and my professors don't say anything.

Still, bullying was tough in middle school. The students were like "say that word again" . . . "say that word again." I hated it! I hated it! That was how it was in middle school. That was really the worst time of my life.

My mom realized this because my grades started to drop and I did not want to go out of my room. I stayed in my room all the time because I didn't want to talk to people, because I felt like they looked at me weird every time I say something. So then I started to just try to talk like them, so like, I pronounced my words like how I'm talking now—formal. So, that's how I usually talk (laugh), I started to say things my way. My mom said, "Maybe you start being yourself you don't have to worry about everybody else bullying you and stuff like that, just talk how, you know we all talk how as a family." So I was like, no (more laughter), that's not working. So then,

I don't know, I transitioned in and out of three middle schools. It was because of a lot of bullying. I went to two to three middle schools and then one high school. It was too much bullying and like, me lashing out at people . . . I had a really big behavior problem in middle school.

I know my language was one of the factors because I would like, go home, cry about it, because no one understood what I was saying. I would just say, "I am speaking English, just like some words different," but people look at me as if I AM DIFFERENT. I know language definitely made me struggle during middle school. After some time, some people began to say, "Oh that's so cool," but other people just look at me weird. Plus, most of the teachers weren't very helpful. They were not even aware of what was going on. They never said anything to me. They never suggested anything but counseling. Nothing. High school had counseling for lots of stuff. Middle school, nothing. My sister though, went to a different school. She went to the school with learning differences. She had a lot of summer courses. Yeah, and she also had foreign exchange students at school.

So, it was easy for her, but I am still considered the problem child. And it's easier for her to make friends than it is for me to make friends. Like I broke down yesterday really bad. I had to call my mom. Just like I was struggling, just like making friends. It is really about making friends. I just felt very alone, just like to myself. No one. So, I just rang up my mom. Just like I was struggling out here. I wanted to come home and move because my mom is planning on moving. She's in Dallas right now, she moved to England from Jamaica and then she'll move back here as soon as we graduate. She's the only thing I have.

About reading though, I hated reading out loud. I feel like they just have me read out loud so I can be embarrassed, people started laughing at me and teacher makes, "Sssshhh" and keep going. I didn't want to read out loud. I was going so slow because I had troubles reading. I would go really slow. There were some words I didn't know because I didn't know much of my vocabulary. But I didn't like it. It was only because of my mom that I got to read confidently and comfortably. My mom, she helped me read at home. My mom is a reader, so she was like you need to read this every night before you go to bed.

She still calls me now: "Do you read the chapter that I sent you?" She's a big educator like . . . She's a nurse; but she's a huge person on education. She has like three masters. I don't want to do that. So I have to meet those standards of hers. Always got all A's. She tried to make me just like, you know, get this word. We would sit up late at night and she said, "Say words for me; so, say this word, say this word, say this word." We would do this every night. I had to do worksheets, math worksheets every night, reading every night before I go to bed. Right through middle school and high school. She was very dedicated.

I started to read at 5th grade. That was strange, but I did every day. Yeah. My mom wouldn't let me out unless I read. I had to summarize the chapter, read it back to her. That's why I hate reading now because she made me read too much! To parents, I would say, "Don't push that much," like every day a week was a lot. Even on the weekend, we would spend hours at the library. But I would say, emphasize reading because reading is one of those things like [it builds] the vocabulary, but [still] I wouldn't push that much. I would say let kids do what they enjoy doing. You don't have to force something upon them because I saw lots of them [with things] forced upon them and if it wasn't too forced upon them, I think they [would] enjoy it more.

Middle school was something but high school was different.

High School Years: "Let Me Change My Voice in Order to Fit in, Make Friends"

In high school I started speaking differently because I was at an all-white high school. So I was like, "Ok, it's immediately I'm the one person to live with that all the time so ok, let me change my voice in order to fit in, to make friends." I got a paper back when I was in high school, saying, "Don't write how you speak." It was my English teacher. I got a bad grade on it because I know I spelled words wrong; it was spelled in Creole's way. It was terrible.

I really had that spelling problem going on a lot. But now it's not that bad because I'm at the college, "th", stuff like that. I'm with the writing center to make sure that it's right the first time. Back in high school, I had a big major paper that I was getting it reviewed, but the lower paper. My counselor she reviewed it because I said, "Hey, can you review my work?" We're still friends and she said she would visit me (laughing).

In high school, I had one best friend and we're still friends 'til this day. She's nice. So whenever I am with her, it does not matter. She's the only who can understand as the family does and can understands me as always. I can walk to her house. It's ok.

College Years—Living in the Dorm: "I Am Not the Type of a Typical Black Person"

When I came here, to college, at the university, I was looking for other caring people. I didn't know anybody here. Just like a brand-new life for me. I can just be myself here and stop worrying about everyone else. I went out with a group of girls and immediately I am the one who is singled out because I can't be myself, talking, and I didn't know about it but my roommate who was African at the time, this girl said her mom said, "Beware of her." That's beware of me, of course. So I was like "What?!" So, I called my mom. She said yes this is going on a long time in Africa but in my mind I am thinking, "But it's like 2015, 2016, does this still happen?"

Well the answer is yes. So, I was excluded from things and this can't be happening again. So then, I ended up moving out at the end of December to move to a different room. I just moved myself and I am no longer a friend to any of them. Mind you, some of them in that room were white, some were African, and others were African American. A few were nice. One of the girls, on my birthday, she said Happy Birthday, or she said Merry Christmas. She was nice, she was sweet. I saw that she was sweet. She treated me like a human. But the other ones were looking, they kept on going.

For me, white people, they are really cool all the time. Again I am not the type of a typical Black person. So, basically, I can't be identified as a certain type of Black person. I don't know any of that. [Like people would say] "Why are you talking to me about that? [Saying] Oh, you're not Black?!" I am still struggling to find what am I because my dad is white.

But I didn't know him. I didn't know him whatsoever. I've always identified with being just Jamaican. But my best friend who is white, she is very understanding. So, I've always felt comfortable around white people; I've never really had problems too much, but African American people, that is my biggest problem. I feel like the African group, they stay with their own culture; white people, they're more curious, I should say some of them, about other different countries and cultures. I was surrounded by that at the International Baccalaureate school. . . . We had foreign exchange students coming there so it was cool. Yea, but the African students, they're very within themselves, and only within themselves. I didn't really know where my place was because in my mind, I thought, "I'm going to join all the Black stuff when I get here at college 'cuz I was in a white school my whole life. So, when I got here, I joined ASA, the African Students Association. [But] I [realized I] got there with too many African people. I don't why I can't do this. [To them] You're very different. They look at you. [So I thought] I am not connected with this. I took myself out of that association. Then the Black Student Association [African American], they're very Black power so I was like, "No, I don't fit in there."

College Years—Interacting With Family and Friends: "But When I'm at Home I Speak Totally Different, Just Like My Mom"

Now, in college, I say something and I guess if I say something different, people won't look at me. I'll correct myself immediately. If I say like rucksack, that means backpack [so] I'll hurry up to correct myself. People look at me for a second. If people don't know, we don't call it out. [If they say], "What? Say that again." I say, "backpack." [Then they say], "No, what you say the first time." [But I ignore it].

I still use my Creole with my mom. Her accent is Jamaican English. She lived like 20 years in England, 19 years in Jamaica. She sounds perfectly normal to me but [people] catch it immediately. "Where's your mom from?" [they ask]. "Well, she's from Jamaica," [I say]. And then they say, "She sounds like it now. She's Jamaican." She sounds more American but she still has problems with saying some difficult words; but when I'm at home I speak totally different, just like my mom. [I can switch] immediately. I can turn it off and turn it on. I got used to that. So, when I'm at home, I am totally comfortable. [Otherwise I] just try to fit in. [But my friend Nisha] catches [my Jamaican Creole] a lot.

But not full flex. Not full flex because she's not like a friend, friend. She's the only one that catches it [outside of my home]. Like . . . I just talk [Jamaican Creole] with her all the way. I'm nervous about this. I don't know how I do this. When I first got here, I merely started talking the way I usually talked, but no one said anything to me. They didn't know me; so, they didn't say anything to me. They just went through with it and they didn't care and people who knew me, they would say something—all the time.

College Years—Literacies for the Future: "You'll Never Hear Her Speak Like Broken; but You Also Hear the Accents"

Now, in college, I only read when I have to, like my reading books for the class. I would read those, but I wouldn't just read a book. My mom sent me a book last week and she said you needed to read this book and you needed to be done by the end of the month. I [will] probably skim through it. She called me. She asked, "Do you read this chapter?" and I quickly look at it and said, "Oh about this." Probably when I get older I will want to read it. I would go to the library and I would find the book that I want to read.

There're a couple good books that I want to read, but I have to choose what I like. Don't give it to me; I'll choose it myself, but if I enjoy. I like reality books, kind of. I like *The Other Wes Moore*. I don't know if you ever heard of it. That's my favorite book. Two kids named Wes Moore, one grew up in poverty and one grew up to be a president and it's like a totally different transition. Like, he went to jail and this one became a president. I think it's probably the differences that attract me to it. They're the same persons. It talked about two different pathways. I just say yeah, "That's interesting." I guess that what intrigues me about two different pathways. If I had to have different paths in my life perhaps, I would literally consider going to university in the Washington, DC. I really applied there but my mom said no. She doesn't want me to be there.

As a college student, I would say to other students like me, I guess, to embrace their own culture and identity and try to fit in with everybody else. There're different ways to fit in like being comfortable with yourself then confident with yourself first.

For example, I go to the support system [at my university]. In that hall, that environment is really culturally diverse and I feel like if there're more places like that [in the university], they will help people more comfortable. If students have supports, they can cope better because they only hear you say "Ok," when [they] need the support strategy. I go to that hall at the university and I'm cool there; I don't have friends but I go to the hall and I do stuff there. I might not have really close friends.

As for parents, if my mom was a little bit encouraging [it would have helped]. [And if I could go back, I would tell my younger self] to just be comfortable with myself for who I am. My mom was thinking about future setting, like me getting a job and stuff like that. And still now, she likes me getting a job. And yeah, [she says] you need to represent yourself like this and speak [proper] like this. She still pronounces her words; you'll never hear her speak like broken; but you also hear the accents. She wouldn't change her accent or sound Jamaican. She hates it. She hates it. She's a proper person. She's very proper. She reads a lot and I think that is kind of changing her. She reads all the time and so, she carries herself at this high level and she wants me to meet that level. She doesn't want me to speak down at this level. I try to just get over it, try to change. I work with her.

I would say that parents need to be accommodating, try to understand. And I think [students like me], they need to educate the ones are from the United States. Like educate them a little bit more about different cultures, about how to embrace different cultures. What are the do's and don'ts stuff in speaking, I guess, to someone else from another culture because it could be offensive. I think we could make the world different, but I feel like if they knew [they would be better off].

College Years—Going "Back Home": "I Can't Speak Full Creole Anymore; but When I Do, They Already Know That I've Been in America"

Oh, my god. When I'm back home [with my immediate family], my mom, my sister and me, we get treated differently from the rest of the family because my mother's the only person that left Jamaica and everyone else stayed and it was just my mom and my grandmother who left to go to England. And then when we come back, they will think, "Oh, we are too good for people." They say, "You speak in this way." My uncles, they are more understanding than my aunts. I don't know. They immediately know we are American. I can't speak full Creole anymore; but when I do, they already know that I've been in America because I sound like American, Creole mixed. They don't say anything. They just accept it. My uncles, sometimes they'll say something smart, but there're still big problems. I don't know.There's something else. Like they think my mom was kind of more privileged than they were.

[Anyway] I'm going back in summer. I like going back. I try going back every year, to my grandmother's house. My grandmother passed away so they now own my mom's house. But I don't know. I want just to be off from my job and go there right now. But I also don't want to live there anymore. It sounds too much, for 3 months. I don't like it too much because I got used to air conditioning and stuff like that [in the US] and the bed is too hard. I don't want to be here anymore. But I went there for a week and I come back. I'll probably never live there. I don't want to live there anymore.

INSIGHTS FROM CHLOE'S AUTHENTIC NARRATIVE

This authentic narrative, "Entanglements of Englishes, Race, and Migration," as presented, reflects a chronological account of Chloe's transnational experiences with languaging and life across the United States and her country of origin, Jamaica.

Becoming Black

As reflected in the authentic narrative, Chloe draws on certain resources while "becoming Black" (Ibrahim, 1999). In doing so, she is affected in differing ways and has to decide whether and how she will *lay claim to the struggle for justice* as exemplified by her Black

American and African peers. I now describe how the authentic narrative highlights this element in Chloe's life.

Laying Claim to the Struggle for Justice. When Chloe says, "For me, white people, they are really cool all the time," and, "Again I am not the type of a typical Black person," or, "Basically, I can't be identified as a certain type of Black person," she makes it clear that there is no clear demarcation in terms of how she can be categorized. To some of her peers who respond by saying, "Oh, you're not Black?!" Chloe appears to be wrestling with how to position herself as someone who is part of the struggle for justice because she is still struggling to find out what she is because her dad is white. Chloe's indication that she's always identified with "being just Jamaican" signals how she has thought of herself both in the United States and beyond. Her feeling of comfort with her white best friend, whom she finds to be "very understanding," is presented in stark contrast to "African American people," whom she describes as her "biggest problem."

When Chloe then explains that she feels like the "African group" stays "with their own culture" or that "they're very within themselves, and only within themselves" and that "to them, you're very different," she is indicating that she sees them to be more accepting of other Black people who look like them, that is, Africans, and less accepting of someone like her who is Black but not perceived as having lived in a country on the African continent. For different reasons, Chloe also finds herself struggling with the "Black Student Association [African American]" and with their focus on "Black power," which causes her to decide that she does not fit in there. Chloe's dissonance is even more impactful given what seemed like a longstanding desire of hers through elementary, middle, and high school to successfully engage with Black populations, indicated by her saying, "I'm going to join all the Black stuff when I get here at college 'cuz I was in a white school my whole life."

According to the Black immigrant literacies framework, opportunities are created for Black immigrant youth like Chloe to lay claim to the struggle for justice as they develop an understanding and as they interact with other Black peers and come to understand how slavery functioned historically in the United States and the Caribbean, as well as how it is linked to the ancestors of Black people in countries within Africa. To lay claim to the struggle for justice, as Chloe seems to want to do by "testing the waters" with her African and African American student peers, she works to develop these understandings. However, she receives limited guidance from knowledgeable others (e.g., teachers) about the ways in which the white supremacist context of the United States has created divide-and-conquer politics, which, in turn, has inadvertently positioned Black peers from the African continent (i.e., African) against Black peers who were born and/or raised in the United States (i.e., African American) or Black peers who have Caribbean heritage (i.e., Afro-Caribbean).

In the absence of a process that engages Chloe critically with Black students from the African American and African immigrant populations to explore literate practices that help them to understand what it means for them to all be racialized as Black because of and in spite of their differences, it is easy for Chloe to look back with regret on her elementary, middle, and high school years of longing for a Black space in which to feel comfortable. However, Chloe's persistence in laying claim to the struggle for justice is re-warded when she finds the Caribbean Student Association (CSA) where she seems to be able to find peers who allow her to fit in.

Teaching the Black Literate Immigrant: Part I. Teachers who wish to enable Black immigrants to lay claim to the struggle for justice must first understand that not all Black immigrant children and youth necessarily understand the ways in which Black American and Black Caribbean populations, many of whom were separated at the Caribbean border upon being brought to a new land, operate as descendants of slaves across geographical, generational, and virtual spaces. Using their literacies to engender a sense of understanding about this process is, therefore, a critical first step in a global dynamic where Black subpopulations such as those from the North American continent and from African countries are pitted against their Black counterparts elsewhere (e.g., Latin American countries such as Brazil, English-speaking Caribbean countries such as Jamaica, French-speaking Caribbean countries such as Haiti).

Teachers of literacy and English language arts who understand the need for enabling Black immigrant youth to develop these key understandings can begin with literacies that explore slavery and colonization across the diaspora. In doing so, they would dem-onstrate similarities and differences with how slavery and colonization were leveraged within the African continent, within the North American continent, and within the Caribbean as well as Latin American countries. They also would indicate how various Black immigrants fit within and across various elements of this dynamic.

Guided by relevant columns of the completed chart presented in Figure 4.1, teachers can provide Black immigrant youth with an opportunity, using Figure 4.2, to use their literacies to explore where they fit as it relates to slavery and colonization, their languag-ing, and their literacies.

Teachers who operate from this element of the Black immigrant literacies framework also can source, create, and use materials based on a matrix such as that in Figure 4.2, which can be presented to Black students. This matrix illustrates to Black youth, regard-less of where they are from or where they live, why they are each positioned and should lay claim to the struggle for justice. The matrix allows youth from each population to position themselves historically in relation to the struggle for justice. Such a matrix also provides an avenue for Black immigrant, Black American, and African youth to explore texts, multimodal and otherwise, as a basis for discussions, student creations, and student advocacy through which Black youth can engage with the struggle for justice together.

Through the completion of this chart, Black immigrant students such as Chloe are positioned to better understand how their struggles are linked with those of other Black youth from various locales across the globe. They also are able to better understand how their Blackness functions as a global construct, which is not only unique to them and their ancestors, but also affected by how other Black subpopulations perceive them. It is only through an emerging understanding of such connectedness that Black immigrant youth can better understand the impetus for solidarity across African, Black American, and Black immigrant populations. Teachers who enable Black immigrant youth to de-velop such understandings position them to develop a sense of shared justice based on

Figure 4.1. Laying Claim to the Struggle for Justice

	African	Black American	Black Immigrant	Caribbean/Latin American
Slavery & Colonization	My ancestors experienced slavery within the continent of Africa. In spite of the fact that most were not enslaved, many were caused to believe that certain tribes and groups were better than others because of colonization. Those who were enslaved and taken were made to believe that my ancestors were primarily responsible for their plight. This caused much division among people across countries with in my continent and across the diaspora that still exists today. I am in my native land, but this has not prevented countries across my continent from being exposed to the results of race wars because division based on apartheid was present in Africa and division based on colorism still exists.	My ancestors experienced slavery within the continent of North America. Many of my ancestors' families were divided at the Caribbean border upon arrival and some were kept in the Caribbean while others were sent to the North American continent. My ancestors were enslaved and treated horribly because of colonization. They were made to believe that they were unfit to be human. This caused much division among my people and Africans that still exists today. I am in a new land because my parents were brought here as slaves, but this does not mean that I am better or worse than the Black immigrants who come here. Understanding that we are all perceived similarly because of our race is important because of the divisions that persist	My ancestors experienced slavery on the islands and in countries of the Caribbean. Many of my ancestors' families were divided at the Caribbean border upon arrival and some kept in the Caribbean while others were sent to the North American continent. My ancestors were enslaved and treated horribly because of colonization. They were made to believe that they were unfit to be human. I am in a new land because I migrated or my parents did but this does not mean that I am better than the African Americans who live here. Understanding that we are all perceived similarly because of our race is important because of the divisions that persist among Africans and African Americans today.	My ancestors experienced slavery on the islands and in countries of the Caribbean. Many of my ancestors' families were divided at the Caribbean border upon arrival and some kept in the Caribbean while others were sent to the North American continent. My ancestors were enslaved and treated horribly because of colonization. They were made to believe that they were unfit to be human but after slavery there was not a significant white presence in my country to daily remind me of my Blackness. Believing that whiteness does not affect me has caused much division among my people, Africans, and African Americans that still exists today. I must understand that being in a new land after my

	I am not better than the African Americans who live in the United States even though there is not a significant white presence in my country to daily remind me of my Blackness.	among Africans and African Americans today.		ancestors were brought here as slaves caused a lot of colorism across countries in the Caribbean, where I live, based on colonization and this still remains.
Language	My ancestors' languages were the main way in which they demonstrated who they were. Colonization caused my ancestors' languages to seem inferior and English to be instituted as the main language used to learn and achieve success across countries in my continent. I come from a lineage of people who had to learn English to be accepted as human beings in a society where many other languages were used daily. This has caused many of my people to believe that speaking and writing English	My ancestors' languages were the main way in which they demonstrated who they were. Colonization caused my ancestors' languages to be stripped from them, and whatever language practices they had left were made to seem inferior. Even though they used English, their Englishes were designated less than acceptable and even after slavery up until the present day, my people's language practices given to us by our ancestors are excluded from pathways for achieving success in this country.	My ancestors' languages were the main way in which they demonstrated who they were. Colonization caused my ancestors' languages to be stripped from them, and whatever language practices they had left were made to seem inferior. Even though they used English, their Englishes were designated less than acceptable. And even after slavery up until the present day, my people's language practices given to us by our ancestors are excluded from pathways for achieving success in this country.	My ancestors' languages were the main way in which they demonstrated who they were. Colonization caused my ancestors' languages to be stripped from them, and whatever language practices they had left were made to seem inferior. Even though they used English, their Englishes were designated less than acceptable. And even after slavery up until the present day, despite the fact that there is no predominant white presence, my people's language practices given to us by our ancestors are excluded from

(*continued*)

Figure 4.1. (*continued*)

	African	Black American	Black Immigrant	Caribbean/Latin American
	well is a requirement for success and those who cannot do this in acceptable ways have many challenges. Despite the fact that there is no predominant white presence across many countries in my continent, many of my people still believe that speaking and writing English 'well' is a requirement for success and those who cannot do this in acceptable ways have many challenges showing how they can do well in schools, universities and at work.	This has caused many of my people to believe that speaking and writing English well is a requirement for success and those who cannot do this in acceptable ways have many challenges showing how they can do well in schools, universities, and at work	This has caused many of my people to believe that speaking and writing English "well" is a requirement for success and those who cannot do this in acceptable ways have many challenges showing how they can do well in schools, universities, and at work.	pathways for achieving success in countries across the Caribbean. This has caused many of my people to believe that speaking and writing English "well" is a requirement for success and those who cannot do this in acceptable ways have many challenges showing how they can do well in schools, universities, and at work.
Literacies	I can use my literacies to support the struggle for justice for all Black people because we have all suffered various forms of discrimination against our bodies and languages as a result of colonization.			

Figure 4.2. Literacies in the Struggle for Justice

	African	Black American	Black Immigrant	Caribbean/ Latin American
Slavery & Colonization				
Who were my ancestors and how did slavery and colonization affect them?				
How did my ancestors' history with slavery and colonization influence other Black people across the world?				
How am I perceived in the land of my birth (and/or migration) because of the history of my ancestors with slavery and colonization?				
How do I relate to other Black people across the world now that I know of my ancestors' history with slavery and colonization?				
Language				
What are/were the languages of my ancestors and how did they use these languages to show who they were?				
How did colonization and slavery affect my ancestors' uses of their languages?				
How did my ancestors come to use Englishes and what did that mean for my people?				
How did the use of Englishes by my people affect how my ancestors lived and also influence how they are perceived across the globe today?				
Literacies				
How can I use my literacies to support the struggle for justice for all Black people based on our shared experiences as a result of slavery and colonization?				

the history of colonization as experienced by all Black peoples across the diaspora, repair their sense of self, and allow them to advocate for one another in more authentic ways.

Becoming Immigrant

As reflected in Chloe's narrative, several overlooked instances are available for her to identify and disrupt the myth of the model minority while "becoming immigrant." Through these opportunities, it is possible to gain insight into how Chloe and other Black immigrant students can be better positioned to use their literacies individually and in relation to their peers. Beyond this, Chloe is also placed in a position to consolidate her local and global experiences through her literacies by acknowledging how her racialization and immigration intersect based on how she uses her Englishes across spaces. Such positioning can prove useful for Chloe and others in recognizing how languaging and its accompanying resistance in relation to racialized users can be mitigated.

Addressing the Myth of the Model Minority. In the authentic narrative, Chloe indicates that she went to five different middle schools. Contrary to the generally held notion of Black immigrant youth as more academically adept, Chloe explains that "in middle school, they pulled me out of the class in the middle of the day and said, 'Oh, time for an hour of English.'" The reason for Chloe's placement in ESL classes was what she described as having "language problems" because her mom had a very "thick accent," which led them to speak Jamaican Patois, and thus Chloe was forced to take English as a Second Language classes up until middle school. Chloe describes feeling like she "was speaking English" when she was in ESL classes but acknowledging that it was "broken Jamaican" (i.e., Jamaican Creolized English). She explained how this caused her and her sister to be bullied by peers.

Chloe recalls hating being made to read out loud in class because of how embarrassing it was and because her peers laughed at her while her teacher overlooked her feelings of shame. Her description of reading slowly because she had challenges and didn't have a clear knowledge of vocabulary further exhibited that Chloe was not a "Black designer immigrant," at least not in middle school. It is intriguing that Chloe describes herself as learning to read in 5th grade, suggesting that this is when she recalls being a competent reader. Even so, Chloe credits much of her confidence and comfort to her mother. This suggests that had her mother, who had three master's degrees, *not* taught Chloe to read and engage in many other literacy practices every night at home, Chloe might have had a different account of her literate experiences as she emerged beyond her teenage years into adulthood.

It is interesting that even as Chloe praises her mother's support, she laments emphatically, "That's why I hate reading now because she made me read too much!" Thus, although Chloe supposedly has "made it" into university, is on target to complete a first degree, and seems like an accomplished student—*successful*, unless her full and complete story is visible, it may be easy for Chloe to be labeled a "model minority."

The account that Chloe presents of her elementary, middle, and high school years is one that stands in stark contrast to what often is presented perceptually about the supposed literate success of Black immigrant youth (P. Smith et al., 2022). Much like Chloe's middle school experience, her elementary school years reflect that her teacher always had to work with her on reading. Chloe references the program Reading Rainbow and recalls struggling with the spelling components of the lesson because of her British English background from the Caribbean context and the contrast to Americanized spelling. Chloe's experience illustrates that she continued to struggle with literacy in middle school where she kept getting words "wrong" and was "pulled out of class" but did not find it beneficial because her writing would reflect how she spoke—using Jamaican Creolized English.

Chloe's experiences as a Black immigrant reader and writer who has faced challenges and does not portray the superior academic performance typically expected of "model minority" Blacks migrating to the United States are not undocumented in the literature. Ukpokodu (2018) has explained how students who are African immigrants have challenges with the performance requirements of schools even though the prevailing belief societally is that they do not.

In response to indications such as this, the Black immigrant literacies framework identifies opportunities for enabling those who work with Black immigrant youth like Chloe, as well as her peers, to disrupt the myth of the model minority. The framework does so by creating opportunities for developing an understanding of how the meritocratic model minority myth, as applied to Black immigrant youth, perceptually or literally, functions based on white supremacy. It illustrates how divide-and-conquer racial politics is created that sustains intra- and interracial divisions between Black immigrant youth and their Black American peers and other minoritized immigrant populations. To address the myth of the model minority would require schools, teachers, and society to support Chloe so that she used her literacies to understand why she might be viewed by certain Black peers and other peers of color in ways that caused her to feel rejected. These supports would have been critical as she emerged as a college student seeking community across Black student groups, even as she recalled having received additional supports beyond the mainstream classroom in her earlier educational environments.

Teaching the Black Literate Immigrant: Part II. Teachers who wish to support Black immigrant youth such as Chloe by addressing the myth of the model minority first must use their own literacies to ask themselves whether they subscribe to this myth. Second, there is a need to enable Black immigrant youth to use their literate practices to identify and become aware of this myth as it is often the case that they and their parents may not be aware of how they are being perceived and positioned by other Black populations or other populations of color. Third, teachers can then use literacies to work to explicitly disrupt the myth of the model minority, as a basis of self in the world, not only for Black immigrants but also for their peers of color and others with whom they interact within and across school systems.

Teachers who operate from this element of the Black immigrant literacies framework can source, create, and use materials based on news stories in social media or otherwise that differentially portray Black Americans and Black immigrants. They can use these materials as a way to allow youth to develop argumentative essays rejecting the model minority myth. Teachers also can collect, use, and curate the stories of white, Black immigrant, and Black American youth as a basis for teaching English language arts concepts in classrooms.

Addressing the Relationship Between the Local and the Global. In her authentic narrative, Chloe reflects an intriguing connection to home. Her description of her mother, sister, and herself being treated differently and perceived as "too good" by their Jamaican relatives is related to how she speaks and the fact that she "sounds American" (i.e., like a white mainstream English speaker). While there are certain family members who seem to accept her regardless of how she uses language, she observes that there are still many "big problems" because the family "back home" thinks her "mom was kind of more privileged than they were." In response, Chloe likes visiting but does not want to live in Jamaica.

Chloe's description of the ways in which she and her family are perceived is reminiscent in part of the discussion presented by Drs. Jonathan Rosa and Nelson Flores (2017) about efforts by the racialized and minoritized to approximate standardized language norms. In Chloe's family, there seems to be a refusal to accept Chloe's as well as her mother's and sister's uses of Englishes in ways that mirror that of white speakers. Much like Rosa and Flores describe the lack of acceptance of these efforts to use language in "proper" ways by the "white listening subject," Chloe's family in Jamaica also resents the approximations. In doing so, they demonstrate the dissonance that becomes Chloe's existence: She fears a lack of acceptance that she is likely to face despite efforts to sound as "proper" as her mother has always wanted, but is also wary of being rejected by her Jamaican family members because of her "privileged" English-speaking and cultural way of being.

The response to languaging based on her racialization thus occurs for Chloe locally in the United States with regard to her Englishes as one who is becoming Black and becoming immigrant as she faces alienation in multiple spaces. In addition, the response to Chloe's languaging based on how her mother teaches her to respond to racialization by becoming "proper" manages to create distance between her and her Jamaican family members. In fact, the family members' refusal to accept her approximations of standardized uses of Englishes in favor of their own use of Jamaican Creolized English suggests that they resist and refuse the white listening subject's crediting of standardized Englishes as the acceptable way to speak and to function within interactions in society.

This dynamic shows how Chloe's global norms for using Englishes, established in her home country, are reinforced in her linguistic repertoire based on her mother's adoption of the white listening subject even while Chloe's family members reject it. This situation also illustrates how Chloe's local norms where she lives in the United States become complicated. Globally, she seeks to show that she can connect to the Englishes used by her family. This is evident when she says, "When I'm at home I speak totally different, just like my mom. [I can switch] immediately. I can turn it off and turn it on," and "I can speak Creole all the way with my friend." Even so, she also seeks to show that she can use Englishes to speak "properly," which she often alludes to in our interactions locally in the United States.

For Black immigrant students like Chloe, opportunities must be present to rethink the global (e.g., "back home") through lived experience with the local (e.g., "in the United

States"). They can do this by recognizing what I have described as duality and hybridity in how racialization is implicitly embedded in the "postcolonial" structures of youth's home countries as they encounter its explicit enactment through hegemonic whiteness and individual racialized encounters within countries of destination such as the United States (P. Smith, 2019; see also Rowe & Schelling, 1991). In the experience presented by Chloe, her mother was the one who perpetuated the use of Englishes globally based on the white listening subject, while others reinforced this locally in the United States. As will be shown in Chapter 6, these white listening subject norms for Black immigrant Englishes often extend beyond parents to societies in students' home countries. Having these expectations for their Englishes interrogated based on how these norms function, whether locally or globally, is critical to how Black immigrant youth thrive.

Teaching the Black Literate Immigrant: Part III. Teachers who operate using the local–global element of the Black immigrant literacies framework can source, create, and use materials based on global portraits, videos, and stories of Black individuals beyond the United States who grapple with racialization that adversely affects their persons and languages. These can serve as a basis for teaching English language arts concepts in classrooms. To facilitate this process, I have presented five steps for creating local–global connections in the International Literacy Association's Literacy Now blog, *Five Steps to Address Anti-Blackness in Language: Black Immigrant Literacies* (P. Smith, 2021).

The first step advises that teachers allow Black immigrant youth to share their experiences with Englishes and their languaging, as well as being Black, in their home countries and the United States. They can do this orally, in writing, and multimodally. Through these creations, teachers are advised to encourage youth to reflect on the variations and how they and others perceive their ethnic, racial, and linguistic backgrounds. During the second step, teachers can invite Black U.S.-born youth to share their experiences with Englishes and languaging, as well as with being Black, in the United States orally, in writing, and multimodally. With these creations, teachers can encourage youth to reflect on varied representations of how they as well as others respond to the ethnic, racial, and linguistic backgrounds they present.

In the third step, teachers are advised to use the literate creations of Black immigrant and U.S.-born youth as a basis for engaging them in reflecting individually about Blackness. Teachers can do so by having Black immigrant youth and U.S.-born youth exchange their various creations and participate in discussions. Teachers might have students reflect on questions such as: "What similarities and differences do you see between your creation and those of your peers? What elements do you not understand?" Teachers can allow all students to write down their responses. In the fourth step, teachers are advised to engage Black immigrant and Black American youth in discussions about their reflections, guided by questions such as: "How did Blackness seem present or absent in creations when peers were born in the United States? How did Blackness seem present or absent in creations when U.S.-born peers had immigrant parents or when their parents were foreign born? What new insights can Black immigrant peers learn about Black American students' experiences and how to respond to negative responses about their languages and literacies?"

Figure 4.3. Literacies Across Local and Global Contexts

Guiding Questions	Local: *Migration Country*	Global: *Home Country*
How do peers, family, friends, and others respond when I use my Englishes and languages in speaking?		
How do peers, family, friends, and others respond when I use my Englishes and languages in writing?		
How do teachers respond when I use my various Englishes and languages in speaking?		
How do teachers respond when I use my various Englishes and languages in writing?		
What do teachers prefer in my reading?		
What do teachers prefer in my writing?		
How do teachers respond to me and to my peers based on the complexion of our skins?		
How do I use reading and writing to communicate with my family, friends, peers?		
How do I use reading and writing online?		
How do peers, family, friends, and others respond when I use my Englishes and languages online?		

In the fifth step, teachers can invite youth to revise their creations as they reflect insights from their Black immigrant or U.S.-born peers. All students can then share their creations with other Black peers in their classrooms, in their schools, and via social media as well as with their parents, friends, families, and caregivers. Teachers are reminded to create opportunities across classrooms and schools for broad discussion about these insights, inviting non-Black peers or peers from the dominant group, who may or may not be Black, depending on the part of the globe in which they live, to be part of the learning and conversation.

Beyond and/or in conjunction with the above steps, teachers are invited to use Figure 4.3 to support Black immigrant indications and descriptions of their uses of Englishes in their countries of migration locally, and globally in their home countries, as they attempt to reconcile expectations across contexts.

Unbecoming a "Native" English Speaker

As reflected in the authentic narrative, Chloe is subtly, if not often, (un)aware of the ways in which her Englishes require her to choose to be someone whom she doesn't want to be. Her awareness or lack thereof is influenced by the fragmented ways that schools, teachers, her mother, peers, and she herself demand literate practice to be demonstrated across multiple spaces. If Chloe were more aware of the fragmentation occurring in her literacies, she could be better positioned to reconcile the literacies she possessed, to validate them, and to embrace her individual linguistic repertoire in ways that could cause her to feel legitimate as a human being in her classrooms and beyond. I now describe how the authentic narrative makes this dynamic clear in Chloe's life.

Addressing Holistic Literacies. In the authentic narrative, Chloe indicates varied subtleties in how her Englishes are fragmented in favor of her use of certain elements of her unique linguistic repertoire over others even as she is unbecoming a native English speaker. And I say unbecoming a "native" English speaker here because we have seen much debate about the use of the term *native* English speaker emerging throughout the past two decades, which point to the problematic nature of this term (Cook, 2015). For Chloe, to *unbecome* a native speaker suggests that she initially would have thought of herself as capable of speaking Englishes in a way that she believed was sanctioned by her mother, whose expectation mirrors that of the white listening subject—the supposed notion of being "native English speaking" (see Rosa & Flores, 2017). Her process of unbecoming based on how she is racialized, even as she juxtaposes her various uses of Englishes, occurs through various interactions she has in the United States.

Chloe explains that she and her sister had "language problems" so they "started talking [Jamaican] Patois." In her understanding, this thus means that their use of the Jamaican Creolized Englishes is deficient. Chloe describes her Englishes, explaining that she spoke "Jamaican broken Jamaican" and equates the use of these Englishes with the bullying she receives. This demonstrates how Chloe has been socialized to accept only certain literacies. She speaks poorly of the Jamaican Creolized Englishes in her repertoire and seems to recognize that she needs to make an effort to privilege certain Englishes as determined by the white listening subject (Rosa & Flores, 2017).

As a result, Chloe's literacies, based on the legitimate languaging she possesses, are fragmented and not holistic. It is no wonder that we see this fragmentation extending beyond just the languaging used by Chloe and beyond her literacies in middle school to her entire being—her personhood—when she says emphatically, "I hated it! I hated it! . . . That was really the worst time of my life." As Rosa and Flores (2017) describe when they talk about personhood, the languaging used by the child is "twinned" with the sense of being a racialized person, causing the two to operate in ways that cannot be detached. In other words, Chloe's rejection of certain elements of Englishes in her linguistic repertoire meant that she also needed to reject elements of herself. I have identified this process as traumatic, detrimental psychologically, and potentially responsible for the emerging challenges with mental well-being of immigrant youth of color (P. Smith et al., 2022).

It is no wonder that with such twining creating fragmentation of Chloe's literacies, she commented, "I stayed in my room all the time because I didn't want to talk to people, because I felt like they looked at me weird every time I say something." It is also not surprising that, given the lack of a holistic process for equally validating all elements of her literacies, Chloe then "started to just try to talk like them," "pronouncing" her words. Even so, Chloe seems to laugh off the formality that she now uses in her typical speech. In addition, her lashing out at people, as well as her challenges with behavior centering around her languaging with her increasingly fragmented literacies, do not go unnoticed. Chloe confirms the basis for languaging in her literacies, saying:

> I know my language was one of the factors because I would like, go home, cry about it, because no one understood what I was saying. I would just say, "I am speaking English, just like some words different," but people look at me as if I AM DIFFERENT. I know language definitely made me struggle during middle school.

The fact that "most of the teachers weren't very helpful," "were not even aware of what was going on," and "never said anything" to her, while some suggested "counseling," which was absent at the high school level for Chloe, perhaps all point to the ways in which the fragmentation of literacies for Black immigrant students does not seem serious or critical enough to warrant "intervention," or even mere attention.

Chloe's indications that this situation of fragmentation of her literacies by schools and teachers persisted into high school are telling. She describes getting "a paper back when [she] was in high school" telling her to "speak how you write, don't write how you speak," meaning that her Englishes for writing, which approximated white listening subject norms, needed to be taken up in her speech. Again, we see Chloe's efforts to obtain equilibrium, always through an effort to appropriate certain literacies that she believed were designed by teachers and others in her high school. She says, "So I was like, 'Ok, it's immediately I'm the one person to live with that all the time so ok, let me change my voice in order to fit in, to make friends.'"

Chloe's recognition of the fragmentation in her literacies as well as the twining of her race and language (Rosa & Flores, 2017) appear to both be visible here. Her efforts to approximate white listening subject norms appear to be made because she wants to be accepted as a person and to have friends in school, even though she never really ends up having more than one or two friends. Chloe is entangled with her racialized Englishes and her racialized Englishes are entangled with her (P. Smith, 2022d). This confirms the theoretical assertions by Rosa and Flores (2017) that even when many racialized youth try to "sound white," they often are not accepted.

Chloe's current continued description of her Jamaican Standardized Englishes as "terrible," even while she sanctions her use of the writing center to "make sure her writing is right the first time," signals her acceptance of this preference for some of her literacies and rejection for others. Chloe's mother inadvertently reinforces the fragmentation of her literacies throughout her entire life by telling her, "You need to represent yourself like this and speak [proper] like this." Speaking of her mother, Chloe explained that "you'll never hear her speak like broken." Chloe's mother retains the British accent and refuses to "sound Jamaican," while insisting on being "a proper person," all of which seems to have made it difficult for Chloe to recognize, as a child, the possibility of holistic literacies in her present or her future.

Chloe appears to subtly allude to the fragmentation in her literacies when she describes her mother's reading, which is "a lot," as "kind of changing her" and causing her to "carry herself at this high level." Even so, Chloe says her mother expects her not to "speak down" at a level of inferiority associated with being "unproper" as signaled by certain Englishes. To Chloe's mother, it seems, the Jamaican Creolized Englishes that she warned Chloe against were "less than," and her intent was to have Chloe "meet that [other] level" of "proper" uses of Englishes at which she was inadvertently approximating whiteness. Chloe's subtle though not explicit recognition of the fragmentation in her literacies often is evidenced in statements such as, "I try to just get over it, try to change. I work with [my mother]."

The basis for Chloe's challenges with the fragmentation in her literacies has long since been acknowledged by literature that focuses on communicative differences, power, and culture, in families and across societies. Scholars such as Dr. Shirley Brice Heath (1983) acknowledged, in their examinations of white and African American children across communities, that although close to one another, children reflected differences based on values of their families as well as patterns of communication. Others, such as Dr. Lisa Delpit, in "The Silenced Dialogue" (1988), observed how issues of power become constructed in classrooms with their accompanying rules for engaging in participatory structures that allow for power. Delpit observed that knowing the rules of the culture of power could allow those without power to obtain it, but that privilege held by those with power often was overlooked by those who wielded it and most acknowledged by those without it. As Delpit showed, the goal should not necessarily be to teach students to adopt a code (e.g., way of using language) different from the one they possessed, but rather to enable them to understand the power associated with the code (e.g., Englishes) they already used as well as the power structures within which their codes functioned in society.

A few years later, Dr. Luis Moll and colleagues (1992) demonstrated how students use their funds of knowledge—practices in the household, including those involving labor and socialization—that are located at the center of learning interactions between children and adults. And Dr. Patricia Edwards and colleagues (1999) have shown how parent stories, and later "family literacies" as well as Parent of Color stories, necessarily work to bridge divides across home and school (Edwards et al., 2022; Edwards & Smith, forthcoming). These strides have been all the more possible because of shifts in the field called for by scholars such as Drs. Kathy Au (1993), Brian Street (1995), and Allan Luke (2012) to make visible the ways in which various literacies operate, through sociocultural practices, across home and school.

Yet, despite the progress made in bridging these gaps, there is still a tendency to utilize terms such as *academic language* and *academic literacy* as juxtaposed against notions such as "informal literacy" and "invisible literacy" in the field and in classrooms. Flores (2020) has argued about the importance of moving beyond dichotomies in the ways in which we describe literacies, viewing some as academic (e.g., formal) and others as not (e.g., invisible, informal; see, for instance, Dyson, 2015; Kiramba, 2019). In his description, Flores (2020) suggests the use of the term *language architecture* as a better way to describe the affordances that students bring to their use of languaging in, beyond, and across home and school. As observed earlier, Flores describes language architecture as a dynamic in which students "manipulate language for specific purposes" (p. 25). Based on this distinction, my colleagues and I have shown how language architecture occurs in the case of a Black immigrant youth, given understandings of "how language choice and meaning are related based on how students are socialized into cultural, linguistic, and . . . racial communit[ies]" (P. Smith et al., 2022, p. 76). And my conceptualization of the term *raciosemiotic architecture* (P. Smith, 2022e) to describe how the many modes of meaning-making (e.g., audio, visual, gestural) are racialized in the literate practices of students of color also provides insight into why Chloe adeptly navigates impositions of race on her language and other broader semiotic resources across borders.

Guided by the notion of language architecture, teachers of Black students such as Chloe, and of all youth, can allow the decision-making associated with using languaging to reside with students based on the literacies required by the tasks in which they are engaged. This is an option that youth are not often provided. Had Chloe been given the opportunity by her mother, teachers, and schools to demonstrate that she could utilize various elements of her Englishes from her unique linguistic repertoire as equally valuable for different purposes, there would have been a reduced tearing of the psyche, and perhaps she would not have felt like she had to select literacies to feel safe even while she rejected others, and thus herself (see P. Smith et al., 2022). And in a situation where schools would have attended to raciosemiotic architecture for youth of color during literacy instruction, it is likely that Chloe, as well as her mother, would have had more supportive mechanisms to reduce the trauma Chloe experienced across schools.

Teaching the Black Literate Immigrant: Part IV. By attending to the ways in which Black youth are positioned to disrupt a lopsided pursuit of literate "success" in classrooms, teachers who operate using the holistic literacies element of the Black immigrant literacies framework can engender a balance in how students draw from their literacies and can decrease the fragmentation that divides the psyche. According to my colleague and me (Smith & Warrican, 2021b), acknowledging that translanguaging occurs in the languages and Englishes of Black immigrant youth affords them opportunities to represent their literacies holistically (see also P. Smith, 2020d). Specifically, for Black immigrant youth like Chloe, it is possible with what we call "translanguaging with Englishes" to enable them to draw fully from their individual linguistic repertoires as they manage a range of linguistic and semiotic devices (e.g., gesture, humor, dress, posture, etc.), even as they recognize and anticipate the resistance that tends to accompany racialized Englishes as they leverage these across multiple spaces in society (P. Smith, 2020a; Smith & Warrican, 2021b). This opportunity creates spaces for all teachers, regardless of the content areas on which they focus, to enable Black immigrant youth to draw from various literacies, including those required in extracurricular areas such as the arts and sports. There, teachers can equally value those literacies as much as they do the subject-area literacies that historically have often been accepted as markers of success (e.g., math, ELA, science). This opportunity also presents a charge to those who work with Black, Black immigrant, and other racialized youth beyond schools, who may themselves be delegitimizing certain literacies in their arsenals.

To facilitate this process, mechanisms can be used that foster holistic literacies of students through Black immigrant literacies. One such mechanism is for teachers to be prepared to reject notions of Englishes as "dialects" and instead to recognize translanguaging with Englishes as a legitimate approach to how racialized Black bilingual and multilingual youth, such as Chloe, from the English-speaking Caribbean emerge with holistic literacies. In the article, "Migrating While Multilingual and Black: Beyond the (Bi)Dialectal Burden," my colleague and I highlight the need for positioning racialized speakers across the globe, and particularly those who are Black, as bilingual/multilingual students who translanguage with Englishes, as opposed to referring to them as dialect speakers (Smith & Warrican, 2021b). To preface this argument, we describe how *bidialectalism*, the systematic use of two different dialects (often one being a non-standardized variety) of the same language, is an underrecognized and unappreciated phenomenon in education across the globe (Antoniou et al., 2016). We explain that in education, bidialectalism often is used to represent the relationship between two dialects of a language where students who speak primarily the nonstandardized variety are taught the target language (i.e., the standardized variety) (Siegel, 2012).

While the field of linguistics does not view any language or language variety as necessarily superior to another, socially there is a tendency to value a "standard," often the target language in education, as more important than the nonstandardized variety. Although in the field of linguistics both varieties (standardized and nonstandardized) are considered dialects, nonstandardized languages tend to be the ones labeled as *dialects* socially. My colleague and I assert that no matter the context, inferiority tends to be attached to languages characterized as dialects, and superiority to target languages (i.e., standardized accepted varieties) (Smith & Warrican, 2021b).

The reason for this inferiority associated with dialects, we argue, is based on raciolinguistic ideologies, which, as described by Rosa and Flores (2017), are ways of thinking that cause certain languages (i.e., dialects) and their speakers to have an inferior status based largely on race (Smith & Warrican, 2021b). We also observe that, individually, buying into the notion of being bidialectal on the part of both the white listening subject (i.e., anyone with expectations for proper uses of Englishes) and the racialized "object" (e.g., Chloe and her mother) creates racialized speakers who in turn reinforce standard language ideologies such as those that Chloe works to reflect in her literacies.

Addressing this challenge that further reinforces fragmented literacies, we urge teachers to rethink the notion of the dialectal racialized speaker and to relabel students/speakers as *bi/multilingual users of Englishes* (Smith & Warrican, 2021b). Bi/multilingual users of Englishes already have the power of legitimacy and do not need to obtain it from the white listening subject, or to make efforts to try to use languages, including their Englishes, based on what is believed to be acceptable according to Eurocentric norms (Smith & Warrican, 2021b). Represented broadly across the majority world (e.g., Africa, Asia, Latin America, the Caribbean), racialized bi/multilingual speakers of Englishes, such as Chloe, have long established and leveraged linguistic repertoires for many purposes; it is restrictions from Eurocentric norms that create fragmentation of their literacies. Teachers can intervene in disrupting fragmentation based on connotations of racialized bi/multilingual speakers of Englishes and languages in ways that delegitimate speakers such as Chloe as racialized "objects." In doing so, teachers allow these speakers to use their often-disregarded Englishes and enjoy legitimacy through languaging associated with labels such as *bilingualism*, *multilingualism*, *trilingualism*, and so on. Teachers who understand how Englishes and languaging function across local and global contexts can change the way their students label languages as (inferior) dialects and can position all students based on asset-based perspectives.

As teachers foster holistic literacies of students through Black immigrant literacies, they can consider avenues such as "Black placemaking" (Tichavakunda, 2020) to think of literacies as they occur across places in the destination and home countries of youth. Tichavakunda describes Black placemaking as a consideration of how Blackness intersects with place, structure, and agency, and as a critical element in discussions of Blackness. According to Tichavakunda, Black placemaking "might be applied to any setting where Black people are present and congregate to create communities, places, and events for themselves" (p. 1). Black placemaking can thus function as a way to foster holistic literacies of Black immigrant youth and their peers.

I have documented my *hybridities of identities and place* as a Black immigrant by examining my pasts, presents, and futures, revealing geo-literacies across my lifetime;

Figure 4.4. Cultivating Holistic Literacies

Guiding Questions	Migration Country		Home Country		Online Across Migration Country & Home Country
	In School	*Out of School*	*In School*	*Out of School*	
How do I use my literacies for the subject areas that I study in school?					
How do I use my literacies as a hobby/ for enjoyment or for personal goals?					
How do teachers respond when I use my literacies for the subject areas that I study in school?					
How do teachers respond when I use literacies as a hobby/for enjoyment or for personal goals?					
How do parents respond when I use my literacies for the subject areas that I study in school?					
How do parents respond when I use literacies as a hobby/for enjoyment or for personal goals?					
How do Black, white, and other peers respond when I use my literacies for the subject areas that I study in school?					
How do Black, white, and other peers respond when I use literacies as a hobby/ for enjoyment or for personal goals?					

agricultural literacies, religious literacies, multilingual literacies, and school-sanctioned literacies in my childhood; family and care-taking literacies in my adolescence and adulthood; and financial literacies and professional literacies as an adult. In much the same way, Black placemaking can allow Black immigrant youth to identify and validate multiple literacies forged through their instantiation of place (see P. Smith, in press). To facilitate their understanding and provide students with opportunities to cultivate holistic literacies as bi/multilingual users of Englishes via Black placemaking, teachers are invited to use the exercise shown in Figure 4.4.

By reconciling literacies as holistic through the use of this activity with students, teachers can facilitate youth's identification of the literacies and languaging that they attach to various senses of place and can help them to interrogate their rationales for these attachments. This process allows youth to center racialization as a basis for their determinations of how place creates affordances for certain literacies based on *their* languaging and Englishes, and not that of others. Through languaging attached to Black placemaking (Tichavakunda, 2020), teachers, schools, organizations, and societies have opportunities to identify the ways in which holistic literacies are fostered and/or fragmented in specific ways based on place across students' home countries and destination countries. In doing so, they can use raciosemiotic architecture to recreate place in ways that support Black students as they draw holistically from their literacies across geographical, virtual, and other contexts.

QUESTIONS TO CONSIDER

1. **For Teachers**
   - What differences do varying Black immigrant students and student populations reflect based on their racialized literacies?
   - How do the metalinguistic, metacultural, and metaracial understandings presenting themselves in and beyond literacy classrooms differ based on Black immigrant students' linguistic, migrant, and racial backgrounds?
   - What barriers do these understandings create between Black immigrant students and their Black, immigrant, multilingual, white, or peers of color?
   - What teaching opportunities for building solidarity do these understandings create between Black immigrant students and their Black, immigrant, multilingual, white, or peers of color?
2. **For Teacher-Educators**
   - How are differences among varying Black immigrant student populations presented across various subject areas in teacher preparation programs based on students' racialized literacies?
   - How can teachers be taught to cultivate metalinguistic, metacultural, and metaracial understandings when approaching K–12 learners across subject areas during practice in the field?
   - How can teachers address barriers to these forms of understandings created between Black immigrant populations and their Black, immigrant, white, multilingual, or other peers?

- How can teachers use opportunities based on these understandings created between themselves and Black, immigrant, white, multilingual, or other peers to build solidarity?

3. **For Policymakers**
   - How can subject-based curricular innovations be used to address distinctions within and across Black immigrant student populations?
   - What accommodations need to be made to allow for students' cultivation of metalinguistic, metacultural, and metaracial understandings in classrooms?
   - Which elements of policies present barriers to these forms of understandings created between Black immigrant populations and their Black, immigrant, white, multilingual, or other peers?
   - How can policies be leveraged that allow schools to use opportunities to build solidarity based on these understandings created between Black immigrant populations and their Black, immigrant, white, multilingual, or other peers?

CHAPTER 5

Teaching Ervin, a Black Bahamian Literate Immigrant

Fostering Peer Interactions

In this chapter I present the "authentic narrative" of Ervin, an Afro-Caribbean immigrant youth of Bahamian descent, who identified as Black and perceived himself as speaking Bahamian Creolized English, Bahamian Standard English, and Standard American English. This narrative illustrates Ervin's transnational experience with migration, racialized languaging, and Englishes, in relation to Black American and other peers from childhood into adolescence and adulthood across elementary, middle, high school, and college as a basis for discussing considerations for teaching literacy. Ervin's authentic narrative is based on the notion of story and, as with Chloe's, it is developed from the transcription of our conversations during my engagement in a research study on Black immigrant languages and literacies, excerpts from which have been presented in part elsewhere (see P. Smith, 2019; P. Smith et al., 2022, for a discussion; see also P. Smith, 2023a).

I chose to present Ervin's story because, as Mohl (1986) observes, Black immigrants from the Bahamas were one of the earliest groups of Caribbean immigrants to give "Miami its special character in the early years of the twentieth century" (p. 271). As I have discussed elsewhere (P. Smith, 2023a), the history of Black immigrants from the Bahamas began with Bahamian fishermen, wreckers, seamen, and traders who often conducted business with the Seminole Indians of Florida during the times when it was less developed and more isolated. Mohl observes that Florida appeared to then have been considered another island by the Bahamian immigrants, but also that certain Black Bahamians had arrived as slaves of the British Loyalists who were fleeing after the American Revolution. A significant number of others migrated to Key West in the late 19th century and to other parts of Florida thereafter. Reverse migration also was a part of this experience, when Bahamian British officials appeared to attempt to bring Black immigrants from the south of America, creating a situation of migration across the mainland and the islands of the Bahamas (Mohl, 1986).

Ervin's story is important historically because it gives voice to the legacy of immigration experienced by his Bahamian ancestors, which in many invisible ways influences his manifestation of self in the world as a Bahamian today. Ervin's story here is also emblematic of the significance of his Black slave ancestors from the Bahamas, whose legacies directly influenced the ways he now comes to be in the United States and the world. Like Chloe's, Ervin's story reinforces the multilingualism inherent in the languaging of Black immigrant youth, a dynamic often overlooked in African American, Afro-Caribbean English–speaking, and African youth. To protect his identity, the name Ervin is a pseudonym.

Ervin's authentic narrative (see next section) is used to highlight three insights that persist regarding elements overlooked when teaching literacy and English language arts in ways that foster peer interactions among Black immigrant, Black American, other youth of color, and white American youth in classrooms: (1) "Black enough" as a basis for belonging while "becoming Black" (Ibrahim, 1999); (2) Englishes that alienate or do not while "unbecoming a 'native' English speaker"; and (3) immigration as both a barrier and a benefit while "becoming immigrant." Each of these insights will be discussed by highlighting how Ervin's narrative illustrates specific elements of the Black immigrant literacies framework. Then, the three insights will be linked to the literature and to guidelines for using literacy curricula, via the framework for Black immigrant literacies, that support racialized Black youth and foster peer interactions in classrooms.

For the first insight, I will show how the "struggle for justice" and the "myth of the model minority" elements of the Black immigrant literacies framework are navigated. For the second insight, I will show how the "holistic literacies" and "transraciolinguistic" elements of the Black immigrant literacies framework are reflected. For the third insight, I will show how the "local–global" element of the Black immigrant literacies framework becomes visible.

ERVIN'S AUTHENTIC NARRATIVE: RAC(E)ING ENGLISHES AS A MULTILINGUAL MIGRANT: "TALKING LIKE I'M GHETTO"

Elementary School: "My Mom Wanted Me to Speak in a Certain Way"

[In elementary school] I spoke broken English, compared to America [American English]. My mom wanted me to speak in a certain way. [In] my primary school, [they expected] the standard British English. I myself personally had a hard time with proper English on paper, but I could speak clearly versus on paper because it's slang. I would spell words wrong. [I would tell myself] I can't mess it up. I can't. [But] I would always find myself mess[ing] it up. So, in private school [my mother] definitely wants me to speak better than most people. She would ask me to read a lot of books. She [made] me read a lot. I had a book—I had some books that I didn't read. About the books . . . I still won't read them. I don't know why. [I'm not interested in reading.]

Reading aloud at schools in the Bahamas was an attack for me because I would read choppy, I'm a choppy reader. [What made me think I was a choppy reader?] The class, me. [They would say] "Pick someone else to read" or something like that. Because if I was to read, . . . I just say something in my head, "The boy was running," and I stop because I would find myself, I think, it has to do more with sight because I would read more lines than I needed and then start reading the line that I need. . . . And I think I would try to focus on two lines. . . . [I stood out because] most of the class, that's a lot of people, they volunteer to read. They were fluent. This was more like 1st grade, 2nd grade, 3rd grade, but then afterwards when I start to read some of the books that my mom got for me and I figured it out, I start to realize I read more fluent, I can take on more multiple lines at a time, be able to register the information and just continue . . . fluent . . .

High School: "I Would Push Back in My Brain the Way I Speak and I Would Try to Bring Back Proper"

In high school, my writing got worse, actually. My writing got worse and then I spoke the same way [broken English]. I spoke with the same slang, the same everything.

And in high school [we didn't have middle school]—we go from primary straight to high school—I met a teacher. She's from England and she told me specifically that my English, it's going down and down. She pulled me aside and she told me, "I've been looking at your essay and you write the way you talk." And if it wasn't for her, my English wouldn't elevate the way it did.

In that conversation [with me], basically it was about my grades, my progress, . . . because I was doing good in everything else except English and during inside the conversation, she had all my essays and then she looked at me, so I said, "I find myself writing [the word] you as y-u." She showed me, "You speaking like you write," and then it opened my eyes and she said, "You go to college soon. You're about to be in America. You can't do that." So, I then found myself when I write my essays, I would go over them a ton of times and I would push back in my brain the way I speak and I would try to bring back proper, the way I should. . . . The way I should be writing in proper English. And then sooner or later, I became more efficient with the writing in high school. [I didn't try to use it with my friends though.] I just kept it in my writing. I continued [speaking the way I spoke], but in my writing I would write proper English and my speaking I just kept it [as is].

She [the teacher had high expectations of me speaking differently], I think. She probably did [but she never corrected every single thing I said]. She's around with Bahamian kids all day so she even started speaking like us afterwards. [Still] my mom would [correct me]. She would. When I said, "Bey," she would tell me, "Stop speaking like that." When I said, "Why?" she would say, "Speak correctly," because she would correlate me talking like that to, like, me talking like I'm ghetto. . . . And so, she would be like, "We're sending you to private school, we're sending you to this school, you need to speak correctly." And she would always say, "I bet that is not what you learn inside your books to talk like that."

Reflecting on Being Back Home: "You Can Point at Anything [and That Would Be a Whibe]"

[Overall] we speak predominantly broken English. So, we chop off words. So, a key word in Bahamas I think is "Bey" B-E-Y. I mean that refers to anyone. So, I don't know someone, I don't know their name. I say, "Bey, come here." [Or] "Yes. Bey." There are a lot of phrases like you say back home that most people in Bahamas can understand. [If] I pointed a series of boxes, I say, "Could you give me a whibe?" W-H-I-B-E. Yes. You can point to anything [and that would be a whibe]. And that's predominantly, I wouldn't say, spoken among adults, but it's also spoken among kids. And I [would] say between like 10 to 20 age ranges, that's the way we communicate with each other.

Initially Getting to the United States: "I Spoke English and They Spoke English, but They Couldn't Understand Me"

I first came to the United States in August 2014, that was the first year here and it was very difficult. I had to adjust really quick because I spoke with such a strong accent . . . I had an accent being around Bahamians my whole life. I would speak and then people asked me, "Could you repeat that? Could you slow down?"

I had two switches, I had a Bahamas accent and I had a clearer, I would say "American accent" if you say so. I slow down so that people could understand what I'm saying. It's quite difficult because I found myself not speaking that much—just listen and then answer. After that I developed, say, a second language, and then I was able to communicate with people more effectively.

It took me an entire first semester to just listen and understand people who really can't understand me. I spoke English and they spoke English, but they couldn't understand me. I was aware of adjustments I had to make. [Mostly I felt like I was the only one required to change the way I spoke.] Yes. Most definitely. The Americans, they spoke the way they spoke, I had to adjust to them, and I still couldn't understand it. I had such a strong accent compared to other people. [I felt it was unfair.] In a way, I mean in a way not because, I don't know. I think this is a factor with my communication skill, I wouldn't say it's poor, but I don't want to talk.

I can share quickly with you what happened in my first chemistry class, you know. I asked my teacher a question. It was in the whole-class group. There were 180 people in that classroom. When I showed my accent, he comes up and I showed it at him and he can't understand me and I was asking him, "Can I do it right? Did I do it right? Can I do it this way?" [so I said] Excuse me, Professor. "Can I do this thing this way?" and I said "Thing." And "thing" is the word that only Bahamian and Caribbean people can understand. I guess me saying, asking the question . . . He said, "What? What?" He asked me after class. I found it intimidating. That was a big shock to me that I really need and try to adjust. So, [that was] something I didn't want to happen again.

Getting Into College: "I Constantly Try to Make Sure That My Second Switch, My Second Language, That's Activated"

[When I came here to the United States, I had to do a test.] I had to do TSI. The rationale. I think [it's] because I am from the Caribbean country. And the TSI test was more like the SAT and the first time I took it I rush to it because always like I'm good at English; it is too easy. I missed the score by 10 points, I think and then I took it again and did better than I did the first time. [It was like comprehension passages.] The comprehension, words, vocabulary, something like that. I don't think I have to write an essay. It's just multiple-choice questions, passages. I was kind of, I don't know.

I was kind of angry [trying to get into the university] because I took SAT and everything. I did take the SAT. My SAT would take me to the college. [Then they asked me to] Show it again. I did [the English component with the SAT but] I think my English component is the reason why I have to take it [again] because my English components were lower than math, but I didn't have to take math. I had to take English. [I had to take an English test and they used the SAT score to determine whether I would need to take TSI.] [There were no speaking components]

So I'm taking [communication classes] right now. It's like a rolling ball. The more ball rolls, the more confident I get because my first speech inside the class, I was very, very timid. I have to speak in front of the class. About 22, 23 people. It's not too bad, but still it's like [the most] nervous [thing] I can experience. I ask myself the same question because I can talk in front of a crowd. With no hesitation, with no issue, but if many doors closed and I have people who one hundred percent focus on me, then I have that issue because once I don't want to say words incorrectly, I constantly try to make sure that my second switch, my second language, that's activated. Afterwards I get more comfortable, more relaxed and then it's [fine]. I've done three speeches so far. Actually, I did one on Monday this week. And it went well. Everyone reacted the way I wanted them to react. They applaud. Everyone could understand me. For my first speech, people commented on my accent. They said, "You say words differently, where you're from." And they said, "I can hear your accent." "Are you from Africa? Are you from Jamaica?"

Anywhere but the Bahamas. I told them I'm from the Bahamas. I was actually, speaking clear, I guess. [My teacher recorded my voice speaking in class.] He sent [the recording] to our Dropbox in Outlook; so we can look at it online. The goal for the course, I guess is to be more skilled, to be more well-versed communicating on the job or inside the office or you have to present a presentation. [But for work] Like I'm at work on the phone and someone calls, I speak like an American and I put on my proper voice and I say all my words correctly. So, I'm looking at a book I say, "Hello," I am answering the phone and say, "Thanks for calling Kellogg's. How can I help?" and I speak correctly.

College Friends: "So, Even I'm Speaking Right Now, Speaking My Second Language With You, They Still Won't Be Able to Understand Me"

[Being in the city where I live is different from when I first came to the United States to visit.] People from Texas can't understand me, even when I speak correctly, they said they can't understand me. I guess I said things two to five times. My name is . . . I spoke to people like this. So, even I'm speaking right now, speaking my second language [Standard American English] with you, they still won't be able to understand me. I find it confusing. So, like I say, I go back to one-word question, only one-word answer, simple question. [I kind of dumb down my speech then because it creates so much a problem for communicating with them.]

[I don't think they realize I'm doing that.] They don't. Like, one of my friends, her name is Jordan. When I speak to her, her name is like people say Michael Jordan. I said Michael Jordan, Jordan. [The emphasis is on the *Jor*]. When me and her speak, I find myself sometimes like, when I start to get comfortable. I slip, I start to talk faster and then she is going to say. "What?" And it's only her because I find myself she gets confused from time to time when I talk when I get so relaxed. She said, "You got to repeat that, say that again." She's like. She keeps asking me, "Huh? Huh? Huh?"

I get annoyed when I know that I'm speaking clear and I find myself not talking as much as I would. I shut down. That's what I do. Like I was in the recreation center. I played basketball and soccer. My friends, they got accustomed to understanding what I was saying on the field too because when I'm playing sports, I'm not thinking about speaking clearly. I'm like, "Give me the ball, bey," or I said, "Pass it here," or something . . . I talked with much emphasis on my accent, at that time, because my brain is now not focusing on speaking clear, but I'm trying to obtain objectives and then when I was at the grocery store too, people can't understand me. I don't know.

College Years: "The Moment I'm With Caribbean People I Go Back to My Accent"

[The biggest change I experienced from the Bahamas to the United States] overall was speaking. Moving to the United States, I guess the adjustment to the culture. It's so different like everyone here, I would say they're not friendly as we are. So, when I first came back home in the United States and said, "Good morning" . . . I find myself, I stop saying good morning as often I would because no one says that back to me. And I'm a friendly person. So, I try to converse with anyone. So, I would say, "Good morning, How it go," and . . . I said, "Your hair is nice," and "How's your day going?" and she was like . . . no response back. [She's like] Yes. "Why is he talking to me?!"

I found it's weird. Back home if I'm in a library and I sit next to a stranger and I made a comment like that in the conversation, I'm not trying to get with a lady or be interested. I'm just trying to [have a] conversation. And we will feel more comfortable if we know each other a little bit more than we just sit in front of each other, we don't know each other. . . . So, that was the biggest thing I had to deal with. The friendliness. I think Caribbean people in general are one hundred percent more friendly. So, I think that was the biggest thing for me. [And the community in the city is just as unfriendly as the university.] It's [also] different. I [found the difference] was with the ethnicity. I guess there's . . . in the United States that . . . me coming here. The girl I'm talking about most, that is a Caucasian young lady. I guess she felt distant because I'm . . . Yeah, I'm classified as Black, African American when I'm not African American. I'm a Caribbean person. She felt [distant] . . . So, [I told myself] I can't do [life] like that.

[About my friends], here I have Bahamian friends, that's all [no others]. To be honest, my first year at [the university], I didn't know anybody. I didn't know any Bahamian, nothing. I had one friend. He's from Thailand and I found a strong connection with him. We both felt eliminated and we made the connection through that. [This was] in the class. He noticed the way I spoke and he came over to me and he said, "Where are you from?" "I'm from Bahamas," and he said, "I'm from Thailand." And we were talking and my first question, because I'm so conscious that people couldn't understand me. Most of my first question is, and I'm surprised, "Can you really understand me the way I'm speaking to you?" and he said, "Yes, I can understand everything clearly." Because I always ask people that . . . to me . . . I ask people "Can you understand me?" and that would leave me slow down and be comfortable. That . . . He could understand me clearly and like [that was a relief].

He would laugh, he would joke on stuff I'm saying, but he would understand everything I say clearly and then after that I met [John], I met all Bahamians and it's even more a relief because now I could cut off all those ties, all those barriers . . . to interact with people who can understand what I'm saying. When I made friends with [John], a Bahamian friend, I speak Bahamian. I'm speaking to [Dr. Z] and some other people, I talked to him and I switched. The moment I'm with Caribbean people I go back to my accent. For the man I spoke to at the door [when I was coming here to your office], I switch back off, I have to speak [Standard English]. [I'm always thinking about my audience, thinking about the people I'm talking to.]

Peer Interactions: "I Do Emotion and Then So, I Guess Girls, They Then React"

[How I see it] I've been just a Black male in the U.S. because I feel, me speaking the way I speak, I'm getting more recognition. I try to have more conversation with people who are more interested. And asking me, "Where are you from? Why do you speak like that?" and they said to me like I talked like an African American. Sometimes intentionally I put on my accent if I'm trying to [call out to] a lady or something like that because I guess it gave me certain pizzaz. So I put on my Caribbean accent. I intentionally just talk Bahamian.

It's more attractive I think and I guess the majority of Bahamian guys, they would say the same thing. [It feels like being more unique.] I wouldn't say it's a privilege, but it's just, I'm like a little special [attraction] with a Bahamian flag on it. When people interact with me, they would pass me. They stay more interested because instead of say our regular apple, you see little blue, black, and gold. [To them there is] something on the apple I would like to know. [In their mind, it's about] "Oh, how come the apple look like that?" [So they always have something to ask about.]

[Like] with African American males and African males in the U.S. [the relationship] It's a good one, I think. In a sense, I want to believe . . . The way we interact, I use my accent with them because [we are] on the field. So, the guys who are from Nigeria, and stuff like that, they speak with an African accent, a hundred percent of times. All the time. When we are on the court, they say, "Hey, . . ." and all of that stuff and all African stuff that I don't understand and I feel more comfortable with my accent interacting with them. But African American guys, for African American, I speak more American with them than I speak with the Africans. [I don't feel less comfortable with them though.] Not necessarily. [But I don't think they would understand my accent.] I think it's because they didn't [get] expose to [it before].

The African, and may be [some of the] African American, they live in a family where parents speak African slang. [Then there are] those other guys, they're just around the African American sound. It's like two different experiences and that can affect their willingness to understand [somebody who's different]. [Now] in conversations with African American women, I talk so that people can understand what I'm saying most of the time. But like in my parties or social events, my accent is there because I'm excited, I do emotion and then so, I guess girls, they then react, the way they look back when we open our mouth, they look back and they said, "Who's that?" Because it sounds different to what they normally hear. What I mean is constant conversation with them, I switch it on and off. With African women from Africa, [it's different] because [I don't have that much experience].

[About sounding American] To be honest, I'm only going to sound American when I'm speaking with [Americans] because I have the issue with the Bahamians who come to America and they come back home and speak like Americans. I think you are not sure who you are. You're going to another country and I guess personally me I identify [this as a] weakness in a way. Because you spoke a certain way your whole life and then you come to America. Me, I switch my accent on and off, but when I go back home, I know I'm from the Bahamas. I'm a Bahamian and I speak like a Bahamian until the day I die, but when you're in America, you have standards, you need to speak properly. Yes. When you're in the Bahamas you need to go back to your root.

[But then again] I think I'm not at all processing the thought inside my mind. I'm thinking. It will be difficult for Caribbean persons who are inside Bahamas with only Americans around them, where you're Caribbean students and you have only Caribbeans around you inside the culture and I'm thinking that Caribbean people are just around Americans all day, they are forced to.

To keep speaking in the same way, you probably would be using language that the Americans are reinforcing. And then like exercise anything that you constantly do and then it becomes a part of you. And I'm thinking when those Bahamian or Caribbean students come back to the Bahamas sensitized in the environment they have been so long, they can't help but speak the way they've been speaking. [Like there are people who don't know how to switch, like] let me see. I only know John. That would be John because he mumbles like he's really quiet while he's talking. And a lot of people can't understand him. I don't know, he might be treated differently.

To be honest, I think he gets more attention. I think he gets more attention. Because him, he intentionally talks inside his accent all the time. He talks inside his accent all the time. I don't think he switches it at all. And then another guy, Andy. He speaks the worst out of all of us because he's from the island. He's from Bahamas but, [ok let's me explain] so, you have the major island and smaller islands. So, he's from one of the smaller islands [which makes him farther away] and they speak even worse than us. I mean he has to switch, but his switch is not as effective as my switch would be compared to his. So, when he speaks to us, we make fun of him, "What do you say?" For instance, me and John, we say *whibe*, he says *vibe*. You see it's the big difference and like another word, I say deodorant, he says deodorant too so, I need to record him when he's speaking around . . . so, you can hear the way he speaks. As a Bahamian person, his Bahamian slang is on a whole other level compared to me.

Except for him [my other friends from the Bahamas] they speak more proper when they're around Americans. They speak with almost even American accent sometimes. [I have no feeling about that.] It is what it is. That what they choose to do, but my switch is more, switch is to understand me, not to switch to sound American. I just want to. My switch is I slow down, I pronounce my words more and I say, I don't talk like American, say like "What's up, bro?", "Hey, man." I don't speak like that. I don't speak like that. I would say it in Bahamian. [For instance] I say when we ask someone, "Ha it go?" instead of saying, "How does it go?" or "How's it going?" I would say, "How are you doing?" I translate it. [Translate it from what it is in Bahamas instead of taking its American slang.] Yes, and it'll be like, "What's going on bro?" I would say I would think it might be American, I say, "What's up?" . . . I say, "What's up? How are you doing?" but I always follow it with, "How are you doing?" after. I think it's now second nature. I don't even think about it. As much as I used to, now it ends up in your [arsenal], just takes such a long time.

INSIGHTS FROM ERVIN'S AUTHENTIC NARRATIVE

Ervin's authentic narrative, "Rac(e)ing Englishes as a Multilingual Immigrant," as presented above, reflects a chronological account of his transnational experiences with languaging and life across the United States and his home country, the Bahamas.

"BLACK ENOUGH" AS A WAY TO BELONG

As reflected in Ervin's narrative, he draws on certain resources to assert himself as "Black enough" as a way to belong while "becoming Black" (Ibrahim, 1999), and he reflects elements of the Black immigrant literacies framework. Ervin uniquely *lays claim to the struggle for justice* and reflects *a transraciolinguistic approach* (P. Smith, 2020d) both in everyday life and during interactions with Black American and African peers. Additionally, he *disrupts the myth of the model minority* during the process and uses his *holistic literacies* as well as the *local–global connection* by determining how he manages systemic efforts of Englishes to alienate him and his languaging.

Laying Claim to the Struggle for Justice and the Local-Global Connection

Ervin's narrative shows that he lays claim to the struggle for justice and reflects a transraciolinguistic approach (P. Smith, 2020d) even as he makes local–global connections in many ways. Ervin's attempt to assert himself as Black enough comes from his ability to assert himself as Caribbean, and specifically Bahamian. He says, "[How I see it] I've been just a Black male in the U.S.," but he also makes the distinction saying, "Yeah, I'm classified as Black, African American when I'm not African American. I'm a Caribbean person."

In alluding to being racialized explicitly in the United States, Ervin makes it clear that he understands how he becomes subsumed into the African American population despite his ethnicity as West Indian. He wishes to maintain his West Indian identity even as he tries to assert himself as legitimate. Here, Ervin is thinking about how he thinks about race—*metaracial understanding*. He knows that he, as well as his languaging and literacies, are viewed as illegitimate because he repeatedly gets this message from a number of individuals and spaces in the United States. For instance, his friendliness is ignored, people insist they cannot understand him in spaces such as the grocery store, and when he becomes comfortable speaking to his friend, she eventually begins to say, "huh, huh, huh," which is annoying to him. Immigration functions as a barrier to Ervin, and he is forced to contemplate how he thinks about language—*metalinguistic understanding*. For Ervin, *metacultural understanding* is also at play as he is no longer just West Indian or Bahamian but is "becoming immigrant."

Ervin is stunned when he asks a newfound friend from Thailand, "Can you really understand me the way I'm speaking to you?" He is shocked when his friend says, "Yes, I can understand everything clearly." This recognition makes it clear to Ervin that there is nothing wrong with his languaging or his Englishes. And in fact, he chooses to make strategic decisions about how he uses his Englishes to achieve goals in interactions with his peers and with those he wants to befriend. He says, "I feel, me speaking the way I speak, I'm getting more recognition," and sees himself as a unique "apple" becoming more appealing when he uses his Bahamian Englishes than when he speaks like an African American or as an American in general. He does the same on the court, choosing to use his Bahamian accent with the Nigerian peers with whom he plays sports. However, he changes his use of Englishes with African Americans to Standard American English because he doesn't think they will understand him. He also does the same when he is on the phone or when presenting orally in class with peers.

Ervin's decision to manipulate his Englishes does not deter him from his conviction of being Bahamian, "Me, I switch my accent on and off, but when I go back home, I know I'm from the Bahamas." For Ervin, laying claim to the struggle for justice as a Black person in America means strategically deciding when he wants to use his Englishes in ways that will get him recognition, allow him to be effective with communication, make friends, and "succeed" in class.

Connecting racialization of language in the local context of the United States with that in the global context of his home country allows Ervin to recognize his power and agency to use his languaging and Englishes as he decides. In this way, his local–global connection helps Ervin to flip the switch, deciding how he reframes the ways that he is positioned—Black in the United States—*locally*—when he uses language. He manages to do this in the same way that he held on to the parts of his linguistic repertoire that were rejected from school spaces—*globally*—in the Bahamas. In other words, Ervin's decision-making shows that he refuses to accept the imposed racialization on his personhood, both locally and globally.

Using a Transraciolinguistic Approach in Conjunction With Holistic Literacies

Ervin's decision-making about his racialized Englishes as he is unbecoming a "native English speaker" is unique but not surprising. As I have shown elsewhere and presented earlier (P. Smith, 2019, 2020a), this uniqueness manifests itself in the lives of Black immigrant adolescents and adults. Black immigrants think about: how they think about their thinking about race, how they think about their thinking about language, and how they think about their thinking about culture, all at the same time. Together, these three forms of understanding—metaracial, metalinguistic, and metacultural—operate as part of what I refer to as a transraciolinguistic approach (P. Smith, 2022b).

In Ervin's strategic decision-making, we see elements of metalinguistic, metacultural, and metaracial understanding all working together. These forms of understanding allow him to position himself in agentive ways. They also allow him to reflect a different response from the typical resistance to institutional norms often discussed by Black racialized subjects. In other words, Ervin uses these forms of understanding despite how Englishes are leveraged to alienate him locally as well as globally across the Bahamas and the United States. Using his metalinguistic understanding, Ervin allows for a disruption of his perception of self as a "native English speaker." The U.S system forces him to identify as someone who is incapable of using English in acceptable ways. Ervin confirms Nero's (2006) assertion that often, it is when Black people migrate to the United States that they first question their legitimacy with Englishes.

It is through a transraciolinguistic approach that Ervin determines how to use his languaging and literacies strategically, to his advantage, as shown above. His metalinguistic understanding allows him to decide he will do so, even in situations where Bahamian Creole Englishes tend to have been racialized, thus repositioning their use to make him seem unique and attractive. And it is through his metalinguistic and metaracial understanding that Ervin becomes aware that there are goals he wishes to accomplish socially, academically, and emotionally, allowing him to leverage the elements of a transraciolinguistic approach skillfully as he uses Englishes carefully to achieve these goals. Ervin understands that relying on just the elements of his linguistic repertoire privileged by the white listening subject would not be enough. His use of a transraciolinguistic approach is critical in enabling him to rely on the parts of his linguistic repertoire that will help him keep his friends, do school 'well', and play sports with his teammates, even though these parts of his linguistic repertoire have been deemed inferior by so many all of his life. In doing so, Ervin is using what García and Wei (2014) describe as his full linguistic repertoire. Ervin also is reflecting that he relies on his holistic literacies.

When Ervin's initial annoyance at not being understood changed after he met his friend from Thailand, it is evident that this was his metalinguistic understanding at play. This understanding caused him to realize that his long-held practice of using his Bahamian Creolized Englishes with his friends was something that he could leverage in the United States. Metacultural understanding enabled Ervin to see that connecting with Bahamian peers in the United States further helped him to feel comfortable using his broad and full range of literacies. Even so, he appeared to fail in using some of his meta-understandings to accept what was regarded as the inferior languaging of a Bahamian peer who spoke "worse" than he did. Notwithstanding, through a transraciolinguistic approach, Ervin's fight in the struggle for justice can be viewed as strategic. His various forms of understanding at play raise questions about how Ervin comes to see himself, in both the Bahamas and the United States, as agentive rather than as a victim. Is it just his personality? How does a child decide to do this? How does an adolescent maintain this? And how can this be a key agentive approach to languaging and thriving as an adult in college?

While Ervin is agentive, it does not diminish the need for schools, organizations, institutions, and society to attend to leverage a transraciolinguistic approach for all students. Maintaining the focus on institutions is critical as it reduces the apparent lifetime of strategizing that has been needed on Ervin's part. In fact, in a society where more individuals can use such forms of understanding as they become familiar with linguistic diversity, much like Ervin's friend from Thailand, there is a greater chance that they too can engage effectively with peers' linguistic, racial, and cultural differences. In other words, if there is any "fixing" needed, I argue that it is the monolingual population that needs significant support with developing metalinguistic, metacultural, and metaracial understanding, and not multilingual, immigrant, and/or "underserved" students (e.g., Hispanic, African American) such as Ervin who are incessantly and unduly targeted in United States schools as "incapable," "underperforming," and "underproficient" based on what is perceived as their deviation from white listening subject norms. For Ervin and others like him who already leverage these forms of understanding, being able to recognize these forms of agency in their lived experiences both in and beyond classrooms is what becomes necessary. Through learning about these understandings and how they become leveraged for solidarity, students from dominant populations are positioned to value the strengths that Ervin and his transnational peers of color bring to U.S. classrooms.

In "A Distinctly American Opportunity: Exploring Non-Standardized English(es) in Literacy Policy and Practice," I make this bold assertion, indicating that our reinforcement of standardized language approaches across the United States is a problem not only because we fail to meet the needs of nonstandardized English speakers (P. Smith, 2016). Rather, as I show, it is a problem also because this practice places monolingual speakers at risk. The world is becoming increasingly globalized and transnationalism occurs daily in virtual spaces or physically as people move across borders. If individuals are unable to engage communicatively with various Englishes, languages, and distinctions regarding how others make meaning or sound, they will find their literacies and languaging incapable of helping them to navigate a globalized world.

Ervin's experience clearly reflects what happens when such a challenge is faced. In the predominantly white context in which he lived and attended school, it was almost impossible for anyone to engage with him. Yet his friend from Thailand could, despite having no previous encounter with Ervin's Englishes or accent. It is possible that this friend may have had experiences with metalinguistic, metacultural, and metaracial understanding as part of a transraciolinguistic approach in his life as well. There is a need for societal attention to schooling that focuses on increasing the capacity of the vast numbers of individuals labeled as "monolingual" in the United States (P. Smith, 2016) to engage with a transraciolinguistic approach. This is critical for bridging the gaps among racially, ethnically, and linguistically diverse populations, and indispensable to addressing the polarization that continue to be exacerbated individually, societally, politically, and otherwise across monolingual and multilingual worlds.

Disrupting the Myth of the Model Minority and the Local-Global Connection

Ervin draws on certain resources to assert himself as "Black enough" to belong while "becoming Black" (Ibrahim, 1999, 2019). In doing so, he reflects how he disrupts the myth of the model minority and leverages the local-global connection, both in everyday life and during interactions with Black American and African peers.

Ervin's progression through elementary, middle, and high school suggests that he struggled when confronted with the white gaze as a basis for the reading and writing imposed on him in schools. This happened both globally in his home country, the Bahamas, and also locally after he migrated to the United States. In this way, Ervin was able to see the local-global connection between how racialization of his language occurred in his home country as well as in the United States. In his elementary years, Ervin experienced how the majority-Black teachers and his parents in the Bahamas subscribed to the white listening subject in what they chose to prioritize as legitimate parts of his literacies. This is visible in Ervin's perception that he speaks "broken English" when he uses his Bahamian Creolized English. It is also noticeable in his mother's expectations for him to speak "a certain way"—Bahamian Standard English—as well as in his elementary school's wish for him to speak "the standard British English."

Ervin describes not being fluent with reading, being a "choppy" reader, and how being made to read out loud in school is "an attack" for him. He explains how his writing got worse after he went from elementary school to high school because he would write with the "slang" that he spoke. He also describes wanting to "bring back proper [English] the way he should" in his reading and writing. Being made to take the TSI even after he had proven that he was capable of using Englishes proficiently based on the SAT in college, and being placed in conversation classes where the teacher expected him to speak Standard American English, further reveal his perceived lack.

The instances presented here all show that contrary to how he might have been perceived as a model minority Black immigrant once he started college, Ervin wrestled with raciolinguistic ideologies for his entire brief life across elementary school, high school, and college. The raciolinguistic ideologies (Rosa & Flores, 2017) that Ervin encounters can be seen both in the Bahamas and in the United States. Similar to Chloe, the white listening subject norms that are imposed on him tell him that his languaging and literacies are not good enough and that he must try to use Englishes in the way the white European subject determined a long time ago that it should be used. Even when he tries to do this and thinks he has succeeded, he gets to the United States and no one seems to understand him even when he seems to appropriate the Englishes deemed acceptable (e.g., White mainstream English). Using his metalinguistic understanding to try to grapple with these challenges, it is not surprising that this makes no sense to Ervin. The barrier that he faces is based on his racialization as a Black immigrant to the United States as much as it is about his way of using Englishes, with an accent that seems un-American and "foreign" to many. In this way, immigration functions as a barrier for Ervin based on both his race and language.

As has been shown, efforts to try to use English in ways that the white listening subject requires, often do not lead to acceptance (Rosa & Flores, 2017). We see Ervin's rejection when his languaging and literacies are excluded by his Black mother and by Black teachers in elementary school in the Bahamas. We see this happen when he says he feels "attacked" by not being able to orally read words in his Bahamian classroom—words that have absolutely no basis in his daily languaging practices. We also see Ervin avoiding rejection from his Bahamian friends when he says, "[I didn't try to use Standard English with my friends though] . . . I just kept it in my writing. I continued [speaking the way I spoke]." We see how the rejection affected his sense of being a person in the United States when he says, "I was kind of angry [trying to get into the university] because I took SAT and everything." And we also see it in the United States when he states, as a result of this rejection, "I get annoyed when I know that I'm speaking clear and I find myself not talking as much as I would. I shut down." Yet Ervin appears to rely on a similar approach when he relegates his Bahamian friend's Englishes as inferior himself.

"Twining" of race and language, Rosa and Flores's (2017) term to explain how these elements of being a person are intertwined, is at play here. It is said that race and language work together, and the connection of the two, based on ways of thinking about language, creates feelings of being illegitimate. Rosa and Flores explain how people of color become "racialized objects" because they are made to feel that their language is not legitimate, while also being led to believe that *who they are* is inferior because of how they use language as part of their personhood. For Ervin, this was visible transnationally across multiple instances both in the majority-Black context of the Bahamas and in the binary-defined Black–White context of the United States. There was no instance where he spoke of a teacher or an institution elevating his Bahamian Creolized Englishes as a legitimate part of him or his linguistic repertoire. And in fact, it was surprising that Ervin kept choosing his Bahamian Creolized English over and over again, as a basis for keeping his friendships in school, and later as a way to preserve his unique Black identity in college.

It is possible that Ervin's repeated use of metalinguistic understanding, both in the Bahamas and increasingly within the United States, allowed him a sense of agency, which in turn created the pathway for him to "succeed"—based not on "academic norms" but on his feeling of "wholeness" as a person. As Ervin uses his metaracial and metalinguistic understanding, he is able to connect the local rejection of his Englishes and self in the United States, which is largely linked to race, to a similar rejection that he received in the Bahamas. With this local–global connection, Ervin positions himself as agentive even while the system, via numerous people, repeatedly perceives him as lacking.

Either way, Ervin's experiences with languaging and literacies seem somewhat similar to those faced by African Americans in the United States (see P. Smith et al., 2019).

While the racialized population of African Americans overtly and daily often grapple with white individuals imposing white listening subject norms, Ervin's challenges with white listening subject norms in the Bahamas are imposed by people like him—individuals who are all Black. When he gets to the United States, this changes, and most of the people imposing these norms are white. This does not change the fact that he is *still* racialized as a Black person by the norms of whiteness across the Caribbean and the United States— norms embedded within systems that come to transnationally reflect their commonalities as perpetrators of white supremacy even as their instantiations are very different. In other words, Ervin's experience based on the local–global connection proves that it is not an individual person whom he meets who is ultimately responsible for the racialized norms to which he is subjected; instead there is solid evidence that the problem is the *institution* of schooling that has prepared him and numerous others to privilege Eurocentric named Englishes over others in their individual linguistic repertoires. This confirms the assertion by Rosa and Flores (2017) that it is institutions such as schools, universities, the academy, and *not* merely individual children, youth, or adults like Ervin, that now need to be the major focus of our efforts for change.

Teaching the Black Literate Immigrant: Part I

In response to the need to focus on institutions, teachers have an increasing moral responsibility (Willis et al., 2022) to Black immigrant students such as Ervin. Teachers often indicate that they do not know the languages of immigrant and transnational students (of color) or how these students use language in classrooms. Yet, racialized students who have crossed boundaries, like their parents, possess the capacity to share their thinking about how they use language, how they think about responses to their cultures, and how they think about their racialization across boundaries. Teachers can interact with racialized students and with their parents through their translanguaging practices as they draw and share intentionally from their languages and other semiotic resources (García & Wei, 2014).

Through such interactions, teachers are in a unique position to use insights presented by racialized families of color as a means of supporting and extending meaning-making in literacy instruction. They can do so based on the assets of youth by centering race as they leverage opportunities for students to use their assets through a transraciolinguistic approach. I have shown that teachers are well positioned to facilitate students by drawing from the 3 Ms—*metaracial, metalinguistic, and metacultural understanding* (P. Smith, 2019). Additionally, teachers stand to gain in-depth insights about the individualized ways of using language that such racialized students bring to classrooms.

Creating Storylines With the 3 Ms in Elementary and Middle School Classrooms. To accomplish the above, teachers of elementary, intermediate, and middle school students can create storylines surrounding the 3 Ms with students by following three steps.

Step 1. Determine Student Responses. In creating storylines with the 3 Ms, the first step that teachers can take to foster a transraciolinguistic approach is to determine the responses through which students will provide information about their racialized language and its intersection with culture and migration in their literate trajectories (P. Smith, 2019). These responses will allow students to provide information about their literate trajectories regarding intersections among (English) language, race, and other elements of their cultures. Teachers can elicit responses surrounding the 3 Ms from each student using the guiding questions in Figure 5.1. For instance, responses may be in the form of an oral interview, written narrative, role-play, multimodal creation, or other similar mechanism through which students reflect the elements on which they draw to make meaning. Figure 5.1 also may function as a template for facilitating students' creation of storylines.

The questions, "How do I think about how I speak, read, and write? How do I think about my family's reactions to how I speak, read, and write? How do I think about others' reactions to how I speak, read and write?" presented in Figure 5.1, help to elicit responses about students' metalinguistic understanding. Similarly, the questions, "How do I think about how I look? How do I think about my family's reactions to how I look? How do I think about others' reactions to how I look?" help to elicit responses about the students' metaracial understanding. And the questions, "How do I think about me being a foreigner in the *United States*? How do I think about my family's reactions to me being a foreigner in the *United States*? How do I think about others' reactions to me being a foreigner in the *United States*?" elicit responses about students' metacultural understanding.

Step 2. Discuss Student Responses. The second step that teachers can take with storylines to foster a transraciolinguistic approach with the 3 Ms is to discuss how students implicitly and explicitly view their racialization in relation to their linguistic and cultural backgrounds as immigrant or transnational youth crossing boundaries (K. C. Bryan, 2020; P. Smith, 2019). Guided by students' responses to guiding questions surrounding

Figure 5.1. A Transraciolinguistic Approach: Creating Storylines With the 3 Ms

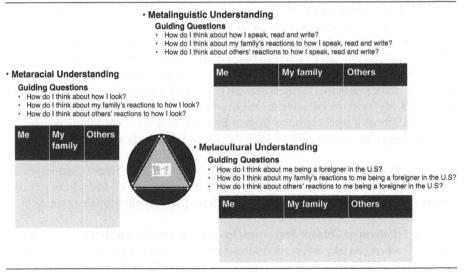

the 3 Ms in Figure 5.1, teachers can discuss responses surrounding the 3 Ms with individual students and/or as a class. In doing so, teachers can allow students to also use the storylines to indicate how institutions such as the school, as well significant and nonsignificant others, position them and their languages when they use these elements while engaged in literate encounters (P. Smith, 2019).

Teachers can support students to identify the underlying racialization of language in the use of their literacies so that students can understand how racialization influences the ways in which their languages and literacies are embraced or rejected by schools and in classrooms. They also can identify and discuss students' reactions to being perceived racially by others and allow students to describe how they respond when others racialize them and their language as they make meaning through their literacies in ways that do not correspond to classroom and school norms. This process will provide each student with the opportunity to gather additional insight about their own forms of metalinguistic, metacultural, and metaracial understanding, and provide opportunities for them to revise and extend their responses about these understandings accordingly.

Step 3. Share and Extend Student Responses. The third step that teachers can take with storylines to foster a transraciolinguistic approach with the 3 Ms is to guide each student to finalize their storylines for sharing with the class, their family, and/or other audience of their choice. Teachers can display storylines on the class wall or in student portfolios, based on student preference, and revisit these intermittently during the school year to further support the student's development of the 3 Ms.

As they revisit the storylines during the school year, teachers can guide students to identify 3 M understandings that they already use to develop a sense of agency in response to how their families, schools, institutions, and others respond to their language and race. During this process, teachers can guide students to describe how schools and teachers might adapt to accommodate their racialized language practices and implement actions that center students' racialized realities (Rosa & Flores, 2017) via meaning-making that extends beyond monolingual, monocultural, and monoracially informed literacy practices. Teachers can support students as they grapple with adjusting their sense of self (i.e., personhood) through meaning-making in academic and social settings based on their newfound understanding of how racialization intersects with both their language and culture in and beyond the U.S. classroom (Ibrahim, 2019; P. Smith, 2019, 2020b). They also can discuss how students might act intentionally to retain a sense of personhood that would allow them to make meaning through literacy beyond traditional code-based (see Luke, 2018) approaches to literacy that often remain visible in schools. In doing so, teachers can guide students to extend their storylines as they further develop their 3 Ms.

Creating Storylines With the 3 Ms in High School Classrooms

I have shown elsewhere how a transraciolinguistic approach can be fostered by teachers and educators of Black immigrant students who "wrestle with a sense of personhood, even while they seem to succeed academically as individuals" (see Figure 1 in P. Smith,

2019, p. 300). This approach also can "be adopted by researchers to better understand how Black immigrant and transnational students, based on their individual and unique trajectories, are positioned in relation to race and language" (p. 300). In addressing the literate practices of Black transnational and immigrant youth of color, such an approach can be elicited by using the following questions, which help racialized students to identify elements that present a sense of agency in their development of a transraciolinguistic approach (P. Smith, 2019).

1. To what degree does the student/teacher/educator/researcher identify and understand the student's racial and linguistic repertoires, their intersections, and by extension, overall cultural identity? How do [varied] others' perceptions influence these repertoires and identity?
2. What steps have been taken by the student to adjust his or her personhood in non/academic settings based on the identification and understanding of the student's racial and linguistic repertoires, their intersections, and by extension, overall cultural identity?
3. What steps have been taken by the teacher/educator/researcher to help the student adjust his or her personhood in academic and social settings based on the identification and understanding of the student's racial and linguistic repertoires, their intersections, and by extension, overall cultural identity?
4. To what degree do the previous steps allow the students to retain a sense of personhood that is aligned with both his or her identity, both racially and linguistically? (p. 301)

The information gathered from these questions can be used to help racialized students use their meta-understandings to develop storylines such as the one in Figure 5.2, which help them to better understand the stories that they have about their racialized selves and languages as well as the stories that (significant) others hold, tell, and reflect about them.

Teaching the Black Literate Immigrant: Part II

There is no reason why literacy curriculum should default to English, to the white gaze, and to the experiences of geographical natives residing in one country over those who have migrated from others in the 21st century. English literacy curriculum worldwide no longer can be steeped in the white gaze and needs to be dismantled in favor of "pursuits" that humanize all racialized students and "cultivate their genius" (see Muhammad, 2020). Teachers of elementary and middle school students are invited to disrupt and rethink Eurocentric literacy curriculum based on the framework for Black immigrant literacies, guided by what Dr. Alice Lee (2022) refers to as "Black epistemological literacy education." They can do so by adapting literacy curriculum to acknowledge the influence of the white gaze and how it is used against immigrants as they leverage their languaging. To do so, it is critical that monolingual, monocultural, and monoracial norms steeped in certain notions of acceptable Englishes are disrupted.

Figure 5.2. Storyline: Ervin and "Proper Language" Across Transnational Contexts of Bahamas and the United States

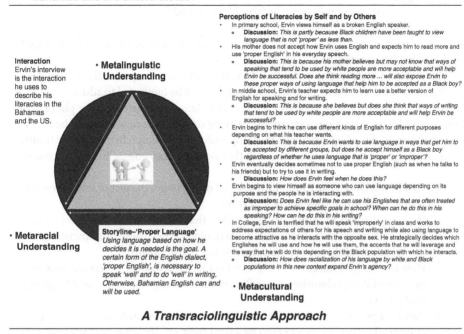

Interaction
Ervin's interview is the interaction he uses to describe his literacies in the Bahamas and the US.

• **Metalinguistic Understanding**

• **Metaracial Understanding**

Storyline–'Proper Language'
Using language based on how he decides it is needed is the goal. A certain form of the English dialect, 'proper English', is necessary to speak 'well' and to do 'well' in writing. Otherwise, Bahamian English can and will be used.

• **Metacultural Understanding**

A Transraciolinguistic Approach

Perceptions of Literacies by Self and by Others
• In primary school, Ervin views himself as a broken English speaker.
   ○ **Discussion:** *This is partly because Black children have been taught to view language that is not 'proper' as less than.*
• His mother does not accept how Ervin uses English and expects him to read more and use 'proper English' in his everyday speech.
   ○ **Discussion:** *This is because his mother believes but may not know that ways of speaking that tend to be used by white people are more acceptable and will help Ervin be successful. Does she think reading more ... will also expose Ervin to these proper ways of using language that help him to be accepted as a Black boy?*
• In middle school, Ervin's teacher expects him to learn use a better version of English for speaking and for writing.
   ○ **Discussion:** *This is because she believes but does she think that ways of writing that tend to be used by white people are more acceptable and will help Ervin be successful?*
• Ervin begins to think he can use different kinds of English for different purposes depending on what his teacher wants.
   ○ **Discussion:** *This is because Ervin wants to use language in ways that get him to be accepted by different groups, but does he accept himself as a Black boy regardless of whether he uses language that is 'proper' or 'improper'?*
• Ervin eventually decides sometimes not to use proper English (such as when he talks to his friends) but to try to use it in writing.
   ○ **Discussion:** *How does Ervin feel when he does this?*
• Ervin begins to view himself as someone who can use language depending on its purpose and the people he is interacting with.
   ○ **Discussion:** *Does Ervin feel like he can use his Englishes that are often treated as improper to achieve specific goals in school? When can he do this in his speaking? How can he do this in his writing?*
• In College, Ervin is terrified that he will speak 'improperly' in class and works to address expectations of others for his speech and writing while also using language to become attractive as he interacts with the opposite sex. He strategically decides which Englishes he will use and how he will use them, the accents that he will leverage and the way that he will do this depending on the Black population with which he interacts.
   ○ **Discussion:** *How does racialization of his language by white and Black populations in this new context expand Ervin's agency?*

"Proper Pronunciation" and "Excellent Spelling"

For phonics, this can be done by revamping standards that function based on white listening subject norms, which don't consider the effects of migration and language difference on students' literacies. Teachers can challenge long-standing and acceptable English literacy practices such as proper pronunciation, proper accent, and accent reduction by acknowledging how the white gaze overlooks spelling difference based on migration, language, and race. They can do so by acknowledging how the home countries and languages of students influence how they present spelling patterns in their writing. Teachers also can do so by investigating how colonial norms in students' home countries affected their prior experiences with spelling in their home countries.

When teaching phonics and phonemic awareness in classrooms, we continue to emphasize proper pronunciation, a proper accent, or accent reduction (i.e., white listening subject norms) over meaning-making and students' legitimate communicative repertories across Englishes or languages. As a result, pronunciation of one word is often differentially accepted based on the race of the speaker. For instance, consider the following video where a Nigerian speaker presents information: https://www.youtube.com/watch?v=UfmqZtvFoSs. Now, consider the following videos where Americans with a variety of Englishes across the 50 United States orally present information:

- https://www.youtube.com/watch?v=riwKuKSbFDs
- https://www.youtube.com/watch?v=OtA1XZVlkIQ
- https://www.youtube.com/watch?v=UcxByX6rh24

American speakers of English who are white are more likely to be regarded as intelligible, credible, and legitimate (see Rosa & Flores, 2017).

A teacher of literacy who recognizes how these differences operate through metalinguistic, metaracial, and metacultural understanding will be motivated to address how raciolinguistic ideologies affect expectations for pronunciation in classrooms. For phonics, the process of taking a running record and identifying oral reading miscues must be focused first on the goals of reading, which are meaning-making and comprehension. Four transraciolinguistic questions that teachers can ask themselves as they engage in this process are:

1. Can I understand the immigrant student or try to get the gist of what they are trying to say when they speak and read?
2. How can I adjust miscue scoring to reflect that the student pronounces words appropriately for meaning-making, particularly when these pronunciations are not based on white mainstream American English norms?
3. How can I adjust miscue scoring to reflect that the student is making meaning, the goal of comprehension, regardless of their immigrant, racial, and language backgrounds?
4. Can I support the speaker to communicate so they are understood without erasing who they are as a person based on their racialization as Black and their perception as an immigrant?

For spelling, we continue to expect and require "correct" spelling in literacy classrooms based on the white gaze. This occurs even though numerous spelling inventions are being developed in online spaces and otherwise by students across the globe on a daily basis. A few years ago, for instance, in response to a text message, my then teenage daughter responded, "meh." Many of you may have an idea of what this seemingly recently "invented word" means, but at the time I didn't. For her, and a large number of teenagers worldwide, this invented word has been legitimized, particularly in online spaces, and evolved too. By expecting correct spelling from students, we overlook how attempts to spell reveal approximations of words, which also can tell us about students' language backgrounds and about their imagination as well as invention of novel ideas. This is not to say that there isn't a time and place for spelling words "correctly" in English depending on the author's purpose. Rather, it simply points to the need for legitimacy to extend beyond one form of correctness as determined by the white gaze.

Teachers can legitimize invented spelling as well as invented words in classrooms as a key part of the beginning stages as well as final stages of students' developmental spelling, depending on who their audience is and the meanings that they wish to convey to this audience. Understanding distinctions in students' use of spelling for developing affinity with their peers via online social platforms allows teachers to consider intentional variations in using spelling for communicating meaning. Inviting Black immigrant youth to intentionally exercise agency over how they use spelling for various audiences, with meaning intact, based on their transnational experiences with languaging, operates as a vehicle for their Englishes, languages, and other semiotic resources to be leveraged in words that they spell. Teachers can do this even when they believe, based on their training, that the words students present are "incorrect" based on white English norms. They can, in turn, praise students for these inventions with an emphasis on the intentions that students have for communicating meaning based on audience. Teachers can use this knowledge about language also, when working on word study tasks to reward student effort and avoid punishing students with bad grades because of supposed inability to spell. It is important that teachers focus on whether students are sufficiently able to communicate ideas and meaning before discarding their writing, even when expectations are based on Eurocentric norms typically expected in classrooms. The goal in this process becomes one where varied named Englishes in students' full linguistic repertoires are deemed as equally leigitimate in classrooms.

In "Prism of Promise: Towards Responsive Tools for Diverse Classrooms," Sara Hajek and I present informal tools that teachers can use to partially engage in this process (Smith & Hajek, 2021). Designed based on gradations of teachers' responsiveness to students' language and cultures across classrooms, the tools provide literacy and ELA teachers with concrete mechanisms for relocating literacies equitably and allowing the assets of children and youth to be drawn upon in classrooms (see Tables 8.3 and 8.4 in Smith & Hajek, 2021). Specifically, the informal tools present: (a) descriptions of teachers' culturally and linguistically responsiveness practices across various levels of culturally responsive literacy practice (CRLP) and linguistically responsive literacy practice (LRLP), (b) examples of teachers' culturally and linguistically responsive practices, (c) factors such as reflection on self and on content that influenced their linguistic and cultural responsiveness, and (d) guiding questions that allow teachers to reflect on the extent to which their literacy practices align with various degrees of CRLP and LRLP. The tools enable literacy educators guide in-service teachers to identify, along a continuum, the areas where they demonstrate multilingual and multicultural awareness for literacy responsiveness in a wide range of literacy instruction and assessment practices such as phonics, word study, comprehension, writing, reading, motivation, word recognition, biliteracy, bilingualism, literature, and fluency. These informal tools also empower educators and teachers who struggle to support underserved students such as Chloe and Ervin who cross cultural boundaries between the home and school.

"Writing Well"

Teachers are well positioned to challenge the notion of "writing well," which so often is ingrained into academic exercises, by acknowledging how the white gaze overlooks differences in writing based on migration, language, and race. Exploring how the home countries and languages of students influence the elements of writing they present at various developmental stages often steeped in research based on English literacy, allows teachers to determine whether Eurocentric mechanisms for valuing writing were imposed and, if so, the degree to which they were emphasized in classrooms, as well as the expectations for writing that students have based on these norms.

In writing, we often view proficiency as a list of abstractions. As I observed in my extensive immersion within schools in Texas (e.g., Smith, 2020c), this perception places little to no premium on the creation of safe spaces for idea generation and the growth of the writer as a person of color. In doing so, we often limit creativity, which is a key goal of writing, because of Eurocentric norms based on the white gaze. Writing can be of a high quality based on the meaning-making processes under development, even when the organization, presentation, and illustration of ideas seem different from what we may be used to based on monolingual, monocultural, and monoracial norms. For students whose racialized language practices have allowed them to develop the capacity for leveraging language in creative ways, what they deem to be high quality often can thus be often overlooked because students are judged based on abstract symbols of writing steeped in Eurocentric norms.

Teachers can accept the writing of students as is, initially, provided that the meaning is intact and that this meaning is conveyed and understood by peers or other audience for whom students are writing. Discussing with students their goals for writing, their audience, and their intended communication in relation to that audience is important. If Black immigrant youth are on social media and wish to communicate about a pressing issue with their broad audiences informally, they may choose not to use formal and sup-posedly "pristine" mechanisms based on typically accepted Eurocentric standards to do so. Teachers who discuss with youth their intended communications and who create a va-riety of audiences with whom they can engage their literacies, can affirm their writing for meaning-making even in cases where it is not deemed to comply with Eurocentric norms that judge the writing proficiency of racialized speakers of color to be deficient in such form. In this way, youth learn how to make strategic decisions about how to draw from the varied Englishes, languages, and broader semiotics in their full linguistic repertoires to communicate the meanings that they wish to share with the world.

If there must be an effort to elicit a translation of students' writing to conform to white Eurocentric norms, teachers would do well to be sure that this translation does not replace the original meaningful production or creation of students, but rather, that it is done in a context where the student writer is given insight, as reasonably as possible, into expectations of the multiple worlds that operate to determine (what is and is not) writing proficiency based on communicative context. In the higher grades particularly, students can be given ongoing insight into how they are being judged based on their language and race in relation to audience so they have agency to respond accordingly across multiple worlds (see P. Smith, 2019). Teachers can reinforce this process by creating spaces for oral language use that deviates from Eurocentric norms and where this racialized language use operates as a vehicle for authentic writing in classrooms.

In "Finding (Radical) Hope in Literacy: Pedagogical Literacy Insights From Culturally and Linguistically Diverse Students" and "Renewing Hope with English Literacies: Insights from Middle Schoolers," I delineate how Black middle school students can be affirmed as they write in ways that allow them to retain hope through their literacies (2018a, 2018b). And in "'Mr. Wang Doesn't Really Care How We Speak!': Responsiveness in the Practice of an Exemplary Asian-American Teacher," I (Smith, 2020c) present the practices of an exemplary middle school teacher working with predominantly Black and white youth, many of whom have immigrant backgrounds. Working with the teacher weekly as part of the second year of a research–practice partnership between a district and university, I highlighted in the study multiple and varied avenues such as "planning and implementing instruction, prompting students to think critically, modeling, conferencing with students, facilitating peer evaluation and support, emphasizing procedural processes, establishing routine classroom practices, and capitalizing on technology and visual aid support" through which this exemplary teacher drew upon culturally relevant teaching practices in the teaching of writing (p. 364).

Similarly, emerging from research conducted in the first year of the same research–practice partnership at the same middle school, colleagues and I illustrate, in "Teaching Writing in the Midst of Fragile Alliances: Insights From Literacy Teacher Educators," how literacy educators in collaboration with ELA teachers used "personal qualities for relationship-building," their "professional characteristics", as well as their "pedagogical practices . . . based on student needs" to foster understanding (P. Smith et al., 2020, p. 349). The study showed that using "real-life experiences to support student writing appeared to be most critical to . . . writing instruction in the partnership" (p. 349).

"Sufficient Vocabulary"

Teachers are well positioned to question notions of "better vocabulary" given the continued indications that the tendency to attribute a non-knowing of words to certain racialized populations of color is based partly on how the white gaze overlooks vocabulary that is different from mainstream norms based on language, migration, and race. They can do so by examining the words that students bring to the classroom and by relying on contextual understandings from the student's countries of origin to gather knowledge about words used synonymously with those that tend to be encountered or expected based on Eurocentric standards. This is highly possible through Parent of Color stories which, as Dr. Patricia Edwards and I show, allow for parents to inform teachers about how youth bring varied literate assets to the classroom. Such assets, we argue, can then be positioned as a basis for designing the curriculum in ways that foster equitable literacy teaching and learning (see Edwards & Smith, forthcoming).

Research has articulated robust tiers of vocabulary (Beck et al., 2013) that students use, which cause them to be more "proficient" regardless of variations in terminology used both in and beyond informal and academic contexts across the globe. Yet words can be the same or synonymous as used by speakers, and still be accepted differently based on the race of the speaker or user. Consider the following video where a white Australian speaker describes this process: https://www.youtube.com/watch?v=xuRrp83jCuQ

It is crucial that literacy teachers make space for the varied words of children and youth of color. A first step is to avoid the deficit thinking that children of color do not have sufficient vocabulary with which to speak legitimately or are impoverished users of language (see Abraham, 2020). Children of color may teach others in their classrooms about words they use at home and how these words may be different from or pronounced differently to those often heard and used in classrooms by white peers. In this way, teachers can enable students to develop metacultural and metaracial understandings.

Teachers also can use shared reading to present opportunities for oral conversations about text. They can ask students, "How would you say this at home?" Teachers can do this by having students write often and share their authentic writing products, with what are considered to be "errors," so that peers in the classroom can see how immigrant children of color use language for literacy.

Teachers can prompt students, particularly racialized students who are also immigrants of color, to share orally during various parts of literacy instruction. Sometimes, the use of multimodal resources may work best for certain students. Then, as students become more immersed in the classroom, they can be prompted to participate. Providing sufficient wait time, as opposed to being dismissive due to students' inability or unwillingness to engage, will be helpful from the onset.

Teachers also can develop their (critical) multilingual awareness as a basis for working with students to support vocabulary in classrooms. As colleagues and I have illustrated, multilingual awareness enhances educators' knowledge of the subject matter of the language—grammar, phonology, vocabulary—and how it impacts literacy. Literacy educators who reflect multilingual awareness have been shown to capitalize on verbal, visual, and written scaffolds to create "opportunities for learning language [and vocabulary] through literacy" and to support "pedagogical and analytic requirements of language in the classroom" (P. Smith et al., 2020, p. 404).

"Making Sense"

The goal of interacting with others and with text through literacy is to make meaning: comprehension. Being able to communicate effectively as language architects (Flores, 2020) who are Black immigrants means being capable of determining which elements of their linguistic repertoires they will use for various situations that they encounter. Teachers who acknowledge how the white gaze causes them to overlook differences in how race, migration, language intersect, are well positioned to support Black immigrant youth. As they recognize how the white gaze obscures these differences, they can modify their literacy teaching as it relates to pronunciation, spelling, vocabulary, writing, and across all areas of literacy and English language arts.

For instance, consider the following video. The video illustrates a Nigerian English–speaking accent as introduced in Google maps: https://www.youtube.com/watch?v=MMs7r9OzVDY. In response, questions can be asked: *Do we understand the speaker? Are we attending more closely to the way in which the speaker presents directions despite understanding what he says? Would we use this speaker's voice for our Google maps? What does this reveal about us?*

To engage deeply with the bases for various responses to the languaging presented in this video, teachers of literacy need what my colleague and I refer to as *critical multilingual awareness, critical multilingual awareness,* and *critical multiracial awareness* (Smith & Warrican, 2021a). It is necessary for all three forms of awareness to work together simultaneously. This is because we have seen that even with a very intensive focus on cultural responsiveness for multiple decades (e.g., Au, 1992; Ladson-Billings, 1999; C. D. Lee, 2001; Willis & Harris, 1997), there is increasingly a backlash emerging against racialized students of color in and across schools in the United States (e.g., Florida, Texas). We argue that it is possible for schools and numerous educators to have undertaken work with increasing populations of diverse students that supposedly was aimed at being responsive, but to have *failed terribly at the same time* to result in a transformation of the self of the teacher and educator. With such critical forms of awareness working together in the lives of literacy teachers, researchers, and educators, we envision a return to disrupting the self as a key basis for authentically and morally—as called for by my colleagues and me—engaging humanely and effectively with immigrant students of color such as Ervin through the framework of CARE (Willis et al., 2022).

Literacy educators who reflected critical multilingual awareness knew both the social and pragmatic norms of English, used a pluralistic approach to teaching literacy that emphasized citizenship based on democracy, and willingly explored and supported the holistic linguistic repertoires of children, allowing for their holistic literacies to emerge. The educators used literacy to present a challenge to histories that were colonial and oppressive, and deployed language as part of literacy teaching to create new social structures in and beyond the classroom and to bring about transformation and change. Similarly, literacy educators who reflected multicultural awareness were shown to value and incorporate varied perspectives while being open to unfamiliar events and people. And those who reflected critical multicultural awareness were unafraid to challenge prevailing norms such as those that Ervin encountered based on the white listening subject. Colleagues and I observed that they centered nondominant viewpoints in their daily lives so they could see the world differently and be capable of and willing to invite their students to daily do the same (P. Smith et al., 2019). Those who wish to reflect critical racial awareness can extend these foci, "revisiting how race positions multiple and intersecting elements of the self as a precursor for responsiveness" (McMillon & Rogers, 2019, p. 5).

Teachers and literacy leaders can use a transraciolinguistic approach to support their peers, as well as administrators and parents, in avoiding enactments of raciolinguistic ideology that damage students, by reminding them of the goal of literacy instruction and assessment. Teachers and literacy leaders also can enhance how they interact with racialized students of color and other racialized individuals, and with racialized languages and literacies presented by these individuals, as they begin to identify and address these concrete enactments of raciolinguistic ideologies in classrooms.

Teaching the Black Literate Immigrant and All Students

A transraciolinguistic approach will not achieve its goals in literacy teaching and learning if it fails to move beyond the racialized students who are often on the receiving end of oppression and if it does not address organizations such as schools that continue to perpetuate raciolinguistic ideologies. Teachers who are responsible for the instruction of nonracialized (i.e., white) elementary, middle, and high school students are also capable of leveraging a transraciolinguistic approach, enabling students perceived as monolingual, monocultural, and monoracial to better relate to racialized peers using metalinguistic, metacultural, and metaracial understanding. I have shown that those who work in contexts with predominantly students of color (e.g., those from Africa, Asia, Caribbean, Latin America), where criticality based on race in literacy often remains invisible in literacy curriculum (P. Smith, 2020a), can also be supported in exploring a transraciolinguistic approach.

The instructional illustration and lesson plan presented next, which I have discussed previously elsewhere (P. Smith, 2022b), shows how a transraciolinguistic approach can be used to redesign literacy and English language arts standards through the 3 Ms—metalinguistic, metacultural, and metaracial understanding.

Transraciolinguistics for Revamping Literacy and ELA Standards

Literacy and English language arts teachers can foster all students' development of the 3 Ms by modifying curricular standards (e.g., Common Core State Standards [CCSS]) in ways that extend and address meaning-making based on racialized language and its corresponding intersectionalities for students in diverse classrooms. An example of how elementary teachers might use the 3 Ms to modify and extend standards that exist in their locales is presented in Figure 5.3.

Four of the standards presented in Figure 5.3 are drawn from the U.S. Grade 1 CCSS to provide teachers in the primary grades, where foundational literacy skills often are emphasized, with an idea of how to teach with standards that rely on a transraciolinguistic approach. One standard presented in Figure 5.3 is drawn from U.S. Grade 4 CCSS to provide teachers of students in the intermediate grades with an idea of how they too might do the same. The standards chosen as examples cut across *foundational reading, informational reading,* and *literature* to reflect the wide range of ELA and literacy content through which a transraciolinguistic approach might be enacted. Teachers can engage in the process above by following three steps.

Step 1. Identify standards for revision. Teachers can first identify the standards preestablished by the school or district for teaching a given topic in literacy or English language arts that they wish to revise.

Step 2. Revise standards based on the 3 Ms. Teachers can then revise standards in literacy and English language arts and reading (ELAR) based on the 3 Ms to explicitly acknowledge and identify knowledge, skills, and appreciation for the literacies of students of color. In doing so, they are positioned to utilize the 3 Ms to disrupt *monoracial, monocultural,* and *monolingual* assumptions often embedded implicitly in ELAR standards across the globe. Revising the standards with this focus can illustrate how the literacy practices of students of color often differ from preestablished Eurocentric standards—racially, linguistically, and culturally.

When revising a standard, teachers may decide to emphasize metalinguistic, metaracial, and/or metacultural understanding. For instance, the Phonics and Word Recognition CCSS.ELA-LITERACY.RF.1.3.A standard, "Know the spelling–sound correspondences for common consonant digraphs," presented in Figure 5.3, inadvertently assumes that there is a common globally acceptable English spelling–sound correspondence for common consonant digraphs and does not consider various forms of accentuation typically leveraged by immigrants, particularly immigrant students of color (see Ramjattan, 2019, for a discussion of raciolinguistics and accentuated language, and Willis et al., 2021, for the raciolinguistic basis undergirding labeling of miscues based on accentuation). As such, the standard in its preestablished form caters to an imagined white, monolingual student who is versed in standardized (American) Englishes.

To move past the imagined student to whom such a standard caters, teachers can revisit the standard so that there is an equitable focus on learners who are immigrant, transnational, multilingual, and/or racialized as students of color. Revising the preestablished standard in Figure 5.3 as, "Know the spelling–sound correspondences for common consonant digraphs used as a linguistically diverse (immigrant) student of color," allows teachers to include within the standard, from the onset, considerations for the lesson that govern students who are racialized, multilingual, and immigrant (i.e., the 3 Ms). Further revising this standard as, "Show the difference in spelling–sound correspondences for common consonant digraphs used as a linguistically diverse student of color in contrast to white, monolingual (and/or American) peers," allows teachers to include within the standard considerations for all students to think about how they think about their language use as well as that of their peers (i.e., metalinguistic understanding). An even further revision, "Value the difference in spelling–sound correspondences for common consonant digraphs presented with confidence as a linguistically diverse (immigrant) student of color," addresses the affective domain, which often is overlooked in classrooms and can be crucial to students' use of the 3 Ms for building mutual understandings among racialized and nonracialized students.

Step 3. Utilize standards based on the 3 Ms. Teachers who have revised the standards to disrupt a monolingual, monocultural, and monolinguistic norm can, in turn, develop specific learning objectives to guide instruction (discussed next) that reflect these revisions. It is expected that incorporating the intersectional realities of racialized students from the onset, through revised standards, will serve as a way to rethink "accommodations" to ELAR lessons that often function as a *final add-on* when planning for instruction.

Through the steps presented above, teachers and schools can work to restructure literacy/ELA standards and curriculum in ways that disrupt a normative and longstanding, yet inequitable, focus of the standards on the imagined monolingual, monocultural, white student as the basis for meaning-making in literate practice, both in the United States and across the globe. Such a process can allow teachers to support students from *all* backgrounds, fostering their metalinguistic, metacultural, and metaracial understanding via a transraciolinguistic approach.

Transraciolinguistics for Revamping Literacy and ELA Lesson Planning

Teachers who wish to use transraciolinguistics as a mechanism for lesson planning can begin with the standards as outlined in the previous section. Following this, they can use the revised standards as a basis for developing learning outcomes that allow for the

Figure 5.3. Revisiting Standards with the 3 Ms

	A Transraciolinguistic Approach for Metalinguistic, Metacultural and Metaracial Understanding				
	Phonics and Word Recognition	**Phonological Awareness**	**Fluency**	**Informational Text**	**Literature**
	Original:	*Original:*	*Original:*	*Original:*	*Original:*
	CCSS.ELA-LITERACY.RF.1.3.A	CCSS.ELA-LITERACY.RF.1.2.A	CCSS.ELA-LITERACY.RF.1.4.B	CCSS.ELA-LITERACY.RI..1.6	CCSS.ELA-LITERACY.RL.4.6
	Know the spelling-sound correspondence for common consonant diagraphs.	*Distinguish long from short vowel sounds in spoken single-syllable words.*	*Read grade-level text orally with accuracy, appropriate rate, and expression on successive readings.*	*Distinguish between information provided by pictures or other illustrations and information provided by the words in a text.*	*Compare and contrast the point of view from which different stories are narrated, including the difference between first- and third-person narrations.*
Revising Standards for Metaracial, Metalinguistic, Metacultural Understanding *Teachers will revise standards in literacy and English language arts (ELAR) based on the 3 Ms by identifying knowledge, skills, and appreciation for the literacies of students of color.*	*Revised:*	*Revised:*	*Revised:*	*Revised:*	*Revised:*
	Know the spelling-sound correspondences for common consonant diagraphs used as a linguistically diverse (immigrant) student of color. **Show** the difference in spelling-sound correspondences for common consonant diagraphs used as a linguistically diverse	**Know** the differences in long and short vowel sounds in spoken single-syllable words that may sound different when used as a linguistically diverse (immigrant) student of color. **Illustrate** how long and short vowel sounds in spoken	**Read** grade-level text orally reflecting differences in accuracy, rate, and expression as a linguistically diverse (immigrant) student of color. **Use** the long and short vowel sounds in spoken single-syllable words as a student of color without hesitation.	**Present** alternative words to those presented in text that correspond to pictures and illustrations as a linguistically diverse (immigrant) student of color.	**Indicate** differences in the point of view of stories narrated when told as a linguistically diverse (immigrant) student of color. **Develop** an alternate story with a point of view that illustrates lived experience as a linguistically diverse (immigrant) student of color.

They will utilize the 3 Ms to disrupt the monolithic, monocultural and monolingual norm often reflected in ELAR standards.

In doing so, they will revise the standards to illustrate how the literacy practices of students of Color differ often from pre-established standards racially, linguistically, culturally.

student of color in contrast to white, monolingual (and/or American) peers.

Value the difference in spelling-sound correspondences for common consonant diagraphs presented with confidence as a linguistically diverse (immigrant) student of color.

single-syllable words are used differently as a linguistically diverse student when compared to (monolingual) white (and/or American) peers.

Read a story to peers using unique long and short vowel sounds in spoken single-syllable words as a linguistically diverse (immigrant) student of color.

Present the alternate story orally as a linguistically diverse (immigrant) student of color to an audience of non-racialized peers.

95

Figure 5.4. Transraciolinguistics in English Language Arts and Literacy for Mainstream Classrooms

---

Example of Mini-Lesson With Revised Standards to Reflect Transraciolinguistics

Name: _____ Date of Mini-Lesson: _____

Grade Level _____ Content_____ Time Frame _____

---

linguistic and cultural assets of immigrant students of color to be leveraged in classrooms. In Figure 5.4, I present an example of what a lesson plan for primary students might look like, with original and revised standards based on a transraciolinguistic approach.

Mini-Lesson Overview

Central Focus:
Students will develop an understanding of the variations that exist in spelling–sound correspondences leveraged by white students and linguistically diverse (immigrant) students of color.

Original Standard:

- Phonics and Word Recognition: CCSS.ELA-LITERACY.RF.1.3.A
  - » *Know the spelling–sound correspondences for common consonant digraphs.*
  - » *Decode regularly spelled one-syllable words.*

Revised Standard (to reflect metalinguistic, metacultural, and metaracial understanding via transraciolinguistics):

- Phonics and Word Recognition: CCSS.ELA-LITERACY.RF.1.3.A
  - » *Know and understand the variations in spelling–sound correspondences for common consonant digraphs used by nonracialized monolingual students and linguistically diverse (immigrant) students of color.*

Rationale/Purpose/Context of the Lesson:

- This lesson is designed to allow students who are nonracialized and/ or monolingual to identify and understand the differences in spelling–sound correspondences presented by (immigrant) students of color who are linguistically diverse. This lesson allows students to move beyond one acceptable notion how accurate spelling–sound correspondences are represented and to envision differences in the sounds of common digraphs when leveraged by different racialized and linguistically diverse (immigrant) populations. This is especially important in order for students of color to feel that their racialized languages and literacies are valued in classrooms. One of the digraphs that commonly are presented differently by certain students from the English-speaking Caribbean and that easily can be assumed to be incorrect in the writing and speaking of the immigrant child of color is the diagraph "th." For this purpose, this lesson is focused on the diagraph "th."

Previous Knowledge:

- Students have already explored the term *consonant digraphs* and are familiar with some consonant digraphs, including the diagraph "th."

Objectives/Learning Outcomes (Include metalinguistic, metacultural, and metaracial outcomes as part of objectives):

- **Identify** spelling–sound correspondences for common consonant digraphs used by linguistically diverse (immigrant) students of color.
- **Differentiate** spelling–sound correspondences for common consonant digraphs used by linguistically diverse students of color as compared with their white, monolingual (and/or American) peers.
- **Appreciate** the difference in spelling–sound correspondences for common consonant digraphs presented with confidence by linguistically diverse (immigrant) students of color.

Instructional Material:

- *Video*

Instructional Procedures and Assessment:

- Teacher introduces students to a video of two children engaged in conversation while playing, one who is a student of color and one who isn't. Students are allowed to listen to and observe both children in conversation for about 1–3 minutes and asked what they notice about the children. Students are prompted to think about how the children look, how they sound, what is different, what they understand, and how they feel about the two children based on how they look and sound.
- Teacher reminds students of what a digraph is: "two letters that make one sound." Teacher presents the spelling–sound correspondence for a common consonant diagraph, "th," guiding students to pronounce the digraph by reminding them of words in which the digraph can be found. Students are then reminded to use a hand signal to illustrate that a digraph brings two letters together to create one new sound. For example: Teacher shows students two fingers then crosses these fingers to illustrate how two become one. Students follow by showing two fingers and then crossing these fingers to illustrate how two become one.

- Teacher replays video and invites students to listen for the digraph "th" as used by children in the video. She prompts students to recognize the differences in how it is pronounced by the child of color and the nonracialized child.
- Teacher indicates to students that many of the people they will meet sometimes say sounds differently depending on how they look and that this is different but okay. Teacher invites students to consider countries where the diagraph "th" might be pronounced differently and notes that it can seem different when it is said by students from different backgrounds.
- Teacher has students draw an image to indicate how they will respond to a child who uses the diagraph "th" differently from them.

Teaching the Black Literate Immigrant to Connect With Peers

There is continued disconnect within and across the Black population worldwide. But there is no reason why literacy curriculum should fail to prepare racialized (Black, immigrant/transnational) middle and high school students of color to interact with Black peers of different backgrounds. English literacy curricula worldwide can no longer obscure this disconnect designed by white supremacy. Institutions must design literacy learning to address prevailing fallacies held by Blacks about one another. Teachers wishing to revamp standards for high school students, while developing instructional modules to connect racialized youth across cultures, can be guided by the instructional module shown in Figure 5.5, which presents a visual depiction of how teachers can design modules that tap into racialized students' assets via metalinguistic, metacultural, and metaracial understanding. Developed using literature suggestions informed by Drs. AnnMarie Gunn and Susan Bennett, the module reflects how teachers intentionally can foster critical conversations that reflect variations in Blackness (Personal Communication, 2021).

Teaching the Black Literate Immigrant and All Students

The final recommendation for teachers in this chapter is simple yet profound. Teachers are invited to have students read and/or listen to Ervin's authentic narrative as a basis for connecting with and having a "mirror" through which to see the life of a Black immigrant as a basis for literate activity in the classroom (see Sims Bishop, 1990). The same can be done with Chloe's narrative. Specifically, it is recommended that teachers read aloud the authentic narrative to students at appropriate grade levels or allow them to read the narrative themselves. Following this, students can use the narrative as a basis for literature response, using what Dr. April Baker-Bell (2020) refers to as "anti-racist Black language pedagogy," and also, in the process, as a mechanism for discussing how Ervin and Chloe leverage metalinguistic, metacultural, and metaracial understanding. Specifically, teachers can have students stop at different points in the narratives to discuss questions from Figure 5.1, such as, "How is Ervin/Chloe thinking here about how they are using language?", "How is Ervin/Chloe thinking here about how people think about their race?", "How is Ervin/Chloe thinking here about how people think about their culture?"

Figure 5.5. Example of Instructional English Language Arts Module Featuring Transraciolinguistics

	English Language Arts and Reading (ELAR) Instructional Module		
	Metacultural Understanding	*Metalinguistic Understanding*	*Metaracial Understanding*
Standards That Foster a Transraciolinguistic Approach	CCSS.ELA-LITERACY.SL.9–10.1.D Respond to diverse perspectives, qualify or justify their own views and understanding, and make new connections.	CCSS.ELA-LITERACY.SL.9–10.1.B Work collaboratively to discuss key issues and different perspectives. CCSS.ELA-LITERACY.RL.9–10.6 Analyze a particular cultural experience from outside the United States.	CCSS.ELA-LITERACY.SL.9–10.1.D Respond to diverse perspectives, qualify or justify their own views and understanding, and make new connections.
Multimodal Text Sets Supporting a Transraciolinguistic Approach	1. Watch *Voices in the Classroom: Black Students Discuss School Practices.* 2. Read a transcription of or listen to the Renee Watson poem on culture encompassing personal, family, and in- and out-of-schooling identities.	1. Read/Listen to article about actor from *Black Panther* fighting to keep African accents in *Black Panther.* 2. View presentation of linguistic dialect differences from American English to Afro-Englishes. Video 3. Read *Cendrillon*, children's book that retells Cinderella from a Caribbean perspective.	1. Read/Listen to article discussing multiracial identities of VP Kamala Harris. 2. Read/Listen to article about BLM protest from Black and immigrant communities. 3. Watch TED Talk: *Everyday Struggle: Switching Codes for Survival.* 4. Watch Harold Wallace talk about how his race impacts how he communicates linguistically and nonverbally.

(continued)

Figure 5.5. (continued)

	English Language Arts and Reading (ELAR) Instructional Module		
	Metacultural Understanding	*Metalinguistic Understanding*	*Metaracial Understanding*
Critical Conversations and Responses Through a Transraciolinguistic Approach *Teachers will use original curricular standards in literacy and English language arts to guide students in expanding their literacies through metalinguistic, metaracial, and/or metacultural understanding via instructional activities.*	***Consider and Indicate in Reading Response Journals*** *1. Differences in point of view of schooling as narrated by Black students in the United States.* *2. Differences in the point of view and cultural identities as narrated by a linguistically diverse woman of color.* **Discuss** *Connecting to self:* *1. How do I view the way I act because of my culture and ethnicity?* *2. How do others view the way I act because of my culture and ethnicity?*	***Consider and Indicate in Reading Response Journals*** *1. Differences in perceptions of Black Englishes and code-switching.* *2. Differences in code-switching in communication styles depending on origin.* *3. Whether language is represented authentically in a children's book written by a white author using standardized American English.* **Discuss** *Connecting to self:* *1. How do I view the way I sound because of my language?* *2. How do others view the way I sound due to my language?* *3. Can white authors using standardized American English*	***Consider and Indicate in Reading Response Journals*** *1. Differences in how multi-identities impact my point of view.* *2. Differences in the point of view of how the BLM movement impacted perceptions of Black youth vs. those of Black immigrant youth.* *3. Differences in personal experiences with microaggressions due to my racial identities.* **Discuss** *Connecting to self:* *1. How do I view the way I appear because of my race?* *2. How do others view the way I appear because of my race?* *3. Have experiences with microaggressions impacted my ways of acting physically and linguistically?*

360 Virtual Reality (VR) Fostering a Transraciolinguistic Approach	Develop	represent the dialect of Black (immigrant) people? Should they?	Develop
		Develop	
The implementation of 360 VR will allow participants to have immersive experiences within situated contexts that allow the engagement needed to enable participants to understand their Black peers' experiences.	1. Revisit my autobiographical narrative: Are there other elements that I believe I can add to the literacies I use for overcoming negative perceptions of my culture?	1. Revisit my autobiographical narrative: Are there other language experiences that can be represented in my narrative?	1. Revisit my autobiographical narratives: How have my experiences with Black peers who are different from me impacted my thinking and ways of being?
	Engage Black immigrant participants in discourses connected to metaculture of their Black American peers, and vice versa.	Engage Black immigrant participants in discourses connected to metalinguistic understanding of their Black American peers, and vice versa.	Engage Black immigrant participants to assimilate new information about African-American populations on metaracial understanding using VR, and vice versa.
	1. Self-reflection.	1. Self-reflection.	1. Self-reflection.
	2. Youth are immersed in VR content evaluation.	2. Youth work collaboratively within a VR environment to establish key issues and perspectives about perceptions of Black peers.	2. Youth work collaboratively to support the creation of 360 VR artifact(s) depicting novel understandings of Black American and immigrant peers.

QUESTIONS TO CONSIDER

1. **For Teachers**
   - How can the 3 Ms be used to elicit storylines of Black immigrant student populations in ELA/literacy and other classrooms?
   - In what ways can multimodal text sets be used based on a transraciolinguistic approach to show how Black immigrant student populations use the 3 Ms as a form of agency?
   - How can the standards addressed in ELA and literacy classrooms be adapted to reflect all students' holistic literacies using the 3 Ms?
   - How can teachers develop the capacity to teach phonics, spelling, vocabulary, and comprehension in ways that address the racialization of language for all students in literacy and other classrooms?

2. **For Teacher Educators**
   - How can the 3 Ms be incorporated into courses taught across teacher preparation programs to elicit storylines of Black immigrant student populations in ELA/literacy and other classrooms?
   - In what ways do courses in teacher preparation programs expose students to literature that can become part of multimodal text sets used to leverage a transraciolinguistic approach?
   - How can courses in teacher preparation programs require teachers to use a transraciolinguistic approach as a basis for decentering Eurocentric monolingual, monocultural, and monoracial norms across ELA/literacy and other classrooms?
   - How can courses in teacher preparation programs serve as the basis for using the 3 Ms to have teachers elicit K–12 students' holistic literacies?
   - How can courses in teacher preparation and inservice programs infuse the mechanisms for teaching phonics, spelling, vocabulary, and comprehension presented in this chapter in ways that address the racialization of language for all students in literacy and other classrooms?

3. **For Policymakers**
   - What text sets should be required across all schools so that all children, including Black immigrants, have access to a wide range of multimodal literature that allows them to see various representations of multiple Black immigrant populations portrayed authentically and in a legitimate way?
   - How can a transraciolinguistic approach be used to revamp ELA/literacy standards so they no longer reflect Eurocentric monolingual, monocultural, and monoracial norms?
   - What policies can be used to require that schools cultivate Black immigrants', and all children's, holistic literacies?
   - How can policies include 3 M understandings to address racialization as the basis for phonics, spelling, vocabulary, and comprehension teaching in literacy and other classrooms?

CHAPTER 6

Bridging Invisible Barriers With Black Immigrant Literacies

Building Solidarity Among Schools, Parents, and Communities

In this book, I have discussed the framework for Black immigrant literacies and its five elements: (1) laying claim to the struggle for justice; (2) disrupting the myth of the model minority; (3) a transraciolinguistic approach; (4) local–global connections; and (5) holistic literacies. I shared the basis for the framework—diaspora literacy, transnational literacy, racial literacy—showing how these three lenses work together to help advance conversations that enable Black immigrant youth to thrive. I discussed the authentic narratives of Chloe and Ervin—of Jamaican and Bahamian heritage, respectively—demonstrating how the life trajectories of these Black immigrant youth across elementary, middle, high school, and college present key opportunities for teachers to address transnational nuances involved in border crossing for youth as they "become immigrant," "become Black" (Ibrahim, 1999), and unbecome what they previously perceived to be "native English" speaking.

Along with each authentic narrative, I explored specific examples of approaches, teaching activities, instructional modules, and lesson plans that teachers can utilize to engage Black immigrant youth across elementary, middle, and high school. My approach to presenting these recommendations was based on the need for institutions to begin to understand and address the ways in which they are often complicit in having Black immigrant, and other immigrant youth of color, bear tremendous burdens that are due to systemic racism as it is embedded within our schools, broader institutions, communities, and societies. Kendi (2019) asserts that we cannot simply be "not racist"; we must be "anti-racist." To do so is, in part, to focus explicitly on anti-racist actions that bring about equity through institutional change. Rosa and Flores (2017) concur that from a raciolinguistic perspective, institutions must be the focus of the work of creating just systems where students of color can thrive, as whole humans, with their languaging intact.

In this concluding chapter, I discuss how teachers, parents, and communities can use the Black immigrant literacies framework to work together in solidarity, across racial, linguistic, and cultural lines, as they address the foregoing as well as other emerging needs of Black immigrant youth. I outline ways in which schools and teachers utilize the Black immigrant literacies framework in conjunction with already-established pedagogical mechanisms to meet the needs of Black immigrant students and to foster relationships among them and their racialized, immigrant, and white peers. I show how institutions can connect nationally across communities in support of Black immigrant youth, and also how local communities might take up the charge in connection with parents, schools, and other institutions to support a broad range of Black immigrant literacies. My recommendations are broad in scope, with the goal of curating a range of resources and organizing them in ways that can help support solidarity building for the Black immigrant community to thrive with peers.

Dr. Vanessa Siddle-Walker (1993) historically has highlighted the value of powerful relationships between communities and schools for students' socialization in ways that lead to learning. And Dr. Patricia Edwards, Past President of the Literacy Research Association, International Literacy Association Reading Hall of Fame scholar, and national and international proponent of family literacy, in her coauthored book, *Partnering With Families for Student Success: 24 Scenarios for Problem Solving With Parents*, has observed that "merely stating a desire for family involvement is not enough; the extent of the responsibility has to be accepted by parents, teachers, the school and the community" (Edwards et al., 2019, p. 2). As a prolific author, scholar, educator, and advocate for parents and families recently inducted as a History Maker, Edwards shared in her book coauthored with Dr. Catherine Compton-Lilly (Edwards & Compton-Lilly, 2016):

> Just as populations change, ideas about how to encourage and work with parents also need to evolve: School officials and teachers must think of new and creative ways in which to welcome, encourage, and involve parents within their schools, and they cannot take a "one-size-fits-all" approach. (pp. xviii–xix)

Guided by this mantra and by these organizing motifs, I offer next a series of ways in which solidarity can be built among schools, parents, and communities in the quest to support Black immigrant youth and foster their relationships with their peers.

PARENTS

Parents of Black immigrant students often profess a similar motive—they migrated to the United States because they wanted a better life for themselves and their children (Kumi-Yeboah, 2018). But a better life often involves giving children the very things that, as the research cited here indicates, can be detrimental to them. Connecting with parents of Black immigrant youth, who themselves are often immigrants, is critical as they "become Black" (Ibrahim, 1999, 2019), "become immigrant," and also "unbecome 'native' speakers," while recognizing that the idea of "native speaking" is not a legitimate construct. Black immigrant parents need to be able to see themselves as sharing the same plight as African Americans—*the struggle for justice*—given the historical and global assault on Blackness of people of African descent and given that many Black populations across the world share a history of colonization regardless of whether they were enslaved.

While this does not minimize the horrors of slavery for any Black population, it allows for a shared understanding of the historical and global basis of colonization and white supremacy as anti-Black. Engaging in the shared struggle for justice on the part of Black immigrants becomes possible as they recognize that they are able to be and live in the United States freely only because of the sacrifices of the former slave ancestors of African Americans in the country within which they now live.

Beyond the above, Black immigrant need ways to feel legitimate even while they learn about the broad range of life pursuits beyond academics that remain possible to all children—*holistic literacies*. They need mechanisms to understand how the historical racial structures among Black immigrants and Black Americans implicitly and overtly position them when they enroll their children in U.S. schools—*disrupting the myth of the model minority*. They are in dire need of supports to clarify how immigration intersects with their racialization and the ways they may often use language to unintentionally obscure or to support their children's potential for using languaging and literacies in self-determination—*transraciolinguistics*. Black immigrant parents, too, need clarity around the ways in which many of the colonially based countries and contexts from which they have migrated, use colonization and racialization in covert ways that also have affected them in their home countries prior to the overt recognition of this in the United States—*awareness of the local-global*. So how can this be done?

Parent of Color Stories

One mechanism that Dr. Patricia Edwards and I have suggested for doing this is Parent of Color Stories, which are "stories told by parents about their children and families designed to present the assets of families of color as a basis for redefining literate presents and futures, within and beyond schools" (Edwards & Smith, in press). We propose the use of parent stories as a key mechanism for understanding the assets that youth of color bring. We propose these also to reshape how teachers and schools engage with students' literacies. Presenting Parent of Color Stories as *stories of imagination, judgmental stories, dehumanizing stories, stories of standardization,* and *evolving stories,* we show how parents can educate teachers and schools about the literate potentiality present in their children's lives. This can allow Black immigrant parents to move beyond a primary focus on academics as they hold hope for their children's futures and enable them to see all pursuits, including the arts, as equally legitimate literacies that Black immigrant youth can and do use. Through Parent of Color Stories, we argue that schools are positioned to accomplish the goals of "family literacies" that position the literate assets students bring to schools as a basis for curricular design and to avoid the longstanding use of deficit lenses during interactions with families (Edwards et al., 2022).

From our collaborative thinking, we believe that "schools and families can make use of opportunities to address the beliefs and ideas regarding who bears responsibility for certain elements of the development of the child" (Edwards & Smith, forthcoming). For Black immigrant youth, Parent of Color Stories can be critical as they allow for insights to emerge which reflect the various elements of the framework for Black immigrant literacies. Schools and teachers can use Parent of Color Stories to invite parents of Black immigrant students to share their languages as well as their views regarding language and literacy. Through these stories, parents of Black immigrant students also can share about their children's lives and the literate assets they possess, as well as about education in their home countries and ways of being.

To elicit Parent of Color Stories from Black immigrant parents, my colleague and I recommend three steps that can be taken by schools and teachers. The first is to allow for avenues through which Black immigrant parents and caregivers of color can offer their stories about their children/youth through writing, oral representation, or photos. Opportunities also can be created for adult children of Black immigrant parents to offer their stories (through writing, oral representation, or photos) about how their parents, or caregivers of color, allowed them to use their literacies. The second step is to use these Parent of Color Stories as a basis for "revisiting, revamping and rethinking curricular processes, standards, content in literacy as well as behavioral responses to children of Color" (Edwards & Smith, forthcoming). The third step is to demonstrate to parents and families how their stories influenced changes in instructional literacy practices and dominant literacy practices, content, and processes in and beyond classrooms.

Critical Book Clubs, Article Clubs, and Video Talks

While teachers and schools can use stories from Black immigrant families to highlight assets, they also must be prepared to extend beyond stories to educate parents about the ways in which their migration, racialization, and languaging intersect to elicit discrimination. The goal is for Black immigrant parents to avoid the cluelessness that often accompanies being immigrant and Black (Simon, 2021). All stakeholders benefit when schools and teachers engage in reciprocal conversations with parents, and schools stand to learn from these processes as much as do parents.

Many schools have teachers and administrators who themselves do not fully grasp the complexities of being Black, multilingual, and immigrant. This is because, as observed in the podcast, "In the Story of U.S. Immigration, Black Immigrants Are Often Left Out," featuring Nana Gyamfi, executive director of the Black Alliance for Just Immigration in the United States, "Black migrants face a lot of challenges that other migrant groups do not face or don't face to the same degree, much of that rooted in the racial inequality, [and] the anti-Blackness that is inherently part of this country" (Simon, 2021). In fact, schools, districts, teachers, and others often operate based on local, national, and global reports such as the Report of the APA Presidential Task Force on Immigration (Bacigalupe, 2012) and the *World Migration Report 2020* (McAuliffe & Khadria, 2019). Reports such as these, while often regarded as complete, may either foreground certain populations and races and/or obscure the presence of Blackness as a key factor in migration, which complicates the ways in which literacy and subject areas need to be addressed for immigrants in schools.

In critical book clubs, article clubs, and video talks, schools can create mechanisms for growth on the part of everyone. Figure 6.1 presents a list of recommended readings (many going beyond those already discussed), organized based on their alignment with elements of the Black immigrant literacies framework, that schools, teachers,

(continued on page 117)

Figure 6.1. A Basic Reading List for Every Parent, Teacher, and School

		Black Immigrant Literacies				
Area of Focus	Article, Book, Podcast, Video	Addressing the Struggle for Justice	Interrupting the Myth of the Model Minority	Connecting the Local to the Global	Leveraging a Transraciolinguistic Approach	Cultivating Holistic Literacies
Literacies	**Article:** *Literary Research Group Seeks Systemic Change on Racial Justice in Field*	★	★	★		
	Article: *Recent and Recommended Books on Improving Black Literacy Selected by the Washington Informer*	★	★	★	★	★
	Article: *Understanding Translanguaging in U.S. Literacy Classrooms: Reframing Bi-/Multilingualism as the Norm*					★
	Article: *Cross-Cultural Approach to Literacy: The Immigrant Experience*			★		
	Article: *Literacy and Racial Justice: The Politics of Learning After Brown v. Board of Education*	★				
	Video Webinar: "Racial Justice in Literacy | David C. Anchin Center for the Advancement of Teaching"	★	★	★	★	★
Literacy Assessment	**Article:** *A Raciolinguistic Perspective on Standardized Literacy Assessments*	★				

(continued)

Figure 6.1. (continued)

		Black Immigrant Literacies				
Area of Focus	Article, Book, Podcast, Video	Addressing the Struggle for Justice	Interrupting the Myth of the Model Minority	Connecting the Local to the Global	Leveraging a Transraciolinguistic Approach	Cultivating Holistic Literacies
Black English Learners	**Article:** *Fact Sheet About English Learners Who Are Black*	*				*
	Article: *Looking Beyond the "Typical" English Learner: The Intersectionality of Black English Learners in U.S. Public Schools*	*				
	Video: "Dr. Ayanna Cooper: Black Immigrants in the United States"	*				
Second Language/ Bilingual Education	**Article:** *Applying Critical Race Theory as a Tool for Examining the Literacies of Black Immigrant Youth*	*				
	Article: *Beyond Anti-Blackness in Bilingual Education: Looking Through the Lens of the Black Immigrant Subject*	*		*	*	
Anti-Black Racism	**Article:** *The Eternal Fantasy of a Racially Virtuous America*	*				
	Article: *If Simone Biles Criticism Doesn't Convince You Black Women Shoulder Too Heavy a Burden, What Will?*	*				
	Article: *The British Empire Was Much Worse Than You Realize*			*		

Resource			
Video: *Cornel West & Myrna Lashley: Antiracism and Academic Freedom*	★	★	
Article: *We Should Not Teach Black and Brown Students That They Need White Acceptance*	★		
Article: *The Rightwing US Textbooks That Teach Slavery as "Black Immigration"*	★		
Article: *Dysconscious Racism, Afrocentric Praxis, and Education for Human Freedom: Through the Years I Keep on Toiling*	★		
Article: *We Are Terrified Police in Our Schools Will Harm Us*	★		
Article: *The Look in Derek Chauvin's Eyes Was Something Worse Than Hate*	★		
Article: *Racelighting in the Normal Realities of Black, Indigenous, and People of Colour*	★		
Article: *A Love Letter to BIPOC Folx Fighting Racism in Predominantly White Institutions*	★		
Article: *Five Steps to Address Anti-Blackness: Black Immigrant Literacies*	★	★	★

(continued)

Figure 6.1. (continued)

Area of Focus	Article, Book, Podcast, Video	Black Immigrant Literacies				
		Addressing the Struggle for Justice	Interrupting the Myth of the Model Minority	Connecting the Local to the Global	Leveraging a Transraciolinguistic Approach	Cultivating Holistic Literacies
Linguistic Racism	**Article:** The Pervasive Problem of "Linguistic Racism"	*				
	Article: Why for Black Speakers, Despite What They Are Told, Using "Standard English" Will Not Lead to Acceptance	*	*	*	*	*
	Article: Hearing Race: Can Language Use Lead to Racism?	*				
	Article: The Reason You Discriminate Against Foreign Accents Starts With What They Do to Your Brain	*				
	Article: Hearing Racialized Language in Josh Inocéncio's Purple Eyes (Ojos Violetas)	*				
	Article: Dr. Geneva Smitherman: Raciolinguistics, "Mis-Education," and Language Arts Teaching in the 21st Century	*				
	Article: Dr. Kate Seltzer: Translating Theory to Practice: Exploring Teachers' Raciolinguistic Literacies in Secondary English Classrooms	*				
	Article: Dr. Jonathan Rosa on Why We Need a Raciolinguistic Perspective	*				

Anti-Black Immigration Law	**Article:** *TAKE ACTION: Urge Congress and Biden Administration to Protect Black Immigrants and Asylum Seekers From Deportation and Family Separation*	★				
De-Essentializing Blackness	**Article:** *Black Is Not a Monolith: An Exploration of How the Black American and Black Immigrant Experiences Diverge*		★			★
	Article: *Black Semiosis: Young Liberian Transnationals Mediating Black Subjectivity and Black Heterogeneity*	★		★		
	Article: *Why Some African Americans Are Moving to Africa*			★		
	Article: *Brazilian: You're Brazilian, Right? What Kind of Brazilian Are You? The Racialization of Brazilian Immigrant Women*	★		★		
	Article: *Bahamian: Migrating While Multilingual and Black: Beyond the Bidialectal Burden*	★	★	★	★	★
	Article: *Dominican Republican: New Blacks: Language, DNA, and the Construction of the African American/Dominican Boundary of Difference*	★		★		

(continued)

Figure 6.1. (continued)

		Black Immigrant Literacies				
Area of Focus	Article, Book, Podcast, Video	Addressing the Struggle for Justice	Interrupting the Myth of the Model Minority	Connecting the Local to the Global	Leveraging a Transraciolinguistic Approach	Cultivating Holistic Literacies
De-Essentializing Immigrant Blackness	**Article:** *Nigerian: Translanguaging as a Gateway to Black Immigrant Collegians' Leadership Literacies*	*		*		*
	Article: *Senegalese: Navigating Black Racial Identities: Literacy Insights From an Immigrant Family*	*				*
	Article: *Ugandan: "I Had to Get Tougher": An African Immigrant's (Counter)narrative of Language, Race, and Resistance;* **Article:** *Applying Critical Race Theory as a Tool for Examining the Literacies of Black Immigrant Youth*	*		*		*
	Article: *Haitian: Living nan lonbraj la: Haitian Immigrant Young People Writing Their Selves Into the World;* **Article:** *Justice for All: Realities and Possibilities of Black English Learners in K–12 Schools;* **Article:** *Haiti: From Haiti to Detroit Through Black Immigrant Languages and Literacies*	*				

Article: Mongolian: Translanguaging, Emotionality, and English as a Second Language Immigrants: Mongolian Background Women in Australia	*				*
Article: Caribbean: Racialized Tensions in the Multimodal Literacies of Black Immigrant Youth	*		*		*
Article: West African: Humanizing the Black Immigrant Body: Envisioning Diaspora Literacies of Youth and Young Adults From West African Countries	*		*		*
Dictionary: St. Lucian: Kweyol Dictionary **Article:** St. Lucia: Centralizing Place as Past(s), Present(s), Future(s): Hybridities of Literate Identities and Place in the Life of a Black Immigrant Scholar	*		*		*
Article: Jamaican: (Re)Positioning in the Englishes and (English) Literacies of a Black Immigrant Youth: Towards a "Transraciolinguistic" Approach	*	*	*	*	*
Article: Trinidadian: "How Does a Black Person Speak English?" Beyond American Language Norms	*	*	*	*	*
Article: Ghanaian: Identity Negotiation in Multilingual Contexts: A Narrative Inquiry Into Experiences of an African Immigrant High School Student	*				*

(continued)

Figure 6.1. (continued)

		Black Immigrant Literacies				
Area of Focus	Article, Book, Podcast, Video	Addressing the Struggle for Justice	Interrupting the Myth of the Model Minority	Connecting the Local to the Global	Leveraging a Transraciolinguistic Approach	Cultivating Holistic Literacies
"Becoming Black"	**Video:** *Learning to Be Black: Navigating a New Identity in Nova Scotia*	*				
Anti-Immigrant Racism	**Articles:** *America's Struggle With Racism, as Told by Immigrants; Black Immigrants to the U.S. are Growing in Numbers, but They Don't Feel Understood; Reporter's notebook: The South is Home to a Growing Black Immigrant Population; Black Immigrants Reflect on Navigating Their Identities in the American South*	*				
Internal Anti-Black Racism	**Article:** *Black Immigrants in the United States: Challenges, Status and Impacts—Boundless Report*	*	*			
	Article: *When Immigrants, Too, Hold Anti-Black Sentiments—New York Amsterdam News*	*	*			
	Article: *A Call to Address Anti-Blackness Within African Immigrant Communities*	*	*			
	Article: *Rice University Breaks Barriers, Appointing 1st-Ever Black, Immigrant President*	*				

114

(continued)

Category	Source			
Anti-Immigration	**Article:** Immigration Coverage Needs More Nuanced Language	*		
	Article: Cop Probed on Immigrant Harassment	*		
Black Immigrant Invisibility	**Podcast:** In the Story of U.S. Immigration, Black Immigrants Are Often Left Out	*		
	Article: Silencing Invisibility: Toward a Framework for Black Immigrant Literacies	*	*	*
Black–Black Peer Relations	**Article:** Ties That Bind? Emerging Race-Conscious Alliances Between African Immigrants and Black Americans	*	*	
	Article: Black Immigrants in the United States: A comparison With Native Blacks and Other Immigrants	*		
	Article: Social Representations of Blackness in America: Stereotypes About Black Immigrants and Black Americans	*		
	Article: Affirmative Action Helps Black Immigrants, But Not Black Americans	*		
	Article: Black Immigrants in the U.S. Face Big Challenges. Will African Americans Rally to Their Side?	*		

Figure 6.1. (continued)

Area of Focus	Article, Book, Podcast, Video	Black Immigrant Literacies				
		Addressing the Struggle for Justice	Interrupting the Myth of the Model Minority	Connecting the Local to the Global	Leveraging a Transraciolinguistic Approach	Cultivating Holistic Literacies
Achievement Gap Narrative	Article: Successful Black Immigrants Narrow Black–White Achievement Gaps		★			★
	Article: One-in-Ten Black People Living in the U.S. are Immigrants: A Growing Share of Black Immigrants have a College Degree or Higher		★			★
	Article: Why Eurocentric Literacy Measures May Be Creating the Illusion That Black Students Are Underperforming	★	★	★		★
Life Pursuits	Article: Exploring the Divergent Academic Outcomes of U.S.-Origin and Immigrant-Origin Black Undergraduates	★				★
Immigrant Peer Relations	Article: National Experts Share Lessons in Community Cohesion and Immigrant Integration	★				
Global Solidarity	Article: A Silent Protest	★	★	★		
Literature	Article: Layering Caribbean Texts and Modalities: Relational Pedagogies for Secondary Language Arts Classrooms	★	★	★	★	★

parents, and others can use for enhancing knowledge to increase intersectional under-standings based on Black immigrant literacies. This list is by no means prescriptive nor is it remotely exhaustive. It merely represents a pathway through which schools, teach-ers, and communities might enter the doorway that leads to accessing the plethora of knowledge useful for supporting Black immigrant youth.

It is important to receive with caution studies such as those by Pinder et al. (2014), the results of which suggest that parents' "discussion of school progress and assistance with homework were some of the factors that significantly correlated with Black immi-grant students' achievement" (p. 49). The study surmises, based on these indications, that there is a Black immigrant advantage for first-generation immigrant students based on achievement in relation to their Black American peers. Yet, as Onyewuenyi (2018) has shown recently, "when care is taken to compare groups that are equivalent in par-ent education," Black Americans perform as well as Nigerians, disrupting what often tend to emerge as inequivalent comparisons within the Black population and beyond. Onyewuenyi observes that attending to such intricacies in comparisons can serve as an "important foundation for future assessments of the Black racial identity and academic achievement of the youth of the African Diaspora" (p. 6).

Comparative narratives presented in the research, although they may be useful for advancing our collective understandings as continuing to be framed by whiteness, may tend to also reinforce unequal comparisons of Black students—immigrant or not—often against a standard of Eurocentric white performance embedded racially in the norms used by institutions to determine the degree to which all students align with this whiteness. My colleagues and I, in our intentional decision to move away from comparing Black students with whites based on a Black-white binary (Willis et al., 2021), and instead comparing Black students with one another, on the Program for International Student Assessment (PISA), illustrated that the achievement of Black immigrants was less than the score estab-lished as an indicator of average performance by this reading literacy assessment despite their supposed "outperformance" of African American youth (P. Smith et al., 2019).

The ability of parents, schools, school districts, universities, policymakers, and com-munities to identify and create mechanisms for enabling racialized students to engage in pursuits that function beyond Eurocentrically driven measures and results is critical. For Black immigrants, this is often a process that must be learned, given that the mechanisms used in many countries of the English-speaking Caribbean are themselves geared toward literacies that uphold approximations of whiteness (P. Smith et al., in press). Developing such understandings can be facilitated via the insights presented in the Appendix. Being conscious of these tendencies in practice and in research can enable Black immigrant par-ents to avoid the continued fostering of divisive rhetoric among themselves and other racialized Black populations, as well as other populations of color, through the perceived "betterness" of certain parents to resist racialization more effectively than others. In this way, the burden for working toward transraciolinguistic justice can be placed squarely where it belongs—on institutions and on the society—avoiding the tendency to inces-santly measure the varied capacities of racialized populations to respond adequately and joyfully respond to trauma (P. Smith et al., 2022).

SCHOOLS AND TEACHERS

It is not enough to read. Schools and teachers have a moral responsibility to also act on behalf of all Black youth (Willis et al., 2022), given the institutional ways in which racialization creates challenges for the acceptance of the languaging and personhoods of youth (Warrican, 2020). Action on behalf of underserved youth of color, as it has always been, is a moral responsibility. As highlighted by my colleagues and me (Willis et al., 2022), this action often is overlooked in the "miseducation of Black children," as a broad array of documented and available scholarship about Black youth literacies remains ignored even when it is clear that this "should inform reading praxis and research."

A more compelling basis for action is needed regarding the subsuming of Black immigrants in the Black American population, much as happens for many immigrants, and specifically immigrants of color, across their corresponding racial subgroups. The tendency for school programming around diversity, and much of the U.S. school legislation on languaging and literacy, to be focused on Latinx populations (understandably and admittedly because of their overwhelming representation in U.S. schools) is another legitimate reason. This situation, although understandable, often makes it almost impossible for schools to extend beyond the myriad populations highlighted for literacy instruction by district, state, and national mandates. As such, there is often a tendency to use established and largely popular diversity frameworks (e.g., culturally relevant pedagogy [Ladson-Billings, 1995], culturally sustaining pedagogy [Paris, 2012]) that are deemed sufficient to reach most youth or that are perceived as catering to the most visible or recognized populations. While this trend is understandable, there are nuances among varied immigrant populations of color, such as Black immigrant youth whose needs remain invisible and whose literacies and languaging largely stand to be addressed through frameworks such as that of Black immigrant literacies.

One way this can be remedied, at least in part, while maintaining the use of already-established frameworks, is to reconcile approaches for diversity that are already in use within and across curricula for "majority populations" in schools, with elements of the Black immigrant literacies framework designed to engage nuances unique to this population. Schools that rely on preestablished and broader mechanisms, such as translanguaging (García & Wei, 2014), culturally relevant teaching (Ladson-Billings, 1999), funds of knowledge (Moll et al., 1992), the four resources model (Luke, 2012), culturally sustaining pedagogy (Paris, 2012), historically responsive teaching (Muhammad, 2020), cultural modeling (C. D. Lee, 2001), and numerous other approaches, can identify the specific ways in which these mechanisms, as they are integrated into literacy and English language arts curriculum, can be complemented by integrating elements of the Black immigrant literacies framework.

To facilitate this process, Figure 6.2 presents a selective list of a broadly used range of approaches, theories, models, and frameworks in the field of literacy and education, providing an indication of how the elements of the Black immigrant literacies framework might be aligned with these preexisting mechanisms. The asterisks corresponding to each element of the Black immigrant literacies framework represent areas where alignment is most easily achievable; therefore, this is where I recommend schools and teachers begin.

The areas where asterisks are absent also represent key opportunities for alignment but will require additional work to integrate the elements of Black immigrant literacies with preexisting frameworks if the needs of Black immigrant students are to be addressed.

For the teacher, principal, or other school district administrator working to address diversity broadly in schools that serve a myriad of populations, the information in Figure 6.2 is intended to allow them to infuse the programming already being undertaken with elements from the framework for Black immigrant literacies. This will be critical for beginning and/or extending explicit conversations regarding inclusivity for Black immigrant student populations. It is also expected that schools that do not already use an approach listed here can extend this list to foster alignment with the Black immigrant literacies framework as needed. While this list is not exhaustive and only a modest and initial pathway to better address the literacy and languaging use of Black immigrant students, it is expected that as the field evolves, curriculum developers, schools, districts, and policymakers will be more attuned to integrating Black immigrant literacy considerations into literacy and ELA practice.

Another compelling avenue for action on the part of schools and teachers is literature. Serving as mirrors, windows, and sliding glass doors, literature can provide an avenue for identifying as well as cultivating metalinguistic, metacultural, and metaracial understandings highlighted in a transraciolinguistic approach across diverse racial, linguistic, and ethnic populations.

COMMUNITY

Community is often one of the most difficult aspects of Black immigrants' lives in their adopted country. Often Black organizations in the United States tend to be African American in focus or largely emphasize issues of diversity unique to Americans. The school can play a critical role in helping Black immigrant youth and their parents to find connections and thrive. One of the main ways that this can occur is by schools maintaining a running list of the local organizations within and across their communities that may serve as a home for Black immigrant families. This can help connect Black immigrants to communities through Black immigrant literacies. Figure 6.3 presents a list of readings and organizations that can provide a basis for schools to begin educating Black immigrant parents around understanding and establishing community as they navigate the overtly racialized landscape of the United States. Figure 6.4, which is available online at www.tcpress.com, presents an overview of literature that can be used to facilitate the development of meta-understandings discussed here.

SUMMARY

In this book, I have provided teachers, parents, schools, and communities with a clearer understanding of the literacies of Black immigrant youth. Specifically highlighting the literacies of two Black Caribbean immigrant youth from Jamaica and the Bahamas, I have

(text continued on p. 132)

Figure 6.2. Complementing Existing Approaches With Black Immigrant Literacies

	Black Immigrant Literacies				
Preexisting Frameworks, Theories, Models, and Approaches	**Addressing the Struggle for Justice:** *Supporting students with understanding where they fit.*	**Interrupting the Myth of the Model Minority:** *Showing students how this myth works to create barriers.*	**Connecting the Local to the Global:** *Enabling students to see race across contexts.*	***Leveraging a Transraciolinguistic Approach:** Supporting equal use of metalinguistic, metacultural, and metaracial understanding.*	***Cultivating Holistic Literacies:** Supporting students' equal use of all literacies.*
Liberatory Caribbean Imaginaries: *Creates opportunities for Parents of Color to share insights about their students' languaging and literacies in ways that highlight assets useful for transforming literacy teaching* **(P. Smith, forthcoming).**	*		*		*
Parent of Color Stories: *Creates opportunities for parents of Color to share insights about their students' languaging and literacies in ways that highlight assets useful for transforming literacy teaching* **(Edwards & Smith, in press).**	*		*		*
Transnational Literacies as a Tool: *Creates opportunities for "immigrant of color literacies" to be acknowledged and centered in transnationality through explicit attention to racialization as a function of institution across nation-states* **(P. Smith et al., 2023).**	*		*	*	*
Decolonial Translingual Pedagogy for Writing: *Creates opportunities to challenge raciolinguistic ideologies in the writing practices of students from a global perspective that addresses language, colonization, and racialization* **(Milu, 2022).**	*		*		
Black Church Pedagogy: *Creates opportunities for the Black Church to serve as a resource that guides educators around best practices in literacy education that address educational inequity* **(McMillon, 2022).**	*				*

CARE: *Developed based on (counter)narratives of African American and Black immigrant scholar-mothers of literacy and undergirded by the idea that access to literacy can eradicate anti-Black mindsets, it illustrates how "Black students, like all students, should be accepted as fully human and worthy of an appropriate, high-quality, and informed (culturally, linguistically, racially) literacy education." CARE is Centered on Black students, reflects Awareness of anti-Blackness—historical knowledge and political knowledge; emphasizes Racial Equity/Justice; and insists on specific Expectations of personnel in school districts, schools, and classrooms* **(Willis et al., 2022).**	*	*	*
Translanguaging With Englishes (While Black): *Creates opportunities for Black students typically regarded as dialectal to be perceived as bi-/multilingual students who rely on their broad range of linguistic repertoires for meaning-making* **(P. Smith, 2020a; Smith & Warrican, 2021b).**	*	*	
Raciosemiotic Architecture: *Creates opportunities for engaging students' multiple modes of meaning-making for particular purposes while centering the often-invisible racialization of these modes based on how students make meaning through multiple modalities across cultural, linguistic, and racial communities* **(P. Smith, 2022e).**	*		
Black Girls' Literacies: *Creates opportunities for centering Black girls' literacies as multiple, tied to identities, historical, collaborative, intellectual, political, and critical across grade levels and contexts* **(Muhammad & Haddix, 2016; Price-Dennis & Muhammad, 2021).**	*	*	

(continued)

Figure 6.2. (continued)

	Black Immigrant Literacies				
Preexisting Frameworks, Theories, Models, and Approaches	*Addressing the Struggle for Justice: Supporting students with understanding where they fit.*	*Interrupting the Myth of the Model Minority: Showing students how this myth works to create barriers.*	*Connecting the Local to the Global: Enabling students to see race across contexts.*	*Leveraging a Transraciolinguistic Approach: Supporting equal use of metalinguistic, metacultural, and metaracial understanding.*	*Cultivating Holistic Literacies: Supporting students' equal use of all literacies.*
Critical Multilingual, Critical Multicultural, and Critical Racial Awareness: *Creates opportunities for literacy teachers and educators to engage critically with the self-first, as a basis for enhancing cultural, racial, and linguistic responsiveness in literacy classrooms* **(Smith &Warrican, 2021a).**	*			*	*
Artifactual Literacies as Austere Love: *Creates opportunities for teachers and teacher educators to foreground relationships, experiences, pasts, and possibilities in ways that acknowledge and extend the already present literacy practices possessed by youth of color for more equitable curriculum and teaching* **(Marciano & Watson, 2021; see also Pahl & Rowsell, 2010).**	*				*
Literacy Futurisms: *Creates opportunities, through a grounding in intersectionality, translanguaging, decoloniality, ancestral/collectivism, and play that facilitates a reenvisioning and reclamation of the future(s) of literacy research* **(Literacy Futurisms Collective-in-the-Making, 2021).**	*				*
Anti-Racist Black Language Pedagogy: *Creates opportunities for examining and dismantling anti-Black linguistic racism and white cultural and linguistic hegemony in English language arts*	*		*		*

classrooms through the use of literature that fosters a study of: (a) Black language and identity; (b) language, history and culture; (c) Black language; (d) language and power; (e) language and racial positioning in society; (f) language, agency, and action; and (g) language and solidarity (**Baker-Bell, 2020,** **pp. 8–10; see also Baker-Bell, 2013**).

Post-White Orientation: *Requires racial reorientations that result in racial literacies—thinking and doing race for human well-being—particularly practices that (a) demonstrate unequivocal regard for "nonwhite" or hyperraced humanity; especially "Black" humanity; (b) demote the inflated ranking of white(ness) as often represented by positionings or status; (c) reject all forms of post-racialism; (d) debunk hierarchical racialization; a1(e) anticipate a post-white sociopolitical norm* (**Croom, 2020; see also M. Croom, personal communication, November 26, 2022**).

Transliteracies: *Creates opportunities for attending to the connections, relationships, and intersections among people and things and to ways in which these happen unequally to support certain learners while disenfranchising others* (**A. Smith et al., 2018**).

Historically Responsive Literacy Framework: *Creates opportunities for teachers and leaders to equitably support learning goals and pursuits via identity development, skill development, intellectual development, and criticality* (**Muhammad, 2020**).

123

(continued)

Figure 6.2. (continued)

	Black Immigrant Literacies				
Preexisting Frameworks, Theories, Models, and Approaches	Addressing the Struggle for Justice: Supporting students with understanding where they fit.	Interrupting the Myth of the Model Minority: Showing students how this myth works to create barriers.	Connecting the Local to the Global: Enabling students to see race across contexts.	Leveraging a Transraciolinguistic Approach: Supporting equal use of metalinguistic, metacultural, and metaracial understanding.	Cultivating Holistic Literacies: Supporting students' equal use of all literacies.
Black Male Literacies: *Creates opportunities for Black male readers, through a focus on categories of vital signs of literacy, of reading, of readers, of literacy instruction, and of educators, which are viewed as critical elements for helping students improve reading to engage meaningfully with texts* (**Tatum, 2018**).	*				*
Black Placemaking: *Spaces created by urban Black Americans as sites representing endurance, belonging, and resistance, which emerge through social interaction* (**Hunter et al., 2016**).	*				
Transnational Literacy: *Creates opportunities for teachers to engage with transnational youth based on the literacies that they present as individuals moving back and forth across borders in schools* (**Skerrett, 2015**).	*		*		*
Translanguaging: *Creates opportunities for students to use their entire linguistic repertoire to make meaning* (**García & Wei, 2014**).	*		*		*
Culturally Sustaining Pedagogy: *Creates opportunities for perpetuating and fostering the linguistic, literate, and cultural pluralism that is involved in schooling as a function of democracy* (**Paris, 2012**).	*				

The Four Resources Model: *Creates opportunities for students to use coding, semantics, pragmatics, and critical resources together in meaning-making* **(Freebody & Luke, 1990).**	*
Cultural Modeling: *Creates opportunities for recognizing and using the language competencies that students bring from beyond schools to construct activity systems in classrooms* **(C. D. Lee, 2001).**	*
Culturally Relevant Pedagogy: *Creates opportunities for addressing student achievement while also helping students to accept and affirm their cultural identity* **(Ladson-Billings, 1999).**	*
Funds of Knowledge: *Creates opportunities for teachers to engage in co-research about the communities they serve so they can use these insights to engage in participatory pedagogy* **(Moll et al., 1992).**	*
ABCs of Cultural Understanding and Communication: *Creates opportunities for autobiographies and biographies to be created about cultural difference and analyzed, then applied to literacy teaching and to home and school connections* **(Schmidt, 1998).**	*

Figure 6.3. Readings and Organizations for Building Community Through Black Immigrant Literacies

Types of Literacies	Black Immigrant Literacies				
	Addressing the Struggle for Justice: Supporting students with understanding where they fit.	*Interrupting the Myth of the Model Minority: Showing students how this myth works to create barriers.*	*Connecting the Local to the Global: Enabling students see race across contexts.*	*Leveraging a Transraciolinguistic Approach: Supporting equal use of metalinguistic, metacultural, and metaracial understanding.*	*Cultivating Holistic Literacies: Supporting students' equal use of all literacies.*
Immigration Literacies	Immigration is a Black issue, American Friends Service Committee: https://www.afsc.org /blogs/news-and-commentary /immigration-black-issue In evolving Charlotte, Black immigrants across diaspora are often overlooked: *The Charlotte Post*: https://www .thecharlottepost.com/news /2022/09/15/local-state/in -evolving-charlotte-black -immigrants-across-diaspora-are -often-overlooked Summit School District drafts new equity policy: https://www .summitdaily.com/news/summit -school-district-drafts-new -equity-policy "Generations of pain": The road to reparations in Evanston:	Bloomberg News: Import More Migrants Because Americans Can't Get It Done: https://www .breitbart.com /economy/2020 /ansjorgomberg -news-import -migrants-americans -cant-get-done			Helping Immigrant Students to Succeed at School—and Beyond: https://www.oecd.org /education/Helping -immigrant-students-to -succeed-at-school-and -beyond.pdf

https://dailynorthwestern.com /2020/05/29/city/generations-of -pain-the-road-to-reparations-in -evanston

Black immigrants are more likely to be denied U.S. citizenship than white immigrants, study finds: https://www.cnn.com/2022/02/23 /us/black-immigrants-citizenship -approval-disparities/index .html#:~:text=About%2094%25 %20of%20White%20women, approval%20ratings%20at%20 around%2086%25.

Report of the APA Presidential Task Force on Immigration: https://www.academia.edu /2903175/Report_of_the_APA _Presidential_Task_Force_on _Immigration

White House Task Force on Black Immigrants:

Policy Recommendations and Priorities for the First 100 Days and Beyond: https://africans.us /sites/default/files/White%20 House%20Task%20Force%20on %20Black%20Immigrants _FINAL_Dec.%2010%202020 %20%281%29.pdf

(continued)

Figure 6.3. (continued)

			Black Immigrant Literacies		
Types of Literacies	*Addressing the Struggle for Justice: Supporting students with understanding where they fit.*	*Interrupting the Myth of the Model Minority: Showing students how this myth works to create barriers.*	*Connecting the Local to the Global: Enabling students see race across contexts.*	*Leveraging a Transraciolinguistic Approach: Supporting equal use of metalinguistic, metacultural, and metaracial understanding.*	*Cultivating Holistic Literacies: Supporting students' equal use of all literacies.*
Media Literacies	Creative Conversations | Reimagining a Black Utopia for the Black Immigrant Communities: https://laundromatproject.org/creative-conversations-reimagining-a-black-utopia-for-the-black-immigrant-communities				What immigrant students can teach us about new media literacy: https://www.sesp.northwestern.edu/docs/publications/20190771245413726982.pdf Wellness, Wellbeing, and Virtual Reality: https://www.youtube.com/watch?v=dokwyRC1N4k Is the Metaverse the New Hope for Mental Health? https://www.linkedin.com/pulse/metaverse-new-hope-mental-health-deepak-chopra-md-official-/?trackingid=L3Ilp17wR6C7mnd9EPvz%2Fg%3D%3D
Indigenous Literacies	Dr. Keisha Josephs on Twitter: "Anyway, everyone is welcome to visit the Kalinago Territory (although maybe not during Covid). I'd especially love more				

	connections between Indigenous people of North, Central and South America and Kalinago. Come visit." https://mobile.twitter.com/home	
Health Literacies	David R. Williams: https://scholar.harvard.edu/davidrwilliams/biocv Racism's corrosive impact on the health of Black Americans: https://www.cbsnews.com/news/60-minutes-disease-black-americans-covid-19-2021-04-18 Now Open at Bok, a New Health Center for Philly's Immigrant and Refugee Population: https://www.phillymag.com/healthcare-news/2021/ansjorgnsjorg-wyss-wellness-center-bok-building	Healthy People 2030 Language and Literacy: https://health.gov/healthypeople/priority-areas/social-determinants-health/literature-summaries/language-and-literacy
Generational Literacies	Protests reveal generational divide in immigrant communities: https://www.conchovalleyhomepage.com/news/protests-reveal-generational-divide-in-immigrant-communities	
International Literacies		Literacy Around the World: https://www.air.org/resource/spotlight/literacy-around-world

(continued)

Figure 6.3. (continued)

Types of Literacies	Black Immigrant Literacies				
	Addressing the Struggle for Justice: Supporting students with understanding where they fit.	*Interrupting the Myth of the Model Minority: Showing students how this myth works to create barriers.*	*Connecting the Local to the Global: Enabling students see race across contexts.*	*Leveraging a Transraciolinguistic Approach: Supporting equal use of metalinguistic, metacultural, and metaracial understanding.*	*Cultivating Holistic Literacies: Supporting students' equal use of all literacies.*
Communicative Literacies					Promoting anti-racist practices through intercultural communication: A collaborative conversation: http://news manager.commpartners .com/tesolicis/issues/2021 -03-11/4.html
Racial Literacies	Why the APA's apology for promoting white supremacy falls short While the mea culpa details many of the past racist practices in psychology, it largely omits a key portion of this history: https://www.nbcnews.com/think /opinion/why-apa-s-apology -promoting-white-supremacy -falls-short-ncna1284229				
Nation-Based Literacies			Brazilian: Literacy, speech and shame: The cultural politics of literacy and language in Brazil:		

https://www.tandfonline.com
/doi/full/10.1080
/09518390701207426

Mongolian:
Translanguaging, Emotionality,
and English as a Second
Language Immigrants:
Mongolian Background Women
in Australia: https://
onlinelibrary.wiley.com/doi/abs
/10.1002/tesq.3015

St. Lucian:
St. Lucian French Creole
Dictionary: http://www.saintluci
ancreole.dbfrank.net/dictionary
/KweyolDictionary.pdf

Guyanese: The future sound of
Black English: https://audio
boom.com/posts/818672-the
-future-sound-of-black-english

Haitian:
The discursive pathway of two
centuries of raciolinguistic
stereotyping: 'Africans as
incapable of speaking French':
https://www.cambridge.org
/core/journals/language-in
-society/article/abs/discursive
-pathway-of-two-centuries-of
-raciolinguistic-stereotyping
-africans-as-incapable-of
-speaking-french/80D24F6C6
65B44836E168F7B292000E2

discussed the nuances that Black immigrant youth face based on race, language, and immigration. Outlining mechanisms for teachers, I have indicated how Black immigrant youth's literacies can be addressed in classrooms where there is diversity and where the needs of Black immigrants often go unaddressed. In keeping with this goal, I have highlighted the need for schools, parents, communities, and organizations to better understand how Black immigrant students can be supported, both in solidarity with other Black students and more broadly as they relate to other racial and immigrant students in the United States.

Overall, this scholarship holds potential for transforming how literacies are considered in the field because it:

1. Advances the novel framework for Black immigrant literacies to revolutionize literacy teaching in ways that draw on all students' literate assets for redesigning, rethinking, and reimagining literacy and English language arts curriculum;
2. Presents the five elements of the Black immigrant literacies framework—struggle for justice, the myth of the model minority, transraciolinguistics, the local–global, and holistic literacies—as mechanisms through which Black immigrant literacies and languaging can be better understood based on the intersectionality of race, language, and immigration;
3. Highlights authentic narratives that center the holistic voices of Afro-Caribbean immigrant youth from Jamaica and the Bahamas to demonstrate how these youth grappled with racialization, with becoming immigrant, and with the responses of others to their use of Englishes in the United States;
4. Highlights the intersectional framework of transraciolinguistics as a basis for teaching all students to equally draw on their metalinguistic, metacultural, and metaracial understanding in literacy and ELA classrooms as they build solidarity across racial, linguistic, and other cultural boundaries;
5. Includes lesson plans, instructional modules, and templates that range in their focus from K–12 to college, and which teachers and educators can use to teach Black immigrants and to build solidarity among all students using each element of the Black immigrant literacies framework; and
6. Presents numerous concrete outlets and mechanisms for schools, districts, policymakers, and researchers to support Black immigrant populations in establishing and sustaining a sense of community across linguistic, cultural, and racial contexts.

Emerging as a love note to Black immigrant students, parents, and peoples everywhere, it is expected that this book centering Blackness, immigration, and languaging will silence invisibility (P. Smith, 2020d) and transform how we plan for and design literacy instruction for Black immigrant youth, for immigrant youth of color, and for all youth in schools.

Afterword

Without a doubt, this publication is right on time! It comes to us at a moment when there is heavy movement of peoples globally and where classrooms in the United States are seeing an increase in Black immigrant youth, hopeful of experiencing that "better" life embodied in the American Dream. As Dr. Patriann Smith highlights in her book, *Black Immigrant Literacies: Intersections of Race, Language, and Culture in the Classroom,* this dream is often crushed when assumptions are made about Black immigrant students by those charged with guiding their education pursuits. The invisible (and sometimes very visible) barriers to the success of these youth are mounted on assumptions that marginalize the learners in the classroom.

Two such assumptions are (1) Black immigrant students have restricted literacy in English as it is used in schools, which functions as a sign of all-round absence of literacy; and (2) the experiences that Black immigrant youth bring with them have little or no value in an American classroom. This book exposes the invisible barriers to success that are fed by these and other assumptions about Black immigrant youth. Dr. Smith highlights the tensions that these youth experience in a context where Black immigrant youth are racialized and where they are forced to position and reposition themselves (Yoon, 2012) to fit into classrooms where whiteness is privileged. They are forced to live double lives in their quest to satisfy their need to identify with their own cultures in one setting, and then to abandon their identity for acceptance into the culture of the school. This enforced schizophrenia is foisted on youth whose forebearers have struggled to establish their identities in the face of the colonial pasts of their home countries, where the notion was instilled that their heritage and culture was deficient compared to Western standards (Thompson, Warrican, & Leacock, 2011). The turmoil that this situation creates for the immigrant youth can manifest in ways that are detrimental to their overall well-being.

The assumptions, barriers, and tensions accompanying Black immigrant youth as described in this book are not unique to the United States and demonstrate the urgency and relevance of this work for global contexts. As a scholar in the Caribbean (a region with a strong colonial past that continues to influence modern education policies and practices), I see similar situations, not only linked to race and language, but also to class. For example, in recent years, there has been much movement across the region as families search for what they perceive to be better economic conditions in neighbouring countries and even extra-regionally. In English-speaking Caribbean countries, all of which are predominantly Black and Brown, the barriers that affect immigrant youth in schools are therefore also linked to nationality, class, and language background. It is not uncommon for these Black youth, especially those from the working class whose first language is likely to be a Creole or English vernacular, to be limited by the invisible barriers created by assumptions like the ones identified earlier. In addition, Brown immigrant youth (usually either Hispanic or Asian) are treated as "Other," neither Black nor White, but often as "defective." For them, the obvious barrier of language is clearly visible, but it is the cultural and heritage differences that support the insidious barriers that often marginalize these learners in the classroom.

Paradoxically, Black immigrant youth from African countries are often most likely to be deemed lacking in literacy and intelligence. This, I believe, is a legacy of the colonial past of the region, where the European colonizers created an education system that designated anything linked to African culture and heritage as inferior to what originated with the colonizers (Thompson, Warrican, & Leacock, 2011). The immigrant youth that tend to fare best are whites of European and North America origin, suggesting that even in predominantly Black settings, whites are still privileged. This, as is largely acknowledged, is part of the legacy of the colonial history of the countries such as Jamaica and the Bahamas in the Caribbean region, from which Black immigrant youth in this book such as Chloe and Ervin originate. As indicated by Dr. Smith, these barriers that affect Black and other non-white immigrant youth are often invisible, existing beyond the consciousness of teachers and school administrators.

A major strength of this publication are the interviews between Dr. Smith and the two Black immigrant youth, Chloe and Ervin. In Chapters 4 and 5, we hear the rich voices of these two youths echoed in authentic narratives as they shared events and experiences of their lives with us. We journey with them as they navigate the unequal world filled with racial, cultural, and linguistic injustices. The appeal of these two chapters is that Dr. Smith makes no attempt to retell, revoice, or rewrite (Smith, 2022) their stories. She lets them tell their stories and make interpretations in their own way, and in the languages with which they are comfortable. The presentation of these narratives helps maintain the identities of the Black immigrant youth, as no attempt is made to thematize or categorize the messages that ring loudly in their words.

Dr. Smith maintained the authenticity of the youths' voices through using the framework of Black immigrant literacies designed to make race central to literacy teaching. Of note are the five elements of this framework:

1. The claim to the struggle for justice;
2. The myth of the model minority;
3. A transraciolinguistics approach;
4. A focus on local–global;
5. Holistic literacies.

The approach encouraged by the framework as demonstrated by the author helps teachers and educators throw off the mindset of Black immigrant youth as individuals who should be grateful for the opportunity to be educated and enlightened (Warrican, 2020) as if their lives prior to moving to the United States were lived in darkness and emptiness. This type of moral licencing obscures the fact that if properly embraced, the diversity that immigrant youth bring to the classroom can enrich the learning experiences of all the students there.

Black Immigrant Literacies: Intersections of Race, Language, and Culture in the Classroom is a worthwhile resource for every teacher and educator who plies their craft in diverse classrooms. A valuable take away is the set of practical resources (lesson plans, instructional modules, and templates that can be used from K–12 to tertiary levels) by teachers and educators. As Dr. Smith points out, these resources can promote equity in literacy classrooms in which Black immigrant youth are being educated. This book is not only of value to teachers and educators in the United States, but it also holds international appeal and will be a useful resource for those in any teaching and learning context in which there is linguistic, racial, and cultural diversity, and where teaching involves bridging barriers that disadvantage some groups while privileging others.

—*S. Joel Warrican*

REFERENCES

Smith, P. (2022, December). Towards a methodological shift for examining racialized entanglements: Interrupting raciolinguistic erasure for transraciolinguistic justice [Conference session]. Literacy Research Association Annual Conference 2022, Phoenix, AZ.

Thompson, B. P., Warrican, S. J., & Leacock, C. J. (2011). Education for the future: Shaking off the shackles of colonial times. In D. Dunkley (Ed.). *Readings in Caribbean history and culture: Breaking ground* (pp. 61–86). Lexington Books.

Warrican, S. J. (2020). Towards caring language and literacy classrooms for black immigrant youth: Combatting raciolinguistic ideologies and moral licensing. *Teachers College Record, 122*(13), 1–22.

Yoon, B. (2012). Junsuk and Junhyuck: Adolescent immigrants' educational journey to success and identity negotiation. *American Educational Research Journal, 49*, 971–1002.

Lessons for "Becoming Black" in a "White" World

Over the years, I have penned a few literary nuggets from my experiences and from the shared experiences of Black immigrants in the United States. I offer these anecdotal insights here to my Black immigrant brothers, sisters, parents, teachers, scholars, educators, friends, and others who are grappling with becoming immigrant, "(un)becoming white" (P. Smith, in press) and "becoming Black" (Ibrahim, 1999) in a white world. For my brothers, sisters, and others from populations of color as well as from dominant populations who wish to engage in shared humanity with Black and other immigrants in countries such as the United States, these nuggets will prove enlightening as they invite a (re)thinking of the common in considering Blackness, its linguistic versatility, ethnic enclaves, and heterogeneity. And for all others who wish to support the Black immigrant, please think on these things. Note that each element in quotes below is reflective of what Black immigrants often may hear from others or what they often might say to others upon migration to a new land. The elements that are not enclosed in quotes reflect explanations and reminders to Black immigrants in the United States.

- "You Speak English So Well!": *Most Compliments Are Not Positive; Don't Mistake Racism for Kindness.*
- "How Can She Write So Well?!": *Your Literacies Are Strengths, Use Them.*
- "Well, You Can't File This Form at This Time": *Everything Someone Tells You About Immigration Policies Is Not Necessarily True—Research All Immigration Laws Yourself.*
- "No News Is Not Always Good News": *Self-Advocate: Your Paperwork Is Not Delayed; Maybe It's "Forgotten."*
- "Just Be a Good Little Immigrant": *Achieving "Highly" Based on Certain Norms Is Not Necessarily Bad; Just Don't Forget That Often, You're Expected to Be Indebted.*
- "You're Perfect for the Position!": *Almost Every Employer Needs a "Token Black"; Decide Whether You're Fine With That BEFORE Accepting the Offer.*
- "What She Did Was Blatantly Wrong!": *Don't Make the Mistake of Speaking Your Mind Without Being Strategic, or Seeming Too Righteous, That's Called Being "Uncivil."*
- "I Swear I Could Kill You Right Now!": *Ummm, No Joke, Never Use a Word That Signals Violence, Not Even If This Was Normal for You "Back Home."*

- "Well She Told Me to Wait Here So I've Been Waiting for 3 Hours and I'm So Tired!": *Use Your Instincts; If It Feels Wrong, It Probably Is.*
- "I Don't Have a Problem With the N Word!": *Really? So Is It Okay That It's Derogatory to Your Black Brother Just Because It Doesn't Affect You?!*
- "You Are Not African American; Do Not Leave Your Immigration Papers at Home": *There Is No Way to Explain Who You Are Without Evidence.*
- "You Not Black; You a Caribbean!": *Don't Accept Compliments That Degrade Your Black American Sisters and Brothers.*
- "Wow! I Like Working With Her on This Project: We're Such Great Friends!": *No One at Work Is Necessarily Your Friend; A Good Colleague, Maybe? Of Course, There May Be Exceptions!*
- "I Don't Feel Comfortable Talking About My Accomplishments": *Really? Because Someone Else Is Always Ready to Talk About Things They Haven't Done: Speak up and Speak out.*
- "No Walls, Build Bridges Instead!": *Sure, Go Ahead and Protest but If You Are Deported for the Slightest Offense Because You Are Immigrant, Who Will Lead the Cause Against Injustice?*
- "She Keeps Me as Her Black Friend So How Can She Be Racist!?": *Most Folks Who Are Racist Have Learned How to Mask It. Identify the Mask; in Time It Will Show.*
- "Mummy, Why Did I Get Called to Be the Cotton Picker in the Play? Is It Because I'm Black?" "I Don't Know, Baby, It's Okay": *No, It's Not Okay for Your Child to Play Demeaning Roles in School; Learn U.S. History and Teach the Child Never to be Bound by Its Shackles. Just Take a Look at Florida!*
- "My Friends at School Call Me "Immigrant Girl" but It's Cool; We're Good Like That!": *Teach Your Child to Establish Respectful Boundaries—Remind, Reinforce, Insist.*
- "I Can Tell, He Sounds Jamaican!": *Most Folks Only Know Jamaica in the Caribbean or Think Africa Is a Continent; Humor Can Be Your Best Friend; Don't Sweat the Small Stuff; Think "Teachable Moment."*
- "I Can't Understand What She's Saying": *You Need Them More Than They Need You; Swallow Your Pride and Slow Down When You Speak. No, You Shouldn't Have to but It's Only for a Time—You Can Soon Trangress Linguistic Norms.*
- "She Thinks She's Better Than Us!": *You Might Not See Your Perceived Arrogance but They Do; Build Bridges, Not Walls; Be Humble.*
- "They're Always Using Their Accent to Get Our Men!": *Show That You Have Much More Than an Accent and That People Fall in Love With Personality; Be Unapologetic About Your Migrant Blackness.*
- "I Know They Act Like This Because They See My Black Face!": *What "They" Want Is for You to Hate You, Only You Can Love You, So Love Your Black Face and See What Happens.*
- "We Must Get Rid of These Immigrants, Taking Our Jobs!": *Never Forget That You Are a Threat; Someone Is Simply Waiting for You to Make That One Mistake or Doesn't Mind Pushing You to Make It; Live a Life of Integrity.*

- "I Will Just Get Over There and Somehow I Will Make It!": *Yes, You Just Might Make It Starting With Nothing and No One in the United States, but Think About How Much You Lose; Plan Ahead.*
- "I Will Just Stay by My Aunt Until I Get a Job!": *Trying to Get a Job in the United States Is a Job; If You Don't Want to Be Kicked Out for Not Helping With Rent, Secure a Job Before Moving.*
- "I Think She From Barbados; I Will Probably Go Chat With Her!": *Not Every Black Person Who Migrates Wants a Black Migrant Friend (Fortunately or Unfortunately); Learn How to Differentiate.*
- "Ma'am, You Are Under Arrest": *Comply Now, Talk (AND I REPEAT), Talk Later.*
- "Jonathan, Would You Like to Take Over the Front Desk While I Go in to Discuss With This Client?": *What the Boss Means Here Is Do What I Just Said, Phrased Like a Question but It's Really a Command; Unless You Don't Mind Losing Your Job, You Probably Want to Adhere to Such Direct Questions.*
- "So What You Meant a While Ago When You Said X, Was It Then Really Y?": *Don't Let Them Get Into Your Head; Keep Calm and Resist the "Noose," the One Created to Make You Hang Yourself.*
- "He Raped Me!": *There Is Always a Likelihood That a Woman (or Man, Yes Man) Will Cry "Rape"; Get Consent, Assured Consent.*
- "Sh#*^!": *That Is Obscene Language, and So Is "Damn"; Choose Your Words Wisely.*
- "Why Do You Always Work So Hard?!!": *"You Got to Work Twice as Hard!": Make That Ten Times Given the Scenario Today; Unless You Work Smart, Whichever It Is, You Do Not Have the Luxury of Living Lazy. But Still, Let Yourself Rest.*
- "Your Daughter Is So Well Behaved, I Didn't Hear Her Speak a Word This Whole Time!": *Translate, Translate, Translate; Is Your Daughter Expected to Be "Loud" (Whatever That Means), Compliments Are Not Always What They Seem.*
- "You Are So Well Dressed Today, Franklin!": *By Your Clothing, You Will Be Evaluated. Yes, Whether You Like It or Not, Pay Attention to Your Clothes, When You Want to, of Course.*
- "So, How Does It Feel to Win an Award That Says You Do Great Work?": *Ummm, It Might Be Best to Switch That Up a Bit and Deflect by Responding: "How Would YOU Feel If You Could Win an Award That Says YOU Do Great Work?" Not Every Question Deserves an Answer.*
- (*in a job search meeting*) "I Believe Janice (Black Woman) Deserves the Job but Sara (White Woman) Has Been With Us Longer So We Can't Help but Give Her the Position": *There Is Always That Moment When You Must Stand up for Something; Let It Be Something Like This, Something That Matters.*
- "(She's African and Smart) I'm Sure She'll Choose Medicine!": *Not All Africans Become Doctors and That's Okay.*
- "I Don't Really Like Blacks but I LOVE Me Some Caribbeans!": *My Friend, That Is Not a Compliment; Think Teachable Moment (Again).*
- "No Matter What I Do, They Never Think I'm Good Enough!": *Your Validation Comes From a Higher Power, Not Man. You Are Already Enough.*

- "The White Kids at This School Always Get All the Awards!": *The World Has Always Been Unfair and It Still Is; Teach Your Child This and Also Show Them Daily What Uniqueness They Bring to the World So They Can Inspire Change, Redefine Responses to Blackness.*
- "I Want to Get a Big House and Live in That Lovely Neighborhood!": *Not All That Glitters Is Gold; Success Can Be Many Different Things to Many Different People.*

References

ABC News. (2020, February 10). *Backlash emerges behind Cynthia Erivo's role in 'Harriet'* [Video]. YouTube. https://www.youtube.com/watch?v=zr3fiKJitmo

Abraham, S. (2020). What counting words has really taught us: The word gap, a dangerous, but useful discourse. *Equity & Excellence in Education, 53*(1–2), 137–150.

Adichie, C. N. (2009, July). *The danger of a single story* [Video]. TED. https://www.ted.com/talks/chimamanda_ngozi_adichie_the_danger_of_a_single_story?lan-guage=en

Aguilera, D., & Lecompte, M. (2008). Restore my language and treat me justly: Indigenous students' rights to their tribal languages. In J. C. Scott, D. Y. Straker, & L. Katz (Eds.), *Affirming students' right to their own language: Bridging language policies and pedagogical practices* (pp. 92–108). Routledge. https://doi.org/10.4324/9780203866986-13

Agyepong, M. (2013). Seeking to be heard: An African-born, American-raised child's tale of struggle, invisibility, and invincibility. In I. Harushimana, C. Ikpeze, & S. Mthethwa-Sommers (Eds.), *Reprocessing race, language and ability: African-born educators and students in transnational America* (pp. 155–168). Peter Lang.

Agyepong, M. (2019). *Blackness and Africanness: Black West African immigrant students' experiences in two New York City high schools* [Doctoral dissertation, University of Wisconsin–Madison]. ProQuest Dissertations.

Alegría, M., Álvarez K., & DiMarzio K. (2017). Immigration and mental health. *Current Epidemiology Reports, 4*(2), 145–155. https://doi.org/10.1007/s40471-017-0111-2

Alim, H. S. (2016). Who's afraid of the transracial subject. In S. Alim, J. R. Rickford & A. F. Ball (Eds.), *Raciolinguistics: How language shapes our ideas about race* (pp. 34–50). Oxford University Press.

Antoniou, K., Grohmann, K. K., Kambanaros, M., & Katsos, N. (2016). The effect of childhood bilectalism and multilingualism on executive control. *Cognition, 149*, 18–30. https://doi.org/10.1016/j.cognition.2015.12.002

Anya, U. (2016). *Racialized identities in second language learning: Speaking blackness in Brazil.* Taylor & Francis.

Au, K. H. (1993). *Literacy instruction in multicultural settings.* Wadsworth Publishing Company.

Au, K. H. (1998). Social constructivism and the school literacy learning of students of diverse backgrounds. *Journal of Literacy Research, 30*(2), 297–319.

Awokoya, J. T. (2009). *"I'm not enough of anything!": The racial and ethnic identity constructions and negotiations of one-point-five and second generation Nigerians* [Doctoral dissertation, University of Maryland]. ProQuest Dissertations.

Bacigalupe, G. (2012). *Crossroads: The psychology of immigration on the new century* (Report of the APA Presidential Task Force on Immigration). https://www.apa.org/topics/immigration-refugees/executive-summary.pdf

Baker-Bell, A. (2013). "I never really knew the history behind African American language": Critical language pedagogy in an advanced placement English language arts class. *Equity & Excellence in Education, 46*, 355–370.

Baker-Bell, A. (2020). *Linguistic justice: Black language, literacy, identity, and pedagogy.* Routledge.

Barth, E.A.T. (1961). The language behavior of Negroes and whites. *Pacific Sociological Review, 4*(2), 69–72. https://doi.org/10.2307/1388674

Baugh, J., & Welborn, A. (2008). The hidden linguistic legacies of Brown v. Board and No Child Left Behind. In J. C. Scott, D. Y. Straker, & L. Katz (Eds.), *Affirming students' right to their own language: Bridging language policies and pedagogical practices* (pp. 65–77). Routledge. https://doi.org/10.4324/9780203866986-11

Beck, I. L., McKeown, M. G., & Kucan, L. (2013). *Bringing words to life: Robust vocabulary instruction* (2nd ed.). Guilford Press.

Birmingham, J. C. (2015). Black English near its roots: The transplanted West African Creoles. In J. L. Dillard (Ed.), *Perspectives on American English* (Vol. 29, pp. 335–346). De Gruyter. https://doi.org/10.1515/9783110813340-024 (Original work published 1980)

Blaché, R. L. (2022). *Teaching to (re)member through an AP seminar with African diaspora content* [Doctoral dissertation, Columbia University].

Blake, R., & Shousterman, C. (2010). Second generation West Indian Americans and English in New York City. *English Today, 26*(3), 35–43. https://doi.org/10.1017/S0266078410000234

Bogle, M. (1997). Constructing literacy: Cultural practices in classroom encounters. *Caribbean Journal of Education, 19*(2), 179–190.

Braden, E. (2020). Navigating Black racial identities: Literacy insights from an immigrant family. *Teachers College Record, 122*(13), 1–26. https://doi.org/10.1177/016146812012201310

Bristol, L. S. M. (2012). *Plantation pedagogy: A postcolonial and global perspective.* Peter Lang.

Brooks, M. D. (2015). "It's like a script": Long-term English learners' experiences with and ideas about academic reading. *Research in the Teaching of English, 49*(4), 383–406.

Brooks, M. D. (2018). Pushing past myths: Designing instruction for long-term English learners. *TESOL Quarterly, 52*(1), 221–233. https://doi.org/10.1002/tesq.435

Brown v. Board of Education, 347 U.S. 483 (1954).

Bruner, J. (1987). Life as narrative. *Social Research, 54*(1), 11–32. http://www.jstor.org/stable/40970444

Bryan, B. (1997). Investigating language in a Jamaican primary school: Perceptions and findings of a group of primary school teachers. *Changing English, 4*(2), 251–258. https://doi.org/10.1080/1358684970040207

Bryan, K. C. (2020). "I had to get tougher": An African immigrant's (counter)narrative of language, race, and resistance. *Teachers College Record, 122*(13), 1–28.

Bryce-Laporte, R. S. (1972). Black immigrants: The experience of invisibility and inequality. *Journal of Black Studies, 3*(1), 29–56. https://doi.org/10.1177/002193477200300103

Busia, A. (1989). What is your nation? Reconstructing Africa and her diaspora through Paule Marshall's *Praisesong for the widow*. In C. Wall (Ed.), *Changing our own words* (pp. 196–211). Rutgers University Press.

Cabrera, N. L. (2018). Where is the racial theory in critical race theory? A constructive criticism of the Crits. *Review of Higher Education, 42*(1), 209–233. https://doi.org/10.1353/rhe.2018.0038

Canagarajah, A. S. (2006). Changing communicative needs, revised assessment objectives: Testing English as an international language. *Language Assessment Quarterly, 3*(3), 229–242. https://doi.org/10.1207/s15434311laq0303_1

Canagarajah, A. S., & Said, S. (2011). Linguistic imperialism. In J. Simpson (Ed.), *The Routledge handbook of applied linguistics* (pp. 388–400). Routledge. https://doi.org/10.4324/97802038 35654.ch27

Carrington, L. (1992). Caribbean English. In T. McArthur (Ed.), *The Oxford companion to the English language* (pp. 191–193). Oxford University Press.

Chow, R. (2014). *Not like a native speaker: On languaging as a postcolonial experience.* Columbia University Press. https://doi.org/10.7312/chow15144

Clachar, A. (2003). Paratactic conjunctions in Creole speakers' and ESL learners' academic writing. *World Englishes, 22*(3), 271–289. https://doi.org/10.1111/1467-971x.00296

Clachar, A. (2004). Creole discourse effects on the speech conjunctive system in expository texts. *Journal of Pragmatics, 36*(10), 1827–1850. https://doi.org/10.1016/j.pragma.2004.05.002

Clachar, A. (2005). Creole English speakers' treatment of tense-aspect morphology in English interlanguage written discourse. *Language Learning, 55*(2), 275–334. https://doi.org/10.1111/j .0023-8333.2005.00305.x

Clark, V. A. (2009). Developing diaspora literacy and *marasa* consciousness. *Theatre Survey, 50*(1), 9–18. https://doi.org/10.1017/S0040557409000039

Clemons, A. M. (2021). *Spanish people be like: Dominican ethno-raciolinguistic stancetaking and the construction of Black Latinidades in the United States* [Doctoral dissertation, The University of Texas at Austin]. UT Electronic Theses and Dissertations.

Cook, A. L. (2015). Building connections to literacy learning among English language learners: Exploring the role of school counselors. *Journal of School Counseling, 13*(9), 3–43.

Cooper, A. (2020). Justice for all: Realities and possibilities of Black English learners in K–12 schools. *Teachers College Record, 122*(13), 1–24.

Craig, D. R. (1999). *Teaching language and literacy: Policies and procedures for vernacular situations.* Education and Development Services.

Crenshaw, K. (1991). Mapping the margins: Intersectionality, identity politics, and violence against women of color. *Stanford Law Review, 43*(6), 1241–1299. https://doi.org/10.2307/1229039

Croom, M. (2020). If "Black Lives Matter in literacy research," then take this racial turn: Developing racial literacies. *Journal of Literacy Research, 52*(4), 530–552. https://doi.org/10.1177/1086 296X20967396

Curthoys, A., & Lake, M. (Eds.). (2006). *Connected worlds: History in transnational perspective.* ANU Press.

Dancy, T. E., Edwards, K. T., & Davis, J. E. (2018). Historically white universities and plantation politics: Anti-Blackness and higher education in the Black Lives Matter era. *Urban Education, 53*(2), 176–195.

Daoud, N., English, S., Griffin, K. A., & George Mwangi, C. A. (2018). Beyond stereotypes: Examining the role of social identities in the motivation patterns of Black immigrant and Black native students. *American Journal of Education, 124*(3), 285–312. https://doi.org/10.1086 /697211

Darvin, R., & Norton, B. (2014). Transnational identity and migrant language learners: The promise of digital storytelling. *Education Matters: The Journal of Teaching and Learning, 2*(1), 55–66. https://journalhosting.ucalgary.ca/index.php/em/article/view/62890

Davies, C. B. (2013). *Caribbean spaces: Escapes from twilight zones.* University of Illinois Press.

De Costa, P. I. (2010). From refugee to transformer: A Bourdieusian take on a Hmong learner's trajectory. *TESOL Quarterly, 44*(3), 517–541. https://www.jstor.org/stable/27896744

De Costa, P. I. (2014). Reconceptualizing cosmopolitanism in language and literacy education: Insights from a Singapore school. *Research in the Teaching of English, 49*(1), 9–30.

de Kleine, C. (2006). West African world English speakers in U.S. classrooms: The role of West African pidgin English. In S. J. Nero (Ed.), *Dialects, Englishes, Creoles, and education* (pp. 205–232). Erlbaum.

Delpit, L. (1988). The silenced dialogue: Power and pedagogy in educating other people's children. *Harvard Educational Review, 58*(3), 280–299.

Delva, R. J. (2019). "Kreyòl Pale, Kreyòl Konprann": Haitian identity and Creole mother-tongue learning in Matènwa, Haiti. *Journal of Haitian Studies, 25*(1), 92–125. https://doi.org/10.1353/jhs.2019.0003

Devonish, H., & Carpenter, K. (2020). *Language, race and the global Jamaican.* Springer International. https://doi.org/10.1007/978-3-030-45748-8

Dillard, C. B. (2012). *Learning to (re)member the things we've learned to forget: Endarkened feminisms, spirituality, & the sacred nature of research & teaching.* Peter Lang.

Dillard, J. L. (1972). *Black English: Its history and usage in the United States.* Random House.

Dodoo, F.N.A. (1997). Assimilation differences among Africans in America. *Social Forces, 76*(2), 527–546. https://doi.org/10.1093/sf/76.2.527

Dovchin, S. (2020). Introduction to special issue: Linguistic racism. *International Journal of Bilingual Education and Bilingualism, 23*(7), 773–777.

Dyson, A. H. (2003). *The brothers and sisters learn to write: Popular literacies in childhood and school cultures.* Teachers College Press.

Dyson, A. H. (2015). The search for inclusion: Deficit discourse and erasure of childhoods. *Language Arts, 92*(3), 199–207.

Editorial Staff. (2022, November 9). UN report highlights discrimination against Black boys & girls worldwide. *St. Lucia Times News.* https://stluciatimes.com/17971/2022/11/un-report-highlights-discrimination-against-black-boys-girls-worldwide

Edwards, P. A., & Compton-Lilly, C. (2016). *New ways to engage parents: Strategies and tools for teachers and leaders, K–12.* Teachers College Press.

Edwards, P. A., Pleasants, H. M., & Franklin, S. H. (1999). *A path to follow: Learning to listen to parents.* Heinemann.

Edwards, P. & Smith, P. (forthcoming). From illiterate assumption to literate potentiality: Harnessing the possibility of parent of color stories. *Journal of Contemporary Issues in Early Childhood.*

Edwards, P. A., Smith, P., & McNair, J. C. (2022). Toward culturally relevant literacies with children and families of color. In R. J. Tierney, F. Rizvi, & K. Ercikan (Eds.), *International Encyclopedia of Education* (4th ed., pp. 180–197), Elsevier.

Edwards, P. A., Spiro, R. J., Domke, L. M., Castle, A. M., White, K. L., Peltier, M. R., & Donohue, T. H. (2019). *Partnering with families for student success: 24 scenarios for problem solving with parents.* Teachers College Press.

Emig, J. (1977). Writing as a mode of learning. *College Composition and Communication, 28*(2), 122–128. https://doi.org/10.2307/356095

Fanon, F. (1963). *The wretched of the earth* (C. Farrington, Trans.). Grove Press. (Original work published 1961)

Ferris, R. (2015, July 31). *World population: Quarter of Earth will be African in 2050.* CNBC. https://www.cnbc.com/2015/07/30/world-population-quarter-of-earth-will-be-african-in-2050.html

Fisher, M. T. (2006). Building a literocracy: Diaspora literacy and heritage knowledge in participatory literacy communities. *The Yearbook of the National Society for the Study of Education, 105*(2), 361–381. https://doi.org/10.1111/j.1744-7984.2006.00090.x

Flores, N. (2013). Silencing the subaltern: Nation-state/colonial governmentality and bilingual education in the United States. *Critical Inquiry in Language Studies, 10*(4), 263–287.

Flores, N. (2020). From academic language to language architecture: Challenging raciolinguistic ideologies in research and practice. *Theory Into Practice, 59*(1), 22–31. https://doi.org/10.1080 /00405841.2019.1665411

Foner, N. (1985). Race and color: Jamaican migrants in London and New York City. *International Migration Review, 19*(4), 708–727.

François, R. (2016). *An investigation of Catholic education and the predicament of democracy in Haiti* [Doctoral dissertation, McGill University]. ProQuest Dissertations.

Freebody, P., & Luke, A. (1990). Literacies programs: Debates and demands in cultural context. *Australian Journal of TESOL, 5*(7), 7–16.

Freire, P., & Macedo, D. P. (1987). *Literacy: Reading the word and the world.* Bergin & Garvey.

García, O. (2009). *Bilingual education in the 21st century: A global perspective.* Wiley-Blackwell.

García, O., & Kleyn, T. (2016). Translanguaging theory in education. In O. García & T. Kleyn (Eds.), *Translanguaging with multilingual students* (pp. 9–33). Routledge.

García, O., & Wei, L. (2014). *Translanguaging: Language, bilingualism and education* (pp. 46–62). Palgrave Pivot.

Gilbert, S. G. (2008). *The relationship of immigrant status to perceptions of reading and reading literacy among young Black students: A test of the cultural-ecological theory of school performance* [Doctoral dissertation, Florida International University]. ProQuest Dissertations.

Guinier, L. (2004). From racial liberalism to racial literacy: *Brown v. Board of Education* and the interest–divergence dilemma. *Journal of American History, 91*(1), 92–118. https://doi.org/10 .2307/3659616

Hamilton, C. (1972). *Apartheid in an American city: The case of the Black community in Los Angeles.* Labor/Community Strategy Center.

Hancock, I. (2015). Texan Gullah: The Creole English of the Brackettville Afro-Seminoles. In J. L. Dillard (Ed.), *Perspectives on American English* (Vol. 29, pp. 305–334). De Gruyter. https://doi .org/10.1515/9783110813340-023 (Original work published 1980)

Harré, R., Moghaddam, F. M., Cairnie, T. P., Rothbart, D., & Sabat, S. R. (2009). Recent advances in positioning theory. *Theory & Psychology, 19*(1), 5–31. https://doi.org/10.1177/0959354308101417

Haughton, G. (2022, January 23). *Research finds the Caribbean provides largest origin source of Black immigrants in the USA.* CNW Network. https://www.caribbeannationalweekly.com/news /research-finds-the-caribbean-provides-largest-origin-source-of-black-immigrants-in-the -usa

Heath, S. B. (1983). *Ways with words: Language, life, and work in communities and classrooms.* Cambridge University Press.

Herdina, P., & Jessner, U. (2002). *A dynamic model of multilingualism: Perspectives of change in psycholinguistics.* Multilingual Matters.

Holm, J. (2015). The Creole 'Copula' that highlighted the world. In J. L. Dillard (Ed.), *Perspectives on American English* Vol. 29, pp. 367–376). De Gruyter. https://doi.org/10.1515/9783110813340 -026 (Original work published 1980)

Hordge-Freeman, E., & Veras, E. (2020). Out of the shadows, into the dark: Ethnoracial dissonance and identity formation among Afro-Latinxs. *Sociology of Race and Ethnicity, 6*(2), 146–160. https://doi.org/10.1177/2332649219829784

Horowitz, R. (2012). Border crossing: Geographic space and cognitive shifts in adolescent language and literacy practices. In H. Romo, C.A.G. de la Calleja, & O. Lopez (Eds.), *A bilateral perspective on Mexico–U.S. migration* (pp. 147–164). Instituto de Investigaciones Histórico.

Hotchkins, B., & Smith, P. (2020). Translanguaging as a gateway to Black immigrant collegians' leadership literacies. *Teachers College Record, 122*(13), 1–29. https://doi.org/10.1177/0161468120 12201312

Hudley, C. (2016). Achievement and expectations of immigrant, second generation, and non-immigrant Black students in U.S. higher education. *International Journal of Educational Psychology, 5*(3), 223–248. https://doi.org/10.17583/ijep.2016.2226

Hunter, M. A., Pattillo, M., Robinson, Z. F., & Taylor, K. Y. (2016). Black placemaking: Celebration, play, and poetry. *Theory, Culture & Society, 33*(7–8), 31–56. https://doi.org/10.1177/0263276416635259

Ibrahim, A. (1999). Becoming Black: Rap and hip-hop, race, gender, identity, and the politics of ESL learning. *TESOL Quarterly, 33*(3), 349–369. https://doi.org/10.2307/3587669

Ibrahim, A. (2019). *Black immigrants in North America: Essays on race, immigration, identity, language, hip-hop, pedagogy, and the politics of becoming Black.* Stylus.

Jackson, J. V., & Cothran, M. E. (2003). Black versus Black: The relationship among African, African American and African Caribbean persons. *Journal of Black Studies, 33*(5), 576–604.

Jackson, R. O. (2007). Immigrants, Black. In W. A. Darity, Jr. (Ed.), *International encyclopedia of the social sciences* (Vol. 2, pp. 564–567). Macmillan.

Jacobson, M. F. (1998). *Whiteness of a different color: European immigrants and the alchemy of race.* Harvard University Press.

Jiménez, R. T., Eley, C., Leander, K., & Smith, P. H. (2015). Transnational immigrant youth literacies: A selective review of the literature. In P. Smith & A. Kumi-Yeboah (Eds.), *Handbook of research on cross-cultural approaches to language and literacy development* (pp. 322–344). IGI Global.

Jiménez, R. T., Smith, P. T., & Teague, B. L. (2009). Transnational and community literacies for teachers. *Journal of Adolescent & Adult Literacy, 53*(1), 16–26. https://doi.org/10.1598/jaal.53.1.2

Joseph, V. (2012). How Thomas Nelson and Sons' *royal readers* textbooks helped instill the standards of whiteness into colonized Black Caribbean subjects and their descendants. *Transforming Anthropology, 20*(2), 146–158. https://doi.org/10.1111/j.1548-7466.2012.01156.x

Kachru, B. B. (1992). *The other tongue: English across cultures* (2nd ed.). University of Illinois Press.

Kachru, B. B., & Nelson, C. (2001). World Englishes. In A. Burns & C. Coffin (Eds.), *Analysing English in a global context: A reader* (pp. 9–25). Routledge.

Kalantzis, M., & Cope, B. (2012). *Literacies.* Cambridge University Press.

Kasinitz, P. (1992). *Caribbean New York: Black immigrants and the politics of race.* Cornell University Press.

Kendi, I. X. (2019). *How to be an anti-racist.* One World.

Kigamwa, J. C., & Ndemanu, M. T. (2017). Translingual practice among African immigrants in the US: Embracing the mosaicness of the English language. *Journal of Multilingual and Multicultural Development, 38*(5), 468–479. https://doi.org/10.1080/01434632.2016.1186678

Kim, E. (2014). Bicultural socialization experiences of Black immigrant students at a predominantly white institution. *Journal of Negro Education, 83*(4), 580–594. https://doi.org/10.7709/jnegroeducation.83.4.0580

King, J. E. (1992). Diaspora literacy and consciousness in the struggle against miseducation in the Black community. *The Journal of Negro Education, 61*(3), 317–340. https://doi.org/10.2307/2295251

King, J. E. (2021). Diaspora literacy, heritage knowledge, and revolutionary African-centered pedagogy in Black studies curriculum theorizing and praxis. In W. H. Schubert & M. F. He (Eds.), *Oxford encyclopedia of curriculum studies.* Oxford University Press. https://doi.org/10.1093/acrefore/9780190264093.013.1566

Kiramba, L. K. (2017). Multilingual literacies: Invisible representation of literacy in a rural classroom. *Journal of Adolescent & Adult Literacy, 61*(3), 267–277. https://doi.org/10.1002/jaal.690

Kiramba, L. K. (2019). Heteroglossic practices in a multilingual science classroom. *International Journal of Bilingual Education and Bilingualism, 22*(4), 445–458. https://doi.org/10.1080/13670050.2016.1267695

Kiramba, L. K., Kumi-Yeboah, A., & Sallar, A. M. (2020). "It's like they don't recognize what I bring to the classroom": African immigrant youths' multilingual and multicultural navigation in United States schools. *Journal of Language, Identity & Education, 22*(1), 83–98. https://doi.org/10.1080/15348458.2020.1832499

Kperogi, F. (2009, March 22). African immigrants now America's new "model minority"? *Notes from Atlanta.* http://www.farooqkperogi.com/2009/03/african-immigrants-now-americas-new.html

Kreps, G. L., & Sparks, L. (2008). Meeting the health literacy needs of immigrant populations. *Patient Education and Counseling, 71*(3), 328–332.

Kumi-Yeboah, A. (2018). The multiple worlds of Ghanaian-born immigrant students and academic success. *Teachers College Record, 120*(9), 1–48.

Kumi-Yeboah A., & Smith, P. (2016). Cross-cultural educational experiences and academic achievement of Ghanaian immigrant youth in urban public schools. *Education and Urban Society, 49*(4), 434–455. https://doi.org/10.1177/0013124516643764

Labov, W. (1995). Can reading failure be reversed? A linguistic approach to the question. In V. Gadsen & D. Wagner (Eds.), *Literacy among African-American youth* (pp. 39–68). Hampton Press.

Ladson-Billings, G. (1995). Toward a theory of culturally relevant pedagogy. *American Educational Research Journal, 32*(3), 465–491.

Ladson-Billings, G. J. (1999). Preparing teachers for diverse student populations: A critical race theory perspective. *Review of Research in Education, 24*(1), 211–247. https://doi.org/10.3102/0091732x024001211

Lam, W. S. E. (2000). L2 literacy and the design of the self: A case study of a teenager writing on the internet. *TESOL Quarterly, 34*(3), 457–482.

Lam, W. S. E., & Warriner, D. S. (2012). Transnationalism and literacy: Investigating the mobility of people, languages, texts, and practices in contexts of migration. *Reading Research Quarterly, 47*(2), 191–215. https://doi.org/10.1002/rrq.016

Lee, A. Y. (2022). Shifting epistemologies amidst whitestream norms: Centering Black language in an elementary literacy methods course. *Literacy Research: Theory, Method, and Practice, 71*(1), 268–285.

Lee, C. D. (2001). Is October Brown Chinese? A cultural modeling activity system for underachieving students. *American Educational Research Journal, 38*(1), 97–141.

Literacy Futurisms Collective-in-the-Making. (2021). We believe in collective magic: Honoring the past to reclaim the future(s) of literacy research. *Literacy Research: Theory, Method, and Practice, 70*(1), 1–20.

Luke, A. (2012). Critical literacy: Foundational notes. *Theory into Practice, 51*(1), 4–11.

Luke, A. (2018). *Critical literacy, schooling, and social justice: The selected works of Allan Luke.* Routledge.

Malcolm, Z. T., & Mendoza, P. (2014). Afro-Caribbean international students' ethnic identity development: Fluidity, intersectionality, agency, and performativity. *Journal of College Student Development, 55*(6), 595–614. https://doi.org/10.1353/csd.2014.0053

Marciano, J. E., & Watson, V. W. (2021). "This is America": Examining artifactual literacies as austere love across contexts of schools and everyday use. *The Urban Review, 53*(2), 334–353.

Martinez, D. (2017). Imagining a language of solidarity for Black and Latinx youth in English language arts classrooms. *English Education, 49*, 179–196.

Martinot, S. (2003). *The rule of racialization: Class, identity, governance.* Temple University Press.

McAuliffe, M., & Khadria, B. (Eds.). (2019). *World migration report 2020.* International Organization for Migration.

McLean, C. (2010). A space called home: An immigrant adolescent's digital literacy practices. *Journal of Adolescent & Adult Literacy, 54*(1), 13–22. https://doi.org/10.1598/jaal.54.1.2

McMillon, G. (2022). MyStory, YourStory, OurStory: Literacy development in the Black Church past, present, & future. *Literacy Research: Theory, Method, and Practice, 71*(1), 40–79. https://doi.org/10.1177/23813377221109538

McMillon, G., & Rogers, R. (2019). Racial literacy: Ebony and ivory perspectives of race in two graduate courses. In K. T. Han & J. Laughter (Eds.), *Critical race theory in teacher education: Informing classroom culture and practice* (pp. 46–58). Teachers College Press.

Miller, E. (1989). Caribbean primary education: An assessment. *Caribbean Journal of Education, 16*(3), 136–171.

Milner, R. H. (2012). Beyond a test score: Explaining opportunity gaps in educational practice. *Journal of Black Studies, 43*(6), 693–718. https://doi.org/10.1177/0021934712442539

Milson-Whyte, V. (2014). Working English through code-meshing: Implications for denigrated language varieties and their users. In B. Horner & K. Kopelson (Eds.), *Reworking English in rhetoric and composition: Global interrogations, local interventions* (pp.103–115). Southern Illinois University Press.

Milson-Whyte, V. (2018). Caribbean Creole-speaking cultures, language, and identity. In J. Liontas & M. DelliCarpini (Eds.), *The TESOL encyclopedia of English language teaching* (pp. 1–7). Wiley. https://doi.org/10.1002/9781118784235.eelt0304

Milu, E. (2022). Toward a decolonial translingual pedagogy for Black immigrant students. In T. Do & K. Rowan (Eds.), *Racing translingualism in composition: Toward a race-conscious translingualism* (pp. 123–142). University Press of Colorado.

Mohl, R. A. (1986). Black immigrants: Bahamians in early twentieth-century Miami. *The Florida Historical Quarterly, 65*(3), 271–297.

Moll, L. C., Amanti, C., Neff, D., & Gonzalez, N. E. (1992). Funds of knowledge for teaching: Using a qualitative approach to connect homes and classrooms. *Theory Into Practice, 31*(2), 132–141.

Moll, L. C., Amanti, C., Neff, D., & Gonzalez, N. E. (2005). Funds of knowledge for teaching: Using a qualitative approach to connect homes and classrooms. In N. E. Gonzalez, L. C. Moll, & C. Amanti (Eds.), *Funds of knowledge: Theorizing practices in households, communities, and classrooms* (pp. 71–88). Routledge. https://doi.org/10.4324/9781410613462

Morrell, E. (2002). Toward a critical pedagogy of popular culture: Literacy development among urban youth. *Journal of Adolescent & Adult Literacy, 46*(1), 72–77.

Morrison, S., & Bryan, J. (2014). Addressing the challenges and needs of English-speaking Caribbean immigrant students: Guidelines for school counselors. *International Journal for the Advancement of Counselling, 36*(4), 440–449.

Muhammad, G. (2020). *Cultivating genius: An equity framework for culturally and historically responsive literacy.* Scholastic.

Muhammad, G., & Haddix, M. (2016). Centering Black girls' literacies: A review of literature on the multiple ways of knowing of Black girls. *English Education, 48*(4), 299–336. https://www.jstor.org/stable/26492572

Myhill, J. (1988). Postvocalic /r/ as an index of integration into the BEV speech community. *American Speech, 63*(3), 203–213.

Nalubega-Booker, K., & Willis, A. (2020). Applying critical race theory as a tool for examining the literacies of Black immigrant youth. *Teachers College Record, 122*(13), 1–24. https://doi.org/10.1177/016146812012201309

Nero, S. (2000). The changing faces of English: A Caribbean perspective. *TESOL Quarterly, 34*(3), 483–510.

Nero, S. (2006). Language, identity, and education of Caribbean English speakers. *World Englishes, 25*(3–4), 501–511. https://doi.org/10.1111/j.1467-971X.2006.00470.x

Nero, S. (2014). Classroom encounters with Caribbean Creole English: Language, identities, peda-gogy. In A. Mahboob & L. Barratt (Eds.), *Englishes in multilingual contexts* (pp. 33–46). Springer. https://doi.org/10.1007/978-94-017-8869-4_3

New London Group. (1996). A pedagogy of multiliteracies: Designing social futures. *Harvard Educational Review, 66*(1), 60–93. https://doi.org/10.17763/haer.66.1.17370n67v22j160u

Njue, J., & Retish, P. (2010). Transitioning: Academic and social performance of African immigrant students in an American high school. *Urban Education, 45*(3), 347–370. https://doi.org/10.1177/0042085909355763

Nolasco, V. J. (2020). *Doing Latinidad while Black: Afro-Latino identity and belonging* [Master's thesis, University of Arkansas]. ProQuest Dissertations.

Obeng, C., & Obeng, S. (2006). African immigrant families' views on English as a Second Language (ESL) classes held for newly arrived immigrant children in the United States elementary and middle schools: A study in ethnography. In M. Firmin & P. Brewer (Eds.), *Ethnographic and qualitative research in education* (Vol. 2, pp. 105–116). Cambridge Scholars.

Okonofua, B. A. (2013). "I am Blacker than you": Theorizing conflict between African immigrants and African Americans in the United States. *SAGE Open, 3*(3), 1–14. https://doi.org/10.1177/2158244013499162

Omogun, L. (2021, February 27). Black, on both sides: Living between my Nigerian and African-American identities. *Medium.* https://humanparts.medium.com/black-on-both-sides-5b262 2e23d13

Omogun, L., & Skerrett, A. (2021). From Haiti to Detroit through Black immigrant languages and literacies. *Journal of Literacy Research, 53*(3), 406–429. https://doi.org/10.1177/1086296 x211031279

Onwuegbuzie, A. J., & Frels, R. K. (2013). Introduction: Toward a new research philosophy for addressing social justice issues: Critical dialectical pluralism 1.0. *International Journal of Multiple Research Approaches, 7*(1), 9–26. https://doi.org/10.5172/mra.2013.7.1.9

Onyewuenyi, A. C. (2018). *The unexplored voices of the "new African diaspora": An examination of the impact of race, ethnicity, and teacher discrimination on academic performance for Nigerian and Black American adolescents* [Doctoral dissertation, University of Washington]. ProQuest Dissertations.

Paris, D. (2012). Culturally sustaining pedagogy: A needed change in stance, terminology, and practice. *Educational Researcher, 41*(3), 93–97.

Pennycook, A. (2021). Entanglements of English. In M. Saraceni (Ed.), *Bloomsbury world Englishes: Ideologies* (pp. 9–26). Bloomsbury.

Persohn, L. (Host). (2021, November 23). A conversation with Patriann Smith (Season 2, Episode 14) [Audio podcast episode]. In *Classroom caffeine* podcast series. https://www.classroomcaffeine .com/guests/patriann-smith

Pierre, J. (2004). Black immigrants in the United States and the "cultural narratives" of ethnicity. *Identities, 11*(2), 141–170. https://doi.org/10.1080/10702890490451929

Pinder, P., Prime, G., & Wilson, J. (2014). An exploratory quantitative study comparing and correlating parental factors with environmental science achievement for Black American and Black Caribbean students in a mid-Atlantic state. *The Journal of Negro Education, 83*(1), 49–60. https://doi.org/10.7709/jnegroeducation.83.1.0049

Pollard, V. (1993). *From Jamaican Creole to standard English: A handbook for teachers.* Caribbean Research Center, Medgar Evers College, City University of New York.

Portes, A., Guarnizo, L. E., & Landolt, P. (1999). The study of transnationalism: Pitfalls and promise of an emergent research field. *Ethnic and Racial Studies, 22*(2), 217–237. https://doi.org/10 .1080/014198799329468

Pratt-Johnson, Y. (1993). Curriculum for Jamaican Creole-speaking students in New York City. *World Englishes, 12*(2), 257–264. https://doi.org/10.1111/j.1467-971x.1993.tb00026.x

Price-Dennis, D., & Muhammad, G. E. (Eds.). (2021). *Black girls' literacies: Transforming lives and literacy practices.* Routledge.

Prou, M. (2009). Attempts at reforming Haiti's education system: The challenges of mending the tapestry, 1979–2004. *Journal of Haitian Studies, 15*(1/2), 29–69.

Ramjattan, V. A. (2019). *Working with an accent: The aesthetic labour of international teaching assistants in Ontario universities* [Doctoral dissertation, University of Toronto]. ProQuest Dissertations.

Razfar, A. (2012). Narrating beliefs: A language ideologies approach to teacher beliefs. *Anthropology and Education Quarterly, 43*, 61–81.

Rickford, J. R. (1985). Ethnicity as a sociolinguistic variable. *American Speech, 60*, 90–125.

Rickford, J. R., & Rickford, A. E. (2015). Cut-eye and suck-teeth: African words and gestures in new world guise. In J. L. Dillard (Ed.), *Perspectives on American English* (Vol. 29, pp. 347–366). De Gruyter. https://doi.org/10.1515/9783110813340-025 (Original work published 1980)

Rogers, R., & Mosley, M. (2006). Racial literacy in a second-grade classroom: Critical race theory, whiteness studies, and literacy research. *Reading Research Quarterly, 41*(4), 462–495.

Rosa, J. (2016). Standardization, racialization, languagelessness: Raciolinguistic ideologies across communicative contexts. *Journal of Linguistic Anthropology, 26*(2),162–183. https://doi.org/10.1111/jola.12116

Rosa, J., & Flores, N. (2017). Unsettling race and language: Toward a raciolinguistic perspective. *Language in Society, 46*(5), 621–647. https://doi.org/10.1017/s0047404517000562

Rose, H., & Galloway, N. (2019). *Global Englishes for language teaching.* Cambridge University Press.

Rowe, W. & Schelling, V. (1991). *Memory and modernity: Popular culture in Latin America.* London.

Rubinstein-Ávila, E. (2007). From the Dominican Republic to Drew High: What counts as literacy for Yanira Lara? *Reading Research Quarterly, 42*(4), 568–589. https://doi.org/10.1598/rrq.42.4.6

Schmidt, P. R. (1998). The ABC's of cultural understanding and communication. *Equity & Excellence in Education, 31*(2), 28–38. https://doi.org/10.1080/1066568980310204

Scott, J. C., Straker, D. Y., & Katz, L. (Eds.). (2008). *Affirming students' right to their own language: Bridging language policies and pedagogical practices.* Routledge.

Sealey-Ruiz, Y. (2013). Building racial literacy in first-year composition. *Teaching English in the Two-Year College, 40*(4), 384–398.

Sexton, J. (2018). Unbearable Blackness. In J. Sexton (Ed.), *Black men, Black feminism* (pp. 75–105). Palgrave Macmillan.

Sharifian, F. (2013). Globalisation and developing metacultural competence in learning English as an international language. *Multilingual Education, 3*(7), 1–11. https://doi.org/10.1186/2191-5059-3-7

Shockley, E. T. (2021). Expanding the narrative of the Black–White gap in education research: Black English learners as a counterexample. *The Journal of Negro Education, 90*(1), 7–25.

Siegel, J. (2012). Two types of functional transfer in language contact. *Journal of Language Contact, 5*, 187–215.

Siegel, J. (2020). Review of the book *Language, race and the global Jamaican*, by H. Devonish & K. Carpenter. https://www.montraykreyol.org/article/language-race-and-the-global-jamaican.

Simmons, A. B. (1999). Economic integration and designer immigrants: Canadian policy in the 1990s. In M. Castro (Ed.), *Free markets, open societies, closed borders? Trends in international migration and immigration policy in the Americas* (pp. 53–69). University of Miami North-South Center Press.

Simmons-McDonald, H. (2006). Attitudes of teachers to St. Lucian language varieties. *Caribbean Journal of Education, 28*(1), 51–84.

Simon, S. (Host). (2021, February). In the story of U.S. immigration, Black immigrants are often left out [Audio podcast episode]. In *Weekend edition Saturday*. NPR. https://www.npr.org/2021/02/27/972056955/in-the-story-of-u-s-immigration-black-immigrants-are-often-left-out

Sims Bishop, R. (1990). Mirrors, windows, and sliding glass doors. In H. Moi (Ed.), *Collected perspectives: Choosing and using books for the classroom* (pp. ix–xi). Christopher Gordon.

Skerrett, A. (2011). English teachers' racial literacy knowledge and practice. *Race Ethnicity and Education, 14*(3), 313–330. https://doi.org/10.1080/13613324.2010.543391

Skerrett, A. (2012). Languages and literacies in translocation: Experiences and perspectives of a transnational youth. *Journal of Literacy Research, 44*(4), 364–395. https://doi.org/10.1177/1086296x12459511

Skerrett, A. (2015). *Teaching transnational youth: Literacy and education in a changing world*. Teachers College Press.

Skerrett, A. (2016). Attending to pleasure and purpose in multiliteracies instructional practices: Insights from transnational youths. *Journal of Adolescent & Adult Literacy, 60*(2), 115–120. https://doi.org/10.1002/jaal.571

Skerrett, A. (2017). The role of language in religious identity making: A case of a Caribbean-Chinese youth. *Literacy Research, 66*(1), 325–340. https://doi.org/10.1177/2381336917718176

Skerrett, A. (2020). Transnational students and educational change. *Journal of Educational Change, 21*(3), 499–509. https://doi.org/10.1007/s10833-020-09369-0

Skerrett, A., & Bomer, R. (2013). Recruiting languages and lifeworlds for border-crossing compositions. *Research in the Teaching of English, 47*(3), 313–337.

Skerrett, A., & Omogun, L. (2020). When racial, transnational, and immigrant identities, literacies, and languages meet: Black youth of Caribbean origin speak. *Teachers College Record, 122*(13), 1–24. https://doi.org/10.1177/016146812012201302

Skutnabb-Kangas, T. (1988). Multilingualism and the education of minority children. In T. Skutnabb-Kangas & J. Cummins (Eds.), *Minority education: From shame to struggle* (pp. 9–44). Multilingual Matters.

Smith, A., Stornaiuolo, A., & Phillips, N. C. (2018). Multiplicities in motion: A turn to transliteracies. *Theory Into Practice, 57*(1), 20–28.

Smith, P. (2016). A distinctly American opportunity: Exploring non-standardized English(es) in literacy policy and practice. *Policy Insights from the Behavioral and Brain Sciences, 3*(2), 194–202. https://doi.org/10.1177/2372732216644451

Smith, P. (2017). Nonstandardized Englishes in mainstream literacy practice. *Oxford Research Encyclopedia of Education*. https://doi.org/10.1093/acrefore/9780190264093.013.18

Smith, P. (2018a). Finding (radical) hope in literacy: Pedagogical literacy insights from culturally and linguistically diverse students. *Literacy Practice and Research*, pp. 5–15.

Smith, P. (2018b). Renewing hope with English literacies: Insights from middle schoolers. *Literacy Today: International Literacy Association*, pp. 34–35.

Smith, P. (2019). (Re)Positioning in the Englishes and (English) literacies of a Black immigrant youth: Towards a *transraciolinguistic* approach. *Theory Into Practice, 58*(3), 292–303. https://doi.org/10.1080/00405841.2019.1599227

Smith, P. (2020a). The case for translanguaging in Black immigrant literacies. *Literacy Research, 69*(1), 192–210. https://doi.org/10.1177/2381336920937264

Smith, P. (2020b). "How does a Black person speak English?" Beyond American language norms. *American Educational Research Journal, 57*(1), 106–147. https://doi.org/10.3102/0002831219850760

Smith, P. (2020c). "Mr. Wang doesn't really care how we speak!": Responsiveness in the practice of an exemplary Asian-American teacher. *The Urban Review, 52*(2), 351–375. https://doi.org/10.1007/s11256-019-00531-4

Smith, P. (2020d). Silencing invisibility: Toward a framework for Black immigrant literacies. *Teachers College Record, 122*(13), 1–42. https://doi.org/10.1177/016146812012201301

Smith, P. (2021). Five steps to address anti-Blackness: Black immigrant literacies. International Literacy Research Association Literacy Now Blog. https://www.literacyworldwide.org/blog/literacy-now/2021/03/17/five-steps-to-address-anti-blackness-black-immigrant-literacies

Smith, P. (2022a). Black immigrants in the United States: Transraciolinguistic justice for imagined futures in a global metaverse. *Annual Review of Applied Linguistics, 42*, 109–118. https://doi.org/10.1017/s0267190522000046

Smith, P. (2022b). A transraciolinguistic approach for literacy classrooms. *The Reading Teacher, 75*(5), 545–554. https://doi.org/10.1002/trtr.2073

Smith, P. (2022c, December). *Racialized entanglements and the promise of liberatory Caribbean imaginaries: An interactive panel presented in response to the Oscar S. Causey address by Dr. Arlette I. Willis* [Panel presentation]. Literacy Research Association Annual Conference, Phoenix, AZ, United States.

Smith, P. (2022d, December). *Towards a methodological shift for examining racialized entanglements: Interrupting raciolinguistic erasure for transraciolinguistic justice* [Conference session]. Literacy Research Association Annual Conference, Phoenix, AZ, United States.

Smith, P. (2022e, December). *Why multiliteracies? Black immigrant literacies as a vehicle for raciosemiotic architecture* [Conference session]. Literacy Research Association Annual Conference, Phoenix, AZ, United States.

Smith, P. (2023a). Black immigrant literacies and the promise of unbroken Englishes: Five things every teacher should know and can do. *The Reading Teacher*. [Advance online publication.]

Smith, P. (2023b). Black immigrant literacies can reinstate Black language and transcend the global myth of invented illiteracy and Black brokenness. LSE USAPP Blog. https://bit.ly/3qz7HTX

Smith, P., Cheema, J., Kumi-Yeboah, A., Warrican, S. J., & Alleyne, M. L. (2018). Language-based differences in the literacy performance of bidialectal youth. *Teachers College Record, 120*(1), 1–36. https://doi.org/10.1177/016146811812000105

Smith, P., Chen, Y., Yin, Y., Michels, J., Leacock, C. J., Hunte, A., & Kumi-Yeboah, A. (2023, April). Beyond dichotomized representations of "language at home" on PISA: Insights from Black immigrant literacies. Paper presented at the 2023 annual meeting of the American Educational Research Association, Chicago, IL.

Smith, P., & Hajek, S. (2021). Prism of promise: Towards responsive tools for diverse classrooms. In G. Li, J. Hare, & J. Anderson (Eds.), *Superdiversity and teacher education* (pp. 139–186). Routledge.

Smith, P., Kumi-Yeboah, A., Chang, R., Lee, J., & Frazier, P. (2019). Rethinking "(under)performance" for Black English speakers: Beyond achievement to opportunity. *Journal of Black Studies, 50*(6), 528–554. https://doi.org/10.1177/0021934719851870

Smith, P., Lee, J., & Chang, R. (2022). Characterizing competing tensions in Black immigrant literacies: Beyond partial representations of success. *Reading Research Quarterly, 57*(1), 59–90. https://doi.org/10.1002/rrq.375

Smith, P., & Murillo, L. A. (2012). Researching transfronterizo literacies in Texas border colonias. *International Journal of Bilingual Education and Bilingualism, 15*(6), 635–651.

Smith, P., Varner, J., Nigam, A., Liu, Y., Lesley, M., Smit, J., Burke, D., & Beach, W. (2020). Teaching writing in the midst of fragile alliances: Insights from literacy teacher educators. *Action in Teacher Education, 42*(4), 328–353. https://doi.org/10.1080/01626620.2019.1658657

Smith, P., & Warrican, S. J. (2021a). Critical awareness for literacy teachers and educators in troubling times. *Literacy Practice and Research, 46*(2). https://doi.org/10.25148/lpr.009638

Smith, P., & Warrican, S. J. (2021b). Migrating while multilingual and Black: Beyond the '(bi)dialectal' burden. In E. Bauer, L. Sánchez, Y. Wang, & A. Vaughan (Eds.), *A transdisciplinary lens for bilingual education: Bridging translanguaging, sociocultural research, cognitive approaches, and student learning* (pp. 102–128). Routledge.

Smith, P., Warrican, S. J., Kumi-Yeboah, A., & Richards, J. (2018). Understanding Afro-Caribbean educators' experiences with Englishes across Caribbean and U.S. contexts and classrooms: Recursivity, (re)positionality, bidirectionality. *Teaching and Teacher Education, 69*, 210–222. https://doi.org/10.1016/j.tate.2017.10.009

Smith, R. (1980). Interrelatedness of certain deviant grammatical structures in Negro Nonstandard Dialects. In J. L. Dillard (Ed.), *Perspectives on American English* (393–402). De Gruyter.

Smith, R. (2015). Interrelatedness of certain deviant grammatical structures in Negro nonstandard dialects. In J. L. Dillard (Ed.), *Perspectives on American English* (Vol. 29, pp. 393–400). De Gruyter. https://doi.org/10.1515/9783110813340-028 (Original work published 1980)

Sowell, T. (1978). *Essays and data on American ethnic groups.* Urban Institute Press.

Steinberg, S. (2005). Immigration, African Americans, and race discourse. *New Politics, 10*(3), 42–54.

St-Hilaire, A. (2011). *Kwéyòl in postcolonial Saint Lucia: Globalization, language planning, and national development.* John Benjamins. https://doi.org/10.1075/cll.40

Street, B. (1995). *Social literacies: Critical approaches to literacy in development, ethnography and education.* Routledge. https://doi.org/10.4324/9781315844282

Stuesse, A., Staats, C., & Grant-Thomas, A. (2017). As others pluck fruit off the tree of opportunity: Immigration, racial hierarchies, and intergroup relations efforts in the United States. *Du Bois Review, 14*(1), 245–271. https://doi.org/10.1017/S1742058X16000394

Tamir, C. (2022, March). *The growing diversity of Black America.* Pew Research Center. https://www.pewresearch.org/social-trends/2021/03/25/the-growing-diversity-of-black-america

Tamir, C., & Anderson, M. (2022, January). *The Caribbean is the largest origin source of Black immigrants, but fastest growth is among African immigrants.* Pew Research Center. https://www.pewresearch.org/race-ethnicity/2022/01/20/the-caribbean-is-the-largest-origin-source-of-black-immigrants-but-fastest-growth-is-among-african-immigrants

Tatum, A. W. (2018). Toward a more anatomically complete model of literacy development: A focus on Black male students and texts. In D. Alvermann, N. Unrau, M. Sailors, & R. Ruddell (Eds.), *Theoretical models and processes of literacy* (pp. 281–300). Routledge.

Theuri, C. (Host). (2022, November 24). The future sound of Black English (Episode 55) [Audio podcast episode]. In *Subtitle.* https://subtitlepod.com/the-future-sound-of-black-english

Thornton M., Taylor R.J., & Chatters L.M. (2013). African Americans and Black Caribbean mutual feelings of closeness: Findings from a National Probability Survey. *Journal of Black Studies, 44*(8), 798–828.

Tichavakunda, A. A. (2020). Studying Black student life on campus: Toward a theory of Black placemaking in higher education. *Urban Education,* 1–28. https://doi.org/10.1177/0042085920971354

Tillery, A. B., & Chresfield, M. (2012). Model Blacks or "Ras the Exhorter": A quantitative content analysis of Black newspapers' coverage of the first wave of Afro-Caribbean immigration to the United States. *Journal of Black Studies, 43*(5), 545–570. https://doi.org/10.1177/0021934712439065

Ukpokodu, O. (2018). African immigrants, the "new model minority": Examining the reality in U.S. K–12 schools. *The Urban Review, 50*(1), 69–96. https://doi.org/10.1007/s11256-017-0430-0

United Nations, Department of Economic and Social Affairs, Population Division. (2015). *World population prospects: The 2015 revision, key findings and advance tables.* https://population.un.org/wpp/Publications/Files/Key_Findings_WPP_2015.pdf

University of the West Indies. (2011, January 5). Regional linguists meet at UWI international conference on language rights and policy to present charter. https://www.mona.uwi.edu/marcom/newsroom/entry/4057

U.S. Census Bureau, American Community Survey. (2013). *English learner (EL) students who are Black: Fast facts* (No. 1066637963). Office of English Language Acquisition.

U.S. Department of Education, Office of English Language Acquisition & White House Initiative on Educational Excellence for African Americans. (2015). *Fast facts: English learners who are Black.* U.S. Department of Education, Office for Civil Rights. Retrieved from https://sites.ed.gov/whblackeducation/files/2013/03/OELA-and-WHIEEAA-Fast-Facts-1-of-2-10.6.15-FINAL.pdf

U.S. Department of Health and Human Services, Office of Disease prevention and Health Promotion. (2022). Language and Literacy—Healthy People 2030. https://health.gov/healthypeople/objectives-and-data/social-determinants-health/literature-summaries/language-and-literacy

U.S. Department of Justice & U.S. Department of Education. (2015). *Dear colleague letter: English learner students and limited English proficient parents.* Retrieved from https://www2.ed.gov/about/offices/list/ocr/letters/colleague-el-201501.pdf

Voice. (2011, January 8). Regional linguists meet at UWI International conference on language rights and policy. http://www.thevoiceslu.com/local_news/2011/january/08_01_11/Regional.htm

VoicEd Radio. (2021). A transraciolinguistic approach for literacy classrooms. https://voiced.ca/podcast_episode_post/a-transraciolinguistic-approach-for-literacy-classrooms-ft-dr-patriann-smith/ University of Calgary.

Warrican, S. J. (2009). Literacy development and the role of the eastern Caribbean joint board of teacher education. *Journal of Eastern Caribbean Studies, 34*(2), 71–85.

Warrican, S. J. (2020). Toward caring language and literacy classrooms for Black immigrant youth: Combating raciolinguistic ideologies and moral licensing. *Teachers College Record, 122*(13), 1–22. https://doi.org/10.1177/016146812012201306

Warrican, S. J., Alleyne, M. L., Smith, P., Cheema, J., & King, J. R. (2019). Peer effects in the individual and group literacy achievement of high-school students in a bi-dialectal context. *Reading Psychology, 40*(2), 117–148. https://doi.org/10.1080/02702711.2019.1571545

Waters, M. C. (1994). Ethnic and racial identities of second-generation Black immigrants in New York City. *The International Migration Review, 28*(4), 795–820. https://doi.org/10.2307/2547158

Watson, V. W. M., Knight, M. G., & Jaffee, A. T. (2014). Beyond #talking and #texting: African immigrant youth's social–civic literacies and negotiations of citizenship across participatory new media technologies. *Citizenship Teaching & Learning, 10*(1), 43–62. https://doi.org/10.1386/ctl.10.1.43_1

Watson, V. W. M., & Marciano, J. E. (2015). Examining a social-participatory youth co-researcher methodology: a cross-case analysis extending possibilities of literacy and research. *Literacy, 49*(1), 37–44.

Wheeler, R. S. (2008). "Taylor cat is black": Code-switch to add standard English to students' linguistic repertoires. In J. C. Scott, D. Y. Straker, & L. Katz (Eds.), *Affirming students' right to their own language: Bridging language policies and pedagogical practices* (pp. 200–215). Routledge. https://doi.org/10.4324/9780203866986-20

Wiley, T. G. (2014). Diversity, super-diversity, and monolingual language ideology in the United States: Tolerance or intolerance? *Review of Research in Education, 38*(1), 1–32.

Williams, K. (2016). Caribbean literature in English. *Soka University English Literature Society, 28*(2), 107–149.

Willis, A. I. (2018). Re-positioning race in English language arts research. In D. Lapp & D. Fisher (Eds.), *Handbook of research on teaching the English language arts* (pp. 30–56). Routledge.

Willis, A. I. (2022a). Revolutionizing literacy: The life of Omar ibn Said, written by himself. The Oscar S. Causey Award Presentation. Literacy Research Association 72nd Annual Meeting, Phoenix, AZ. https://literacyresearchassociation.org/news/arlette-willis-to- speak-at-lra2022/

Willis, A.I. (2022b). Arlette Willis to speak at #LRA2022. Literacy Research Association 72nd Annual Meeting, Phoenix, AZ. https://literacyresearchassociation.org/updates/arlette-willis-to -speak-at-lra2022/

Willis, A. I., & Harris, V. (1997). Preparing preservice teachers to teach multicultural literature. In J. Flood, D. Lapp, & S. B. Heath (Eds.), *Handbook of research on teaching literacy through the communicative and visual arts* (pp. 460–469). Routledge.

Willis, A. I., McMillon, G. T., & Smith, P. (2022). *Affirming Black students' lives and literacies: Bearing witness.* Teachers College Press.

Willis, A. I., & Smith, P. (2021). Advancing antiracism in literacy research. *Literacy Research: Theory, Method, and Practice, 70*(1), 152–169. https://doi.org/10.1177/23813377211027554

Willis, A. I., Smith, P., Kim, J., & Hsieh, B. (2021). *Racial justice in literacy research.* Literacy Research Association.

Windle, J. A., & Muniz, K. (2018). Constructions of race in Brazil: Resistance and resignification in teacher education. *International Studies in Sociology of Education, 27*(2–3), 307–323. https://doi.org/10.1080/09620214.2018.1444504

Winer, L. (2006). Teaching English to Caribbean English Creole–speaking students in the Caribbean and North America. In S. J. Nero (Ed.), *Dialects, Englishes, Creoles, and education* (pp. 105–118). Erlbaum.

Wingate, U. (2015). *Academic literacy and student diversity: The case for inclusive practice.* Multilingual Matters. https://doi.org/10.21832/9781783093496

Wingate, U. (2018). Academic literacy across the curriculum: Towards a collaborative instructional approach. *Language Teaching, 51*(3), 349–364. https://doi.org/10.1017/s0261444816000264

Wolfram, W. (1971). Black–White speech relationships revisited. In W. Wolfram & N. H. Clarke (Eds.), *Black–White speech relationships* (pp. 139–161). Center for Applied Linguistics.

Yosso, T. J. (2005). Whose culture has capital? A critical race theory discussion of community cultural wealth. *Race Ethnicity and Education, 8*(1), 69–91. https://doi.org/10.1080/136133205 2000341006

Young, V. A., & Barrett, R. (2018). *Other people's English: Code-meshing, code-switching, and African American literacy.* Parlor Press.

Zaidi, R, & Hurley, S. (Host). (2021, March). A transraciolinguistic approach for literacy classrooms [Audio podcast episode]. In *Shifting linguistic landscapes.* voicEd Radio. https://voiced.ca /podcast_episode_post/a-transraciolinguistic-approach-for-literacy-classrooms-ft-dr -patriann-smith

Zong, J., & Batalova, J. (2016). *Caribbean immigrants in the United States.* Retrieved from http:// www.migrationpolicy.org/article/caribbean-immigrants-united-states

Zong, J., & Batalova, J. (2019). *Caribbean immigrants in the United States.* Migration Policy Institute. https://www.migrationpolicy.org/article/caribbean-immigrants-united-states-2017

Index

About the Author

Associate Professor **Patriann Smith** is a well-known researcher in the fields of language and literacy at the University of South Florida (USF). As a former teacher of ELA/literacy in St. Lucia, Trinidad and Tobago, and the United States, her research considers how literacy teaching, research, assessment, and policy are influenced by the intersection of race, language, and (im)migration. She draws from the Black Englishes, Black literacies, and languaging of Afro-Caribbean immigrants, other Black immigrants in the United States (i.e., African), and Black American students (i.e., African American) to propose solutions that advance transraciolinguistic justice in literacy. She also explores the Englishes of Black populations in their English-speaking Caribbean locales to make recommendations for advancing literacy teaching across local, national, and international boundaries. She has proposed solutions such as "a transraciolinguistic approach," "raciosemiotic architecture," "translanguaging with Englishes," "racialized entanglements of Englishes and peoples," and the framework for "Black immigrant literacies" to clarify how literacy can be reenvisioned and taught to all students (e.g., monolingual, bilingual, multilingual students) in and beyond classrooms. Her expansive body of research has been published in journals such as *The Reading Teacher, Reading Research Quarterly, American Educational Research Journal, Journal of Black Studies, International Multilingual Research Journal,* and *Policy Insights From the Behavioral and Brain Sciences.* She has served as guest editor for the 2020 special issue of *Teachers College Record,* "Clarifying the Role of Race in the Literacies of Black Immigrant Youth," and is coauthor of the book *Affirming Black Students' Lives and Literacies: Bearing Witness,* published by Teachers College Press. She currently serves as an elected member of the Board of Directors of the Literacy Research Association (LRA) and as a member of several editorial review boards including those of *The Reading Teacher* and *Reading Research Quarterly* (International Literacy Association [ILA]), *Journal of Literacy Research,* and the *International Multilingual Research Journal.* She is associate editor of the international journal *Linguistics and Education* and of the *Caribbean Educational Research Journal.* Dr. Smith serves as coprincipal investigator of the USAID-funded "RISE Caribbean" initiative designed to establish an educational research center that enhances research-based decision making in the Caribbean. She is an ILA 2013 Reading Hall of Fame Emerging Scholar Fellow, LRA 2017 STAR Fellow, and a recipient of the 2015 American Educational Research Association Language and Social Processes SIG Emerging Scholar Award. She is the recipient of numerous university awards in research and teaching, including USF's 2022 Global Excellence Research Award and USF's 2021 Faculty Outstanding Research Achievement Award in Research and Innovation.